RAINING
SIDEWAYS

Published by RedDoor
www.reddoorpress.co.uk
© 2022 Sally Vincent

Excerpt from 'Little Gidding' from FOUR QUARTETS by T.S. Eliot,
published by Faber and Faber. Reproduced with permission

Excerpt from 'Little Gidding' from FOUR QUARTETS by T.S. Eliot.
Copyright © 1942 by T.S. Eliot, renewed 1970 by Esme Valerie Eliot.
Reprinted by permission of Mariner Books, an imprint of HarperCollins
Publishers LLC. All rights reserved

978-1-913062-94-1

A CIP catalogue record for this book is available from the British Library

Cover design and typesetting: Megan Sheer

Printed and bound by Clays Ltd, Elcograf S.p.A

RAINING
SIDEWAYS

A Devonshire
Diary of Food
and Farming

SALLY VINCENT

Red Door

To my beloved family, all my wonderful friends and all animals,
past and present, with whom I share my life!

CONTENTS

FOREWORD
BY JOSCELINE DIMBLEBY

Towards the end of the 1960s my new husband took me to a village beside the River Dart in South Devon where his family had spent holidays for several years. At the end of the long drive from London – no motorway then – we turned off the main road for my first experience of Devon's twisting, high-hedged lanes, just wide enough for one car. Finally, from a high point between steep velvety green hills, we saw the gloriously beautiful river below, looking like a nineteenth-century print.

I gasped in wonder. But shortly before arriving at the village of Dittisham I noticed something that made me feel even more that I had come to a timeless and magical part of England. It was an unusually tall, very old house with a large monkey puzzle tree in front of it. Although clearly decaying the house was still elegant and evoked mystery and romance. Every time I drove past it afterwards to shop in Totnes, I felt entranced by it.

I became friends with Dorothy and Desmond, the unmarried brother and sister who had always lived together in their childhood home, the now crumbling Brambletorre. I visited Dorothy each time we were in Devon and often bought a goose from her at Christmas until, more than ten years later, she and Desmond felt it was time to downsize. I remember meeting the new owners, Sally and Paul, standing underneath the monkey puzzle tree, and feeling instinctively that they would be able to save the whole place, and retain its magic. And they have done. Together and against many odds Sally and Paul have achieved the miracle of restoring Brambletorre without losing any of its romantic character, and created an imaginative garden packed with the loveliest flowers and shrubs, with all sorts of features, different aspects and areas to explore. Despite years of hard work and constant battles with the Devon weather, it looks now as if someone simply waved a magic wand over the house and garden and this vision was created in seconds.

When Thames Television, where Paul had worked in London, lost its franchise and he was made redundant, it brought an opportunity for Paul and Sally to re-invent themselves. Bravely they decided to try farming on the almost vertical hills their house is surrounded by. They seem to have such a good relationship with the animals they rear that I wondered if after their children grew up and began to lead independent lives some of the animals became part of the family too.

Before the Vincents moved to Devon Sally worked as a chef, but it is as an imaginative home cook, fired by the enthusiasm she has for everything she creates, that she excels. Inevitably she and Paul soon made a vegetable garden where the produce thrived as much as the garden flowers. Not only did they have the best and freshest ingredients, including eggs, for Sally's delicious dishes but they began to sell the produce for miles around so countless others could share the pleasure. Throughout the years Sally has recorded her culinary ideas, and has explained them simply and clearly here so that we can all benefit.

This visually enticing book will bring inspiration and joy to anyone who cooks, gardens, farms, rears animals or is nostalgic for country life. Or simply wants to get vicarious pleasure from reading the story of a dream, achieved through determination and passion.

INTRODUCTION

This is a diary of my everyday life in a quiet valley in Devon, a story of food, farming and friendship in South West England. For many years now, I have been searching for local produce both cultivated and wild. I have been exploring old culinary traditions and lost skills, hoping to hold them for a moment longer by recording them before they vanish for good.

I have lived in this beautiful valley for many years now. My story is, quite literally, of farming, food, fire and flood. It is about how it was and how it is now, and how it may become. It is about arriving in the valley, coaxing an old house back to life, restoring a garden and reuniting the farmland with the house. It is about producing food naturally and preserving old skills while watching culinary traditions vanish. It is about starting a business, raising chickens for the table and turkeys for Christmas, of growing vegetables and herbs and gathering the wild food from the hedgerows. It is about Dexter cows and donkeys, about breeding Whiteface Dartmoor sheep, lambing time and harvest. It is about a deer farm and rare breed pigs and my Chilean chickens that lay pale blue eggs. It's Brixham Fish Quay at four in the morning and salmon fishing on the River Dart. But above all it is about my kitchen and my love of cooking.

It is a long time ago now that I worked as a chef in London. Over the years I have watched both country life and our diet change dramatically and stealthily. There was a time when we shopped at the butcher, baker, grocer for whatever was available. Most of our food was local and seasonal. We grew herbs and fruit and vegetables in our gardens in the country or on our allotments in the town; we joyfully harvested our little crop. Country people bought direct from local farmers and hunted wild game. They fished in local streams and rivers and searched the seashore for delicacies. In our little local town, we still have a wonderful market, greengrocer, local butcher and fish straight from the sea.

But over the years things began to change. Supermarkets arrived. How exciting we thought as shelves filled with unfamiliar produce, out-of-season fruit and vegetables and ready meals from far away. But gradually the novelty waned and thankfully, the pleasure, the old skills and the spontaneity of gathering and preparing our own food is slowly creeping back, making it even more important to try to record the traditional ways just in case they do, one day, vanish forever.

Sally Vincent

HOW IT ALL BEGAN

New Year's Day came in on the heels of the wind. Dogs and I walked up to the highest fields and watched huge clouds scud across an angry sky. The wind blew so hard I could lean back against it without falling. The sheep cowered in the hedgerows cleverly picking the most sheltered spot. Rain filled the valley below me masking distant Dartmoor. It raced along the rivers' way like a huge sideways curtain lashing horizontally through the hills and valleys, wrapping everything in its path. The wind changed and the rain caught up with us. Dogs put their heads down and their ears back and scurried at my feet.

Min, the ageing, delinquent Cairn, looked even smaller than usual, half-drowned in the torrent but enthusiasm quite unabashed. The smallest, fastest and deadliest of the ratting team, very little dampens her spirit, so, to her annoyance, she stays on a lead a great deal of the time being quite unable to give up on a scent, once sniffed. I have spent hours crawling through woodland, brambles, gorse, riverbank, water, in pursuit of her. I've pulled her by her tail, unceremoniously, from badgers' sets and watched as she struggled with a determination unequalled across a two-acre field dragging her prey — on this occasion a very large, unfortunate rabbit. It took her two hours to bring her trophy to the farmyard. Once on the trail nothing detracts her. At home she is the sweetest, gentlest little dog, adored and adoring of the children: a real little Jekyll and Hyde.

As I struggled down to the farmyard below, buffeted by wind, rain slamming into my face, my mind began to wander back across the years. What had brought me here I pondered. How on earth had I come to have this truly wonderful way of life?

It was February 1982 when our lives changed forever. We travelled west in search of lost friends. We found our friends and fell in love with a poor old battered farmhouse up the road. On the day of completion we arrived early. We sat patiently on the grass pondering our future. In time an old tractor trundled up and Desmond, the farmer, handed over a key; I gazed at it in wonder, just one enormous, rusty, unused old key – the key to our new life. Just then we were startled by the Red Arrows flying overhead. Some welcome we thought, then realised it was the Port of Dartmouth Royal Regatta and the honour was not exclusively for us!

The house was built in 1767 by the local rector for his daughter. Over the last two hundred and forty years it had been home to either churchmen or farmers. The Reverend Francis Lyte, 'Poet and Priest of Brixham', lived here for a year or so before moving across the river. Maybe he even wrote 'Abide with Me' during his short stay here. The deeds are lost so there is much we will never know but we do know that the family from whom we bought it had farmed here since 1922.

Our arrival was eventful. First the removal lorry broke down on the motorway. And then, as I had predicted in several high-decibel phone calls to the removal company, it was far too big to fit through the narrow Devon lanes, too big, indeed, to reach the house. Everything once more had to be decanted unceremoniously into a small hired van in the middle of the village right outside the shop – a good place for passers-by to get a look at the belongings and the people who had bought 'Dorothy's House'.

Deathwatch beetle, wet rot, dry rot and flourishing fungi meant we had no floorboards on which to arrange this furniture. All our belongings, everything but the most basic necessities, had to be stacked high in the farm dairy. They would remain there for the next nine months. We began to forget about them; things we had deemed so essential simply weren't missed. As the months passed I soon learned that black mould is permanent and green mould can be brushed off!

The dairy, now a cosy study, was a cold north-facing addition, circa 1820. The deep slate shelves all around the room still remain. Each shelf has a gully, which held a trickle of cold water that acted as the cooling system, keeping hams and cheese, milk and cream fresh – a nineteenth-century 'refrigerator'.

For months we all camped downstairs, sleeping on plastic-covered mattresses. The children were ecstatic. They climbed around the house balancing precariously on the joists, exploring every corner and bagging a future bedroom each. They spent hours happily picking wet wallpaper off damp walls. They counted dead flies and compiled a scrapbook of the amazing interior decoration. They recorded all details of yellow and orange staircase, pea green panelling in the little Georgian sitting room and the beautiful iron fireplace steeped in cream paint. They explored the overgrown garden and made camps in the orchard. They tramped across fields, arriving home wet and muddy with happy exhausted dogs.

There was no hot water in the bathroom and the lavatory perched on high near the kitchen was inclined to give those brave enough to use it a fairly substantial cold shower when flushed. Fortunately there was another one upstairs that was less eccentric, but journeying to it meant balancing once more on those ceiling joists.

I loved the solid fuel Rayburn. It stood cream and battered in the corner of the old kitchen. It hadn't been used for years but it was the only source of heat we had. All the chimneys were blocked up either deliberately or by years of nesting birds. So, to cook our food, give us a little hot water and keep us warm, I set about bringing it back to life. I called the chimney sweep, scrubbed the old thing, bought some 'nuts' to feed it and fired it up. If the wind was in the right direction, it was a marvel. But, as the hills rise high behind the house, on grey days the smoke was returned unceremoniously down the chimney. I began to understand why it had been out of action for so long! It began to rule our mealtimes. Would it roar into life and cook lunch or would thick cloud, hanging heavy in the sky, make us wait until supper time for the fire to draw?

The old kitchen had no sink or drainage of any kind. A modern breeze block extension housed a metal sink whose waste pipe ended in mid-air. Water flowed first on to the floor then trickled optimistically towards a little drain hole: sometimes it disappeared; sometimes it didn't. It was a long, wet walk from cooker to sink with a saucepan. Cooking was a challenge.

In November the builders arrived and the restoration process began. The pantry vanished together with the waterfall lavatory. Suddenly a large space appeared that would in time become the new kitchen. Ceilings fell down, new ones replaced them. Heating and plumbing appeared, water, no water, heating, no heating. And, of course, things got so much worse before they got better.

Christmas approached and after much discussion we decided to make a valiant effort and celebrate in the shell that was to be our home. We hung a curtain across the bathroom door for Granny who whistled to indicate her occupancy; new floorboards in place made her journey slightly less hazardous.

Rubble was barrowed out of the kitchen; the floor was levelled. A shiny new sink appeared, then taps, hot water. What more did I need! A Christmas tree acted as camouflage and a few decorations lit up the occasion.

The dear old Rayburn came up trumps and cooked a turkey to perfection. Chairs and table were pulled out of storage and dusted down. Table laid, crackers in place and friends and family sat down together for the traditional festive feast in somewhat unconventional surroundings. My father gave me a long look and asked if I thought we had been altogether wise. I just smiled.

As months passed, we made progress. Paul returned to work in London saying: 'Now, don't start taking the staircase to bits…' I made a plan with my new friends, the builders. Terry borrowed a pig trough from farmer Richard. I filled it with caustic soda and washing powder and we were in business. Terry dismantled the staircase piece by piece. I dipped each spindle into the pig trough and scraped and dipped, and scraped and rinsed again until years and years of old paint was gone. I handed them one by one back to chippy Chris who reassembled everything. What a team! By the time Paul returned the job was done. Not a trace of orange or yellow paint anywhere.

Decorating next and along came 'Les the Decorator'. We chiselled off the distemper and hosed down the stairs together, all three floors. As Les transformed each room, I sat on the sitting-room floor for days on end pickling paint with caustic soda and soap then carefully picking it off the cast-iron fireplace as it softened. As I worked the beauty of the metalwork emerged. A jeweller for many years myself, I was lost in admiration at the depth and detail of the design. Soon carpets arrived and curtains were hung and our wonderful team departed. Our worldly belongings emerged from the damp dairy and the house came to life once more. Best of all I had the most beautiful kitchen I could possibly have imagined.

For the next ten years Paul and I lived strangely separate lives, meeting at weekends. I worked in Devon and he travelled east each week to his television life. Children finished school and went their separate ways. The precious time we had together was spent in a flurry of activity restoring the garden.

As we cleared and dug, dug and chopped, cleared and dug, the basic structure of a garden, long forgotten, began to emerge. Someone, sometime had cherished it. Down fell the derelict old greenhouses, broken glass threatening to chop off our heads. Down came the great tin tractor shed, in went the pond, out went the fencing made of gas stove and corrugated tin. In went banks of shrubs, out went broken outhouses and bindweed and dead trees. In went roses and camellias, beech hedges. Up popped swathes of bulbs and wild flowers. Stifled for years beneath the undergrowth, they took their chance to break free at last. Slowly, slowly as we worked, a garden began to re-emerge in the valley.

Then one day we awoke to find the world had changed again. Paul stopped going to London each week. By complete coincidence, if you believe such things exist, at exactly the same time as Thames Television lost its franchise to broadcast, we had the opportunity to buy back the farmyard and some of the farmland that had previously belonged to the old house. I call it synchronicity! And, once more another new life had begun!

In came the animals. First came Truffles, the brown Labrador and Minnie, that aforementioned delinquent Cairn. They were swiftly followed by Phyllis and Madge, two Jacob ewes, named by their previous owner after her mother's Bridge partners. Charming Whiteface Dartmoor sheep joined them, a tiny pedigree flock in fact. It wasn't long before we needed Meg, the sheepdog, to give us a hand. Then, whoops, her Mensa-intelligent daughter, Wellie, joined her. Dexter cows and calves, visiting bulls, Sussex steers, numerous chickens, geese and turkeys followed. Oh, and of course, my beloved donkeys. So, the story unfolds.

SUNDAY

An east wind is hurling itself through the valley and still it rains. Some hope things would warm up as we enter March and move towards spring! Freezing rain drops hammer on the window. Dogs curl up round my feet, turning their noses from the door; donkeys stand dejectedly in their stable.

The sheep are coming in at night now as lambing time approaches. Every evening they're queuing at the gate eager for tea. The ewes become so quiet and gentle before they lamb. It always puzzles me to hear people say sheep are stupid. Compared to whom or what, I wonder? They are such caring careful mothers, each ewe recognising her own lamb's call and each lamb recognising its mother's gentle baa. They know their job as we know ours.

Since the recent foot-and-mouth epidemic we have reduced our numbers drastically. Never again do we want to have ewes about to lamb trapped on barren fields far away from home, leaving us unable to move them to our own land without a licence, as helicopters fly overhead spying to make sure we all comply with panic regulations. Never again do we want to go through the daily terror of losing our healthy sheep to the contiguous cull because of an outbreak somewhere nearby. And we were the lucky ones. Other shepherds suffered unbearably, losing all their beloved stock and generations of skilled breeding. How fortunate we were.

Soon it will really be spring and the whole cycle will start all over again.

Suddenly the weather has changed again. The stream, running through the valley, turns from a sedate crystal flow into a boiling, brown, frothing torrent. Ewes come in as usual for tea, but with heads down through driving sleet and snow. Lambs are arriving. What a sharp contrast to the warmth of the womb. Almost immediately the first twins are born, two small sad little lambs. We lose one despite our best efforts. The survivor is tiny and frail; he may or may not make it. Two more ewes follow close behind. Their single offspring are tough little chaps. Once cleaned by their mothers, they quickly struggle to their feet and find their own way to the food source.

Every year I have to remind myself that a ewe knows if her lamb is sound or not. But it is still heartbreaking to see a mother neglect a sickly lamb and let it die. Year after year I gather them up, put them by the warm range in the kitchen and struggle to get them to suck a bottle. Inevitably they eventually die. Their mothers know best. Mary lived the longest, about twelve weeks. She settled down in the kitchen with the dogs and even made outings to the village with our Labrador who wanted to show her a bit of life, dustbins mainly, food being Truffles' life obsession. I had a few funny phone calls that spring!

Occasionally a ewe really can't cope; she may have triplets and simply not enough milk or maybe she's just young and flighty and needs some help with her new maternal role. Then of course the chances of hand rearing are much better. Some hand-reared lambs do survive; take my old Jacob ewe, Hazel, too old to lamb now and so tame, I sometimes think she's not sure if she's sheep or dog.

It seems a long time ago that we got our first two sheep, those two Jacob ewes, Phyllis and Madge. I knew very little about sheep and it took me some time to understand that sheep speed and human speed are very different. I had no idea how to catch the two of them and rushed madly about the field finally grabbing poor Madge by the horns only to be taken downhill very fast on my stomach. As she protested at my inappropriate efforts my husband looked on quite unable to help, paralysed with laughter! Oh how quickly I learned to slow down and show respect. We added a few more Jacobs to our little flock, two Suffolk crosses, Hazel of course and then Maisy, a stout woman who had lived in someone's back garden. She, like Hazel, was a bit confused about her identity until she joined a flock of something similar to herself.

Those were the early days. How things have changed. Now we have a beautiful flock of pedigree Whiteface Dartmoor sheep and, I'm glad to say, a much more professional approach to animal husbandry.

The Whiteface Dartmoor sheep, registered 'At Risk' with the Rare Breeds Survival Trust, have been on Dartmoor and parts of Exmoor for hundreds, possibly thousands of years. The Whiteface Dartmoor Sheep Breeders' Association is thriving, breeding and promoting the breed and the meat. Most breeders are still up on the Moor and need to be as hardy as their sheep. This year it is Paul's turn to be chairperson, a huge honour for a Cornishman who does not live on the Moor and has only lived in Devon for some twenty years. But he has worked very hard to develop our flock and, in so doing, has become exceedingly knowledgeable about the breed.

The rain is easing up at last. Soon I will go to the yard, clean out the stables, feed the donkeys and go in search of blue eggs laid by the Araucana hens. Spring simply must be on the way because they have started laying their beautiful blue and turquoise eggs once more. An ancient Chilean breed, they can be traced back hundreds of years to the time of the Spanish Conquistadors and before. Some of my hens are lavender, some black and two of last year's chicks are white speckled with black.

Of course I have too many cockerels and am planning a trip to the local rare breed poultry sale in a few weeks. The trick is to sell mine without being tempted to buy others!

The Marans have started laying again too, so has my funny little Chinese goose, Idi, who has strange sticking-out wings. She was a gift from a friend who thought Humphrey, my grumpy, lame gander, needed a companion. They make a funny pair marching round the yard among our large flock of free-range orange-feathered egg factories.

This is the time of year to pickle eggs and make large comforting goose egg tortillas and, of course, goose confit. Idi and Humphrey would be far too tough for the pot, fortunately for them, but a recent bit of barter put a couple of younger geese into my deep freeze.

Not much around in the garden to eat now! The herbs and vegetables are few and far between. Some salad leaves are still standing in the polytunnel and Brussels sprouts and leeks defy the wind and rain outside. The spinach looks a bit sad but purple sprouting is just beginning to show tiny blue tips. In among the flowers in the orchard I see the first signs of wild garlic. The leaves and flowers will cheer up our winter salads and add some zing to boring sandwiches. Maybe I'll dig up some garlic bulbs, chop them and mix with butter and spread in crusty bread to eat with leek and potato soup.

As I look at the winter landscape, I realise how little we have to depend on the food of each season any more. We don't even have to limit ourselves to local produce. We can buy whatever we fancy whenever we like, flown in from all over the world. Strawberries, figs, peaches, cherry tomatoes, peppers, aubergines, melons and so on and so on – all of it out of season. We can simply please ourselves and eat whatever takes our fancy at any time of the year. In some ways at first sight, it seems marvellous: more choice for everyone, a more interesting diet, less drudgery in the kitchen. But is it?

I fear there is a price to pay. Local producers are struggling to compete, quality is compromised by mass availability and, above all, old skills are vanishing. We simply don't need to know 'how' any more, or do we? Who will cook cassoulet, carbonnarde of beef, steak and kidney pud, gardener's chicken or coq au vin to warm you up on a cold dull February night when you've struggled home on train or tube, walked through icy streets, driven along slippery lanes, or maybe even climbed down from the top barn having safely delivered those first new lambs!

It is just so satisfying to be able to use that carefully preserved cornucopia of autumn. Meat we raised ourselves or bought from our neighbours is in the deep freeze. Fruit and vegetables have been frozen too or made into jams, jellies, chutneys and preserves. Some vegetables and fruits are bottled. Eggs are pickled, meats are potted. Terrines and pâtés add variety to our winter diet and we're lucky enough to have fish delivered to our door once a week, provided the fishers can get out to sea: all good things to cheer winter meals for us and unexpected guests.

And a tin of confit of duck in the larder or, better still, sometimes my own homemade confit in the fridge leads to Cassoulet for supper. In these rain-sodden days even an English version of the French classic is comforting. I hear a sharp intake of breath from across the Channel but, yes, I did make a fair Anglicised version recently, all be it taking a few shortcuts!

First, I stood the tin of confit of duck in a pan of hot water to soften the fat. In a big frying pan, I browned the duck in some of that fat until golden. Then I added skinned and chopped belly of pork and a Toulouse sausage. If I can't find a Toulouse sausage, I use a good coarse butcher's sausage.

I set aside the browned meat while I softened a large onion and a couple of crushed cloves of garlic in the same fat. In went half a tin of haricot beans followed by a tin of tomatoes: the latter a somewhat contentious addition in France! Next, I stirred in some good chicken stock, a bouquet garni of fresh herbs and a bay leaf.

Then I cheated again and opened a large tin of haricot beans. I put half into a casserole pot together with the tomato, onion and garlic. The duck and pork went on top covered by the remaining beans. Finally, I covered it all with a thick layer of breadcrumbs.

I cooked it uncovered in a slow oven for a couple of hours. Every so often I checked it, added a little more stock if necessary and more breadcrumbs. When the meat was tender, I scattered the final layer of breadcrumbs on the top, pressing in pieces of sausage. A further 30 minutes or so and it was ready to serve. Rich and deliciously unctuous, it cried out for a crisp refreshing salad.

A knuckle of pork, some pork skin, a piece of bacon, diced mutton or lamb, there are so many variations, but this one works for me!

The rain has stopped at last!

VENISON

'Marconi is wireless now,' said Richard obliquely as we trundled across a muddy field in his jeep, leaving a trail of feed on the ground behind us for the hinds. 'Yes?' I replied, waiting. 'He got some high tensile wire wrapped round his antlers a while ago, I've no idea how,' he continued. 'I couldn't get anywhere near him for days. Then suddenly there he was standing quietly beside me waiting for me to release the wire with my huge wire cutters. It made quite a bang when I cut it but he just stood patiently until I'd finished. I thought it might make him easier to approach but no, once more he won't come near me. But he's wireless now…'

The jeep has been ingeniously adapted so that by opening the driver's door and pulling on a piece of bailer twine the feed is released down a shoot from a tea chest where the back seat should be! The hinds saw us coming and raced towards us, forming a neat crocodile as they reached the food. Marconi trotted up and down the fence forgetting, as he does every day apparently, where the gap is, making him habitually late for tea.

Richard and Leslie have been here for four years, farming just up the road near the little village of Blackawton. Richard grew up on a farm in Cornwall where, as a small child, he remembers being chased from the house and knocked over by boisterous tame lambs. He went on to intensively farm beef, finished in twelve months for the supermarkets. Next came intensive pigs, followed by Dorset sheep, lambing three times in two years. All that's behind him now; he says he 'harvests' deer rather than farms them.

Beyond the gentle-feeding hinds stretches two hundred acres of natural farmland. In the distance I can see the reed meadows; cut only once a year now, they give such good cover for the deer. In the past they were cut more often for thatching. Below these meadows is wet woodland. Here a brook rises that feeds a huge wildlife habitat on its way down to the sea.

The farm is part of the Countryside Stewardship Scheme. No chemicals are used anywhere, no fertilisers and even farmyard manure is not allowed back on the fields. Richard and Leslie let the red deer live as naturally as possible in two large groups with a stag in each group. Tall wire fences keep the animals from jumping onto the road. They also separate the stags who fight fiercely for dominance from August to March. Antlers can weigh as much as five kilograms each. Without them they are very vulnerable as they wait for the new ones to grow. Even the hinds bully them a bit while they're 'in velvet', knowing it's safe.

The hinds calve in about May and June after a gestation period of about five months but this depends on the weather. Leslie and Richard have never had to help a hind and have never lost one during calving. The culling is done by a specialist marksman who picks out animals of eighteen to twenty-four months old from the herd. The carcasses go at once to the local abattoir and then are returned to the farm. Here they are hung in the farm butchery for seven to fourteen days. Venison in the wild is often hung for longer to tenderise the meat of older animals. All the meat is butchered on the farm for specialist shops and farmers' markets.

While I was visiting, I met some of their charming pigs too: as well as the deer, they still keep some pedigree Saddlebacks that will finish in four to six months. The bacon is excellent, dry cured and not too fatty, unlike that of their Gloucestershire Old Spots. In November they bought some Oxford Sandy and Blacks. They are about fifteen weeks now and will also finish at four months. These little chaps are particularly interesting because the breed is in danger of becoming extinct and these youngsters are the early examples of an attempt to reintroduce them. I have arranged a barter of a lamb for a pig for the deep freeze!

COOKING VENISON

Venison is a very lean meat much in favour as we become ever more aware of our cholesterol level and fat intake. Now that we can buy the sort of meat that the Goodman's produce and no longer have to go into the forest ourselves to shoot an animal of uncertain age, we can also employ modern cooking techniques more in line with our changing taste in food.

But the debate still rages: to marinate or not to marinate? We've been eating venison in Europe for hundreds of years. Of course most of the early recipes – by that I mean those of the Middle Ages – deal with salted meats. The old recipes required a bag of oatmeal in the cauldron, a 'frumenty' to absorb the salt. A thick pudding of wheat and almond milk thickened with egg yolks and coloured with saffron is probably not our first choice as an accompaniment to venison in the twenty-first century! Refrigerating meat now gives us much greater freedom of choice!

The purpose of the marinade is to moisturise and tenderise the meat, and to a certain extent preserve it for an extra day or two. Some modern chefs cook their venison like spring lamb, never marinating or slow cooking. This is I believe only possible if you are very sure of the source and the age of the animal.

In 1865 Eliza Acton advised covering the meat with flour and water as well as thick paper before cooking. Or maybe simply lardons of bacon or pork fat instead. Favourite additions are traditionally juniper berries, redcurrants, rowan berries, rosehips and pears.

'Apparently, venison takes longer to cook than other meats and must not be rushed – and the pies look very jolly with redcurrant jelly!'

When I cook a venison roast, I do start with a marinade. For a haunch of venison weighing about 1.8kg, I mix together oil, white wine vinegar, chopped carrot and onion and a piece of celery. I include a bouquet garni: a small bunch of herbs that includes parsley, thyme and bay leaf and any other herbs I have, relevant to the recipe, all wrapped in a little piece of muslin.

I put the meat in the marinade in the fridge for a day or two. When I'm ready to cook it, I preheat the oven to 230°C and strain off the marinade, which I set aside. I dry the meat with kitchen paper, lard it with 225g of bacon strips and a little olive oil and roast for 1 hour. I turn it and baste it a couple of times during cooking, then reduce the heat to 180°C and cook for another 30 minutes or so. It depends how rare or well done I want the meat to be. When it's cooked just as I want it, I take the meat from the roasting pan and let it rest for at least 10 minutes while I make the sauce. I put the pan back on a gentle heat and, stirring and scraping, add the reserved marinade. I let it simmer for 8–10 minutes.

All roasted meat improves with resting. It makes it much easier to carve and gives me time to finish the sauce, cook the vegetables and enjoy a glass of wine with friends!

Braised Venison is delicious too. For this I make up a similar marinade as for the roast haunch of venison but I add 6–8 crushed juniper berries, a sprig of rosemary, a clove of garlic and some crushed peppercorns. Then I cut up 1kg of braising venison and put it into the marinade. It goes into the fridge, as before, for a day or two, no more.

When ready to cook I strain off the marinade as before and save it for later. I brown the meat in hot oil in a heavy-based pan. I find it best to do this in small batches to give the oil time to reheat and ensure the meat seals rather than sweats. The meat then goes into a heavy casserole dish with a lid. I fry some sliced onions or shallots in the remaining oil. When they are softened and beginning to brown slightly, I sprinkle with a little flour to take up any remaining oil and stir in some stock together with the marinade. I bring it to the boil, stirring all the time, and pour it over the meat: then into a preheated moderate oven for 1½–2 hours.

I test the meat with a skewer to make sure it is tender and, if necessary, thicken the gravy with a little beurre manié: a spoonful of softened butter mixed with a spoonful of flour stirred bit by bit into the hot liquid. Sometimes I add vegetables during cooking: a carrot, celery, mushrooms maybe, adding them according to their cooking time so they are not overdone when the meat is ready.

This makes a delicious supper with a crisp green salad.

PAINT, PRIMROSES...
AND NETTLE PUDDING!

It is Easter week, Holy Week, Passover, spring! Suddenly winter is behind us and we're racing into spring at last. The valley has burst into life once more. It all seems to happen overnight; one minute we're bracing ourselves against wind and rain, sliding around in the mud as we struggle up to the farmyard and the next minute the clocks change, the evenings are lighter and we're plunged into the new season. We're awash with flowers, singing birds, trees with buds bursting, ewes fussing over their lambs, ducks shouting on the mill pond; everyone's in a hurry!

And everything is clothed in green. The high hedgerows flanking narrow Devon lanes leap into life, turning themselves into multicoloured tunnels winding their way up and down steep hills. Every so often a farm gate opens up a breathtaking view of river, moor or sea. A dancing mass of stitchwort, bluebells, ramson and red campion vie with one another for attention. Thrusting my hand deep into the hedge I feel the soil through my fingers, dead twigs snapping, insects burrowing and I am immediately involved in the whole life cycle. Birth, life, death, decay and birth again right here beneath my fingertips. But there is no doubt that the most thrilling sight to me are the bluebells drifting in blue waves along roads, through woodland, over banks and now, even scrambling up through our own steep cider apple orchard.

Seeds are germinating and begging to be pricked out, flowerbeds need digging, vegetables need planting and all I can do is paint, paint, paint the holiday cottage in time for the first summer visitors on Good Friday. The winter tenant left it perfect but the time has come for a new coat of paint, and, oh, how I hate being trapped inside with brush in hand when the sun shines!

I had my best ever phone enquiry from holiday makers yesterday: did I have some chicken's eggs that the children could hatch over Easter while staying on the farm? They would give me back the chicks on their return to London! Oh, I wish, but nature doesn't quite work like that, I tried to explain, birds and bees, etc.?

The hedgerows have already started to give of their summer-long wild harvest. The banks are covered with bright yellow primroses. *Primula vulgaris*, or common primrose, has been used for hundreds of years as a medicinal herb mentioned by both Pliny and Culpeper. Pliny recommended it for gout and paralysis while later Culpeper urged city ladies to use it to enhance their complexion! Now I think it's probably best to stick to crystallising the flowers to decorate the Easter Simnel cake or scatter a few flower heads in salad. I noticed yesterday several clumps with all the flower heads nipped off: a bullfinch or a field mouse, perhaps, someone else who appreciates the sweet taste of the nectar.

Cowslips, *Primula veris*, are now so rare that they are best left to reseed wherever possible. I have gone to great lengths to replant them in my garden and nurture each plant, hoping they will one day spread again. Gone are the days of cowslip wine. Cowslips are just one more casualty of modern farming, insecticides and so on. Fortunately wild flowers are protected by law now so we can only pick from our own gardens, which helps them replenish themselves in the wild.

Sweet violets, *Viola odorata*, are just visible on grassy banks, their minute flower heads poking through to the light. They are famous for their scent but also have a large number of culinary and medicinal uses. These days they are used principally as a dye or perfume. In Roman times violet-flavoured wine was hugely popular; Horace is said to have complained that more time was given to growing violets than olives! Legends abound about this tiny flower. When Jupiter turned his beloved Io, daughter of King Argos, into a white heifer for fear of Juno's jealousy, 'Ione', the Greek name for violet, sprung up from the ground to feed her! And of course, famously, Napoleon's nickname was Corporal la Violette, a secret name used by his supporters when toasting their hero. Like the primroses, they are wonderful candied and used as decoration but I'm loathe to pick them in large quantities, even here in my Devon garden.

And then, of course, there are the stinging nettles, masses and masses of them rampaging everywhere despite my best efforts. Wherever my chickens go the common nettle, *Urtica dioica*, appears, in the hedgerows, banks, ditches, round the perimeter of the fields, absolutely everywhere. Nettles give safe haven to some of our most beautiful butterflies and moths. So it is just as well they make such wonderful soup! Nettle beer is another traditional country tipple as well as nettle risotto and nettle-flavoured gnocchi!

In the 1930s Mrs Grieve talks of a nettle pudding mentioned by Samuel Pepys in 1661: Take 1 galleon of nettles, 2 leeks or onions, 2 heads of broccoli or a small cabbage or Brussels sprouts and a quarter of a pound of rice, she says. Chop and mix all the vegetables together and place in a muslin bag in alternate layers with the rice. Tie the bag tightly and boil in salted water until the vegetables are cooked. Serve with butter – very good apparently! I wonder!

Nettles have no end of medicinal uses listed at length by Mrs Grieve and of course they were used to make cloth for hundreds of years. So now maybe I shall feel kindlier towards them as they march through our land!

Add dandelions to your salad now, but not too many; as their old name, *pis-en-lit*, tells us, they are an excellent diuretic. Fat en,

Alexanders and sorrel are all appearing too. I use all with care and make sure I have identified them correctly. Watercress, so tempting at the edge of the stream, is to be avoided despite its delicious taste. Liver fluke is a real hazard, so we give that one a miss.

So what an Easter feast we will have. Soup of nettles, spinach and sorrel, Simnel cake decorated with wild flowers and maybe violet ice cream too!

In the last few weeks newspapers and glossy magazines have been full of enthusiastic recipes for spring. Here are exciting ways to prepare the new season's vegetables, spring lamb, asparagus, fresh peas, tiny broad beans in their pods and so on and so on. And then I walk round my garden so thrilled at the progress of my new vanguard of this year's planting brought on so fast by the mild weather. The pea plants I planted out last week are tearing away and are at least three inches tall! It will be some weeks therefore before I have a pea to harvest! Broad beans are winning though at a good eight inches high! But no sign there of a bean yet either! Even in this mild part of England I will have to wait a little while for my new harvest!

All the vegetables so eagerly written about are flown in from hotter climes or forced into life under 'plastica' on a diet of chemicals, or both. I prefer to wait and as far as possible eat the foods of the season or the produce I have stored since last year. I am just coming to the end of last year's tomatoes frozen as soon as they were picked. Defrosted and whizzed in the food processor, they take the place of tinned tomatoes throughout the winter. We still have some beans left too, as well as plums, damsons and gooseberries. The purple sprouting is still tender enough to pick and I noticed the rhubarb is poking its head above the old drainpipe that protects it, bringing me tender early stalks. In the polytunnel there are still just enough leaves left to scrape together a spicy little salad: rocket, chicory, Japanese mustard and tiny coloured chard leaves.

So now, early peas, broad beans, asparagus, herbs, shallots and artichokes all begin life in the vegetable garden once more. Sweet peas and dahlias will provide the cutting flowers for the house, a throwback for me to the days when I used to spend hours and hours with my granny's gardeners in her kitchen garden when I was small, oh, so many years ago. This was indeed a haven of wonder to a lonely, only child and is probably where my passion for all this came from. I often think of Mr Potter and Mr Cox and thank them so much, so often for their patience and kindness and the gift they unknowingly gave me.

The new fruit cage promises fruit for us instead of the birds this year. And I've started to dig beds ready for French beans, runner beans, leeks, chard, beetroot, Italian cabbage and, of course, the invaluable potatoes to 'clean' the ground.

Tomato plants line the length of the polytunnel – seven varieties this year. Tigerella, Sungold and Red Pear I've grown before, but I've added Auriga, Costoluto Fiorentino, San Marzano and Sun Belle for the first time. We'll see.

Carrots are proving reluctant to appear as usual; my Devon soil is really too heavy for them, even though I try to coax them into life by mixing sand into the seed compost. The first lettuce seeds are germinating and I await land cress, pak choi, chicory, lamb's lettuce and Lollo Rosso. I will cut the leaves when still small to make my own salad packs. Last year they sold before they reached the village shop!

Here in the valley I find the promises of summer.

NETTLE SOUP

A friend of mine, who has recently had to take over the family cooking for the first time, looked at me in a puzzled way the other day and said, 'When you're making soup where does the liquid come from?' If you have never cooked before it's a very good question! I laughed and explained about making stock. Take the meat off the cooked chicken, I said, put the carcass in a pot, fill the pot with water, add a bay leaf, some herbs, a carrot, an onion and put the whole thing in the bottom of your kitchen range and go to bed! 'Goodness, as simple as that?'

Just then we were interrupted, but I overheard him pursuing the subject with a professional photographer I know. 'Where do you get the liquid from?' he asked again. 'A stock cube, of course!' I laughed to myself. Take happy snaps on your phone or work for hours in the dark room printing to perfection. So horses for courses: I make stock or use a cube!

The basis of soup is the same. I gently sweat my chosen vegetables in a little butter and oil over a low heat in a covered pan until they are soft. The oil prevents the butter burning. If I want a thick soup, I add a potato or some rice and stir in a little flour. When the vegetables are just tender, I stir in the stock and any further ingredients and simmer gently until all is cooked. Depending on my choice of ingredients, I either liquidise the soup to a smooth consistency, or simply season and serve.

For the nettle and spinach soup, I take a large bag of young nettles, some spinach leaves and a little sorrel. I sweat a chopped onion, a medium potato, a carrot and a crushed clove of garlic. Next, in go the well-washed nettles with the spinach and sorrel. When they have wilted in the oil and butter, I add the stock or stock cube. I bring it gently to the boil and simmer for 5–8 minutes before puréeing in the liquidiser. Then into the pan again to warm through gently while I stir in a little cream or crème fraîche, season and sprinkle with chopped herbs. It really is a wonderfully fresh summer soup.

THE NEW FISH QUAY, BRIXHAM

It is 3.50 a.m. and the first birds are just beginning to sing. I climb
out of bed, rub my eyes, quieten the startled dog and jump into
the clothes I have been instructed to wear: jeans, T-shirt, sweater,
white coat, baseball cap and Wellington boots. A quick cup of
coffee as I gather up three cameras. I'm not taking any chances.
Then into the car and off to Stoke Fleming to the Old Telephone
Exchange. Mark Lobb is already there. It's now 4.45. If we leave
now, we will be in good time for the fish quay at Brixham. Too
early though for the Dartmouth ferry over the river, so we must
take the long way round.

I have known Mark for many years, ever since we worked for
some time on a government youth employment project. Even
so it was with some trepidation that I asked him if I could visit
the fish quay with him. It is not open to the public and is made
up of a close-knit group of fish traders unused to new faces,
particularly a woman's! 'We boys all grew up together: they'll
look at you and wonder if you're some sort of government
official! You stay near me.' I will I thought!

The early morning air was sharp despite the heat of recent
days. Dawn was breaking as we parked on the quay and fishing
boats, all shapes and sizes, were emerging from the night
shadows. I climbed from the van, gathered up my cameras, two
very small, one very large, took a deep breath, put my shoulders

back and prepared myself. 'Sorry in advance for the language' but there was little to worry about!

We walked into a huge hall where men in the required 'uniform' similar to mine milled around crates of fish. At first I was surprised at the inactivity: a slow drift round each catch. Crates were peered at, fish was picked up, smelt, thrown back, crates kicked. I soon realised the idea was to look as disinterested as possible.

Mark explained that the boats had come in the previous evening. All night a team had sorted, gutted, cleaned and crated the fish. Octopus is kept separately to prevent the ink contaminating the rest of the catch. Scallops have their own place too, 'a special market' apparently. The rest of the catch from each boat is sorted and crated by the boat's name. I was amazed at how the quantities varied: masses of crates from some boats and just a few from others.

The Beamers had come in that night too. These are the boats that go to sea for up to five days at a time. But the high tides and the exceptionally hot weather meant the catches were low even for the best of them. There would be no more Beamers in until the end of the week so the next few days would rely on the short haul boats that go out for the night only. How sparse it all looked.

I have read so much about the troubles of the fishing industry and here it was before my eyes: too many traders trying to buy too little fish. No wonder they try to look casual to keep the price down. And then there's 'that guy over there'. Mark points him out. He's wearing 'two hats', both boat owner and fish trader. It's in his interest to keep the prices up. Gradually I begin to realise the complexities beneath the surface.

And then the auction begins. As I watch the twitch here, the wave of a hand there, the eyebrow raised, the price moving up: it is incredibly hard to see who is bidding for what. All part of the skill, of course. These old hands have it down to a fine art.

My mind begins to drift back over all I have read about the history of fish and fishing. The Romans are said to have had amazing food markets. They knew how to make ice so could keep food fresh. Tanker ships brought the fish to shore. Huge fish ponds were fed by the aqueducts that brought water to the cities. Carts carrying water tanks took the live fish to market. I have seen the same in modern Japan. A lorry driving through Tokyo on its way to deliver fresh fish to restaurants, the whole vehicle one huge tank with fish swimming round for all to see.

In the Middle Ages the Pope made eating fish on Fridays compulsory, Lent and Saints days too. Fish was supposed to cool the blood unlike red meat. Trade grew up between north and south. Fish was dried in Scandinavia with salt from North Germany. Saltfish came to be the staple food stuff of the poor across Europe. Feudal lords gave fishing rights on their lakes and ponds for fresh fish as a privilege to the rich and powerful.

Louis XV offered 9000 francs to anyone who could find a way to bring fresh sea bream to Paris. A little later in 1775 Louis XVI first reduced and then abolished certain taxes to enable the poor to eat saltfish in Lent. Unfortunately no one remembered this when they cut off his head in 1789!

Our own fishing tradition goes way back, too. It wasn't until the 1880s that fishing became industrialised. Some two hundred years earlier Henry VIII had forbidden the purchase of cod from foreigners in an effort to encourage the English to fish the abundance in Newfoundland. Settlers went there with the fisherman, shipwrights and merchants whose descendants are there to the present day...

Even while in this reverie, my camera is clicking. I don't want to miss a thing. 'Who are you?' 'Would you like a coffee?' 'Who are you with?' Mark was right. Who on earth is this woman in our midst? I just smile and say I'm with him over there, and I'm going to write an article about fish. Some move on and others talk about the difficulties facing the industry now. They complain about the mass of regulations that traders and fishers wrestle with. They talk of the Common Fisheries Policy of the European Union, fishing quotas, offshore limits, boats called 'Rule Beaters', satellite communication and how it was back in the old days.

Then, suddenly, Mark is beside me saying: 'Quick take a picture of that.' Alas, I'm too late. A trader is standing on a crate and there right behind him is 'Environmental Health' in a white nylon trilby and mauve hairnet. Fisherman and merchants are suffering from the same well-intentioned, frustrating bureaucracy as the farmers. Many regulations are sensible and helpful, some are not. Unfortunately the latter often eclipse the former and tempers fray.

Gradually all the crates are sold, each trader gathering his together and marking them with his own ticket. In come the fork-lift trucks to load the lorries and vans. I jump out of their frenzied path. Mark goes to load ice on the quay from the huge ice maker. The boats fill their holds from here before they go to sea.

Over there are the Beamers. There are the old-fashioned netters and inshore trawlers that go to sea for short spells. Oh and there are the notorious 'Rule Beaters', big powerful boats 'cut down' in order to make them legal to fish within the inshore limit.

Eventually ice and fish are in our van and it's time for a wonderful and welcome breakfast at the Mission to Seafarers. This is a particular thrill for me, not just because I'm very hungry by now, but because I've heard so much of this splendid organisation from both naval grandfather and husband. So many have been given food and shelter by these great people over the centuries because, as Mark reminds me, they must always be placed on the quay *between* the water and the pub!

Just as the rest of the world is beginning to move into a new day, we return to the van and set off to collect crab meat from the 'crab factory' in another part of Brixham.

Then it's back to Mark's depot, the Old Telephone Exchange. On the way we pass Darren already out on a delivery round for Mark. We check he has all he needs and top up with some of today's catch. Once back at the depot the fish is unloaded and iced. It goes into the chill room and the cutting and filleting begins. Now it's ready for the next delivery round or the market. And the whole process starts all over again. I leave feeling awed and privileged to have been allowed such an insight into a world I think perhaps I have taken for granted.

There is a very fine balance between over- and underfishing. Both take their toll on the fish stocks. It seems like common sense not to catch immature fish or take the breeding stock from the sea but sadly that common sense is often lost due to competition and a fight for survival. The waste is terrible too. It is said that about one-third of the catch is thrown back for one reason or another. That is some forty million tonnes a year – fish, dolphins and sea birds all destroyed in the process.

Add to that the changes in sea temperature. The warming process has accelerated dramatically since the 1960s, bringing different varieties of fish to our waters. Off Plymouth the sea temperature is half a degree warmer than it was a hundred years ago and research shows the fish species are changing and fish are generally getting smaller. Global warming and modern fishing policy is having a profound effect on marine life and, if we're not careful, the world will soon be deprived of one of its greatest sources of protein. We must remember that fish is the world's last great wild food resource.

COOKING FISH

When old friends arrived from France recently, I ordered sea bass, one of my favourites, from Mark. I placed the fish on a big piece of oiled tinfoil, covered it with fennel fronds, drizzled over Pernod and wrapped the fish up tight. I baked it for 20 minutes in a hot oven and served it with Hollandaise sauce, new potatoes and a salad from the garden; so simple and quite delicious! For me, simple is best when cooking fish. When buying fish the flesh must be firm, the eyes bright and the gills deep red. If this is not the case and the fish smells fishy, then I would rather cook something else! Fresh fish cooked simply and quickly is my rule.

I love to cook a whole gutted fish quickly under a hot grill, or on the barbecue with fresh lemon and olive oil. Sometimes I may fill the cavity with herbs or porcini mushrooms, season with salt and pepper, rub with oil, wrap in foil and bake. I always check after 10 minutes because the cooking time will vary according to the size and variety of fish. The flesh should be just opaque and firm, not separated and dry.

Fillets of haddock or cod are great skinned with a sharp knife, dipped in a little beaten egg, then flour and herbs and fried quickly in butter or olive oil.

Scallops or tuna steaks seared in a hot pan for no more than a couple of minutes on each side are delicious too. I add chopped fennel or sage, or flame a little gin and crushed juniper berries over the scallops. The tuna is good just with black pepper, lemon juice and a sharp green salad with plenty of rocket or with a pile of boiled noodles and a dash of soy sauce. The possibilities are endless but fresh, quick and simple are the key.

HARVEST BEGINS

The June sun baked down on us in an unseasonably early heatwave. The grass turned brown and the sprinkler whirred endlessly as I struggled to keep vegetables and flowers alive. Frequent seed sowings in the polytunnel failed as seedlings fried as they germinated! And then the weather changed. Storms raged for days on end. Rain and wind lashed the valley. Paul sailed to France and I struggled through the gale force winds to check the sheep on the top of the hill. Even the dogs were reluctant to join me.

Rose petals filled the air as the wind stripped them from *Rosa* 'Seagull', the huge white climber by the pond. Trees bent double; the stream swelled as the water poured off the parched cracked earth. Trees came down up the valley and power cuts followed.

I kept donkeys and chickens inside out of the weather but nevertheless the badger paid two disastrous visits in the same week – blood and feathers everywhere and my Araucana broodies gone just as the eggs were about to hatch. Just one flustered terrified hen with one little chick escaped: bantams that I've had for years massacred too. Only one forlorn little lady was left, her cockerel and offspring stolen from a stone barn. The hungry creature burrowed under wire fence, concrete blocks and door, removing bodies to a nearby set where the cubs doubtless feasted. Sad though it is I know I must find a way for us all to live together. I share the valley with badgers and foxes, buzzards and innumerable beautiful birds. Squirrels, rats and mink abound too; some are a little harder than others to welcome!

But despite all this destruction Saturday found me at Newton Abbot poultry sale buying two beautiful hens each with a clutch of chicks. Two Welsummer laying hens and four little White Sussex poults came home with me too. The rest of the weekend was spent housing them safely.

We have a respite now from the storms. Breeze, cloud, sun, showers follow one another in rapid succession day in day out. The extremes of heat and wet have changed the landscape early this year. Hedges have grown up hiding familiar landmarks; the lanes have become furry green tunnels only to be shaved close by huge cutting teeth mounted on the back of tractors. The grass in the orchards is suddenly three feet high; it seems like only minutes ago wild flowers covered the ground between plums and apples.

Remarkably I have the best sweet peas ever! I saved seed from last year and have an abundance of long-stemmed, sweet-smelling flowers that somehow survived the buffeting. Not so successful are the peas, mangetout, tough and leathery through lack of water, are now swelling with regular peas. I left them to see what would happen. Broad beans got similarly battered but we've enjoyed a small but delicious crop. Beans, both French and runner, are late, held back by the heat too. Shallots on the other hand already look fat and bronzed; they obviously thrived under the sun.

I was too late to get the strawberry plants into the new fruit cage this year. So I took a chance and covered them with a piece of black netting from the farmyard and had the best crop ever. I even made a little jam, whisking a few away before the family devoured the lot! Gooseberries are ready to pick and the black-, white- and redcurrants, now safely protected from the birds, are looking very promising. New raspberry canes are a little sad but they've given us a few bowlfuls; better next year, I hope.

Beautiful French apricots arrived in the market just as the elderflowers burst into flower so I made more jam. The elderflower scent seems to lift the flavour of the apricots to new heights. It's wonderful with gooseberries too but the blossom is nearly over now and tiny green berries are beginning to form. They'll be ripe in November in time for the game season!

Tomatoes plants are heavy with trusses of fruit gradually beginning to ripen. The delicate flavour of home-grown tomatoes never fails to surprise me; they simply bear no resemblance to those bought in a shop. I'm really not sure why. I wonder if it is the variety, the cultivation, the time between harvest and distribution. Whatever it is the taste of a tomato straight from the plant is unbeatable.

Courgettes are in abundance now too. They, of course, love the rain and swell almost before my eyes. If I'm too slow I have a glut of marrows. Fortunately chicks love them!

So the pickling begins. I supplement what I have in the garden with vegetables from the market. Some cauliflower and celery for piccalilli and sweet peppers, baby carrots and spring onions go into the spiced courgette. I experimented with one over-large round courgette. I hollowed it out and salted it in the usual way and filled it with chopped, salted mixed vegetables and immersed it whole into boiling spiced vinegar. If it holds together, it may make a striking accompaniment for a winter feast of cold meats. Confit of duck perhaps, or more likely, confit of cockerel!

Bottling, pickling and preserving will continue now as summer leads into autumn and stores are put together for the winter months. Nothing pleases me more than an autumn storecupboard and larder filled with jams and chutneys, pickles and jellies, confit and rillettes.

CHUTNEY

My chutney making is very random. I simply use whatever I have in the garden: each year's glut! This time it was, of course, tomatoes, both red and green plus loads of apples. So, I chopped 250g of onions, with 500g of peeled and cored apples, 750g of tomatoes and a couple of lemons and threw them into a large stainless-steel pan.

As the fruit softened gently, I added 250ml of cider vinegar, 500g of light brown sugar, a couple of finely chopped chillies, a tablespoon of mustard seeds and a tablespoon of coarse sea salt. Next, I put in a spice bag: apple skin, apple cores, some peppercorns, coriander seeds, cloves and allspice berries.

I let it all cook gently for up to an hour until the liquid evaporated and the mixture had become thick and rich but not too jammy. Then I took out the spice bag and ladled the chutney into warm sterilised jars being careful not to burn myself. Once sealed, I labelled the jars and kept them in a cool dark place for a few weeks to mature.

Chutney adds deliciousness to so many things: cold meats, bread and Cheddar cheese, warming winter curries! Wonderful.

WHITEFACE IN AUTUMN

It's 1 September and the valley is already glowing in golden autumn sun. The early morning sky is a transparent blue as the first skein of geese arrives and swallows leave. The geese fly overhead in a perfect V formation, squealing excitedly as they spot possible winter quarters in the shiny mud of the creek below. They wheel around abruptly and make their hilarious ungainly landings, sticking out feet in front to act as brakes. I love to watch them paddling and sloshing about in the water by our gate. They've come a long, long way and deserve a rest.

Flying lessons, conducted overhead on telegraph wires, have been going on for some time now. I call out hopelessly, 'Don't leave yet, stay a little longer, maybe we'll have an Indian summer…' But the first cohort of house martins, swifts and swallows have already left – a sure sign that the summer is drawing to a close.

Early mornings are sharp. I need layers of clothes in the farmyard only to cast them off later as the sun comes up. Today the valley was swathed in a chilling thick mist and donkeys faded from sight as they climbed the hill. Grazing sheep seemed to float on the hillside. Thick dew covered the ground and cobwebs glistened in the first light.

All the sheep are separated now. Wethers are finishing for meat. Young rams, picked as potential sires, graze quietly in one meadow while ewe lambs, away from their mothers, settle in another, preparing for their future role. Meanwhile the old pros graze the orchard and build up their strength ready to meet our new boy, Junior, and start the whole cycle again.

Since the foot-and-mouth outbreak, the annual Dartmoor Whiteface Sheep sale, a regular August event, is no longer allowed to be held on the gently sloping field at the edge of the Moor. Now we must go to market in town. There trailers can be washed, feet (human) dipped in disinfectant and all manner of new regulations adhered to. It's one more tradition stealthily lost, a small one perhaps, but a sad loss after hundreds of years of the breed's history. This is how we are losing so many country events, traditions and skills. A kneejerk, frightened, urban reaction rather than a respect for the knowledge of the people who have been farming the land and breeding animals for generations; it makes me sad and just a little angry.

Despite all this we had a good day at Newton Abbot Livestock Market. Best of breed was judged and sheep were auctioned. To everyone's relief ewes and lambs have begun to fetch good prices again. But too many rams and too few buyers meant their prices were low and beautiful animals went home unsold. 'Junior', a handsome full mouth boy, came home with us, however. He will bring new blood to our pedigree flock.

The Whiteface Dartmoor is believed to be one of England's most ancient breed of sheep. In early times it was found not only on the Moor but also all over Devon and in West Somerset too. As land became enclosed, the breed was driven back to its origins on Dartmoor where it flourishes today. Needless to say these are the very hardiest of sheep, capable of surviving on the poorest pasture. On the Moor most grazing is 500–2000 feet above sea level and the majority of the flocks stay out from May to December. The ewes have a reputation for their excellent mothering skills and some off-the-moor farmers don't even bring them in at all but let them lamb in the field. We bring ours in more for our convenience than theirs!

NAVARIN OF LAMB

Today I plan to cook some Whiteface 'Angel Meat'! A shoulder of our own spring lamb will become a sort of Navarin à la Printanière. A little late in the season perhaps! I'll take time and pleasure to prepare this traditional French country classic with garlic and rosemary accompanied by young vegetables from the garden. I'll dig up some potatoes, pick mangetout peas and see if I can find a few little carrots. This is not a dish for stewing lamb. It calls for tender, lean meat that will cook gently but quite quickly. I prefer to cut up a shoulder or even use a boned-out loin.

After trimming off any fat and sinew, I cut the meat into fairly small pieces and brown it in batches in butter and a little oil in a heavy ovenproof pan. I add the oil to stop the butter burning and becoming bitter. When the meat is browned and sealed, I take it out and set it aside.

I add a chopped shallot and a crushed clove of garlic or two to the buttery juices in the pan and, heating gently, allow them to soften slightly. In goes a spoonful or two of flour, scraping up the meat juices to make a thin paste, followed slowly by the stock and a little tomato purée.

Back goes the browned meat. As I heat gently, I adjust the consistency, which should be creamy, by adding more stock if necessary. Once it has come slowly to the boil, I cover the pan with its lid and place in a moderate oven for about an hour. I test the meat with a skewer to see if it is tender. If not, I return it to the oven for a little longer but I am very careful not to overdo it.

Meanwhile, I prepare some young fresh root vegetables: new potatoes, very young turnips and whole baby carrots. Once the meat is tender, I add these and cook for a scant half an hour without the lid. I top and tail some mangetout or shell some peas and broad beans, slice my first runner beans or harvest the early French beans; I use what I have in the garden or whatever I can find in my local farmers' market.

When I have blanched the vegetables very briefly in plenty of boiling water, I drain them well and add to the lamb. I heat through, skim off absolutely any remaining fat, taste and add salt and freshly ground black pepper. Serve on warm plates with hot, crusty bread – delicious!

WIDECOMBE FAIR

It's Widecombe Fair again, a Tuesday in September. I rang sheep farmer Colin Pearse on the Moor to find out the time of his book launch. 'In the Sheep Heritage Marquee 12.30.' 'Yes, Colin, but which Tuesday?' An amazed silence, then, 'Well, second, of course, always has been, has been since the Fair started back in the 1850s.' Colin has taken four years to write a history of the Whiteface Dartmoor sheep and, published at last, it is to be presented at this year's Fair. It's the perfect setting, a celebration of this fine old rare moorland breed on its own territory.

So on the second Tuesday in September we race round the farmyard, feeding here, mucking out there, letting out, shutting in, cosseting, cosseting everyone so they'll be safe until we're back. Old dogs, lab and cairn, climb resignedly into their baskets, yawn and go to sleep. Young sheepdog Meg and Wellie her dotty black-and-white collie lurcher daughter, bounce into the back of the muddy Land Rover.

It's a fair way up onto the Moors from us. We drive through narrow lanes, leaving the sea behind us onto what our old erstwhile neighbour used to call 'they big roads'. Then on through Ashburton and up and up until we eventually cross the cattle grid and leave the trees behind us. The Moor spreads out as far as the eye can see. Ground, covered in heather and gorse, reflects the scudding clouds. The wind is strong; sharp rain and a watery sun follow each other as we climb higher and higher.

Each way we turn the landscape is identical, sweeping away to the horizon. Turn around three times and you will completely lose your bearings. No coincidence the old prison was built up here. One day last year I walked some fifteen miles across a corner of the Moor with friends who know the landscape well and, even then, we briefly lost one of our party. She bent to tie a shoelace as we strode on unnoticing. She looked up a moment later only to find us gone, but in which direction.

Sheep, mostly Scotties, but some Whiteface, doze on the verges or wander unconcernedly along the road. Dartmoor ponies graze quietly with their foals, fat and shiny after the summer grass. Never before has their future seemed so precarious. Not because of the usual scarcity of winter food but once more they, like so many animals, are the subject of new government edicts. Fortunately conservation groups are flexing their muscles, hard enough, I hope, to prevent the Dartmoor ponies becoming another endangered rare breed like the Exmoor ponies.

We follow the one-way signs to the Fair, park in an already slippy, muddy field and are grateful for our four-wheel drive. I wonder how many cars will have to be pulled out by tractors by the end of the day. The fairground is already full. Sheep are being judged in the sheep tent. Rows of rams, tied to the fence, wait patiently for their turn. Horse boxes disgorge ponies of all shapes and sizes. In the ring some of the very smallest horse men and women I have ever seen sit on their mounts in enormous crash helmets, little legs so short they stick straight out from the saddle. It's a solemn business becoming the equestrian sports people of the future.

Dogs of every shape and size mingle in the crowd. I spot one having a very cushy ride in a pushchair. Others wait with owners by the bar, noses twitching, eyeing the succulent beast turning on the spit. And some are just hanging out being dogs. They wait to enter the dog show: prettiest dog at the show, the dog the judge most wants to take home, most agile dog, even the dog with the kindest eyes. That must be my beloved Wellie, but she's a bit too silly for the show ring this year.

There are multicoloured tractor seats for sale, shepherds' crooks, handmade children's clothes, local cheese, weather vanes, ice cream, hot dogs, pasties, pies, beer, cider. And, of course, there are many references by Tony Beard, The Wag of Widecombe, in his commentary to the Beer Tent.

Should I take part in the Cow Pat competition or throw a horse shoe onto a stake. In the craft tent the sponge cakes are definitely the real thing, no *Calendar Girl* Marks & Spencer specimens here! The biggest beans, carrots, onions have been judged and sport their rosettes. Art displays line the walls and plants and flower arrangements await the critical eye of another judge.

Just then I catch site of Auld Uncle Tom Cobley on Tom Pearse's 'Grey Mare'. Yes, really, there he is 'all along, down along, out along lea'. Someone told me he had problems with insurance this year…then I see Bill Brewer or is it Jan Stewer or Peter Gurney, Peter Davey, Dan'l Whiddon, Harry Hawk? One of them is still searching for Auld Uncle Tom Cobley an all. I hadn't realised until today that after the poor old mare died, she 'doth appear ghastly white' at night on the Moor 'midst skirlin' an' groans' an' 'er rattlin' bones.' In the Churchyard at Spreyton is a gravestone that simply says, 'Thomas Cobley, Gent – 1844 Spreyton'.

Widecombe Primary children are all set for the maypole dance. It's getting so crowded I have to sneak to the front to get a good view. Round and round they whirl, weaving their ribbons in and out in traditional, intricate patterns. How amazing to grow up and be able to say, 'I danced at Widecombe Fair.' Will it even still exist when they've all grown up, I wonder.

An old restored pump engine, tap gushing water is proudly displayed, as is the diesel engine and the flour mill. Mr C. Westcott was delighted to have his picture taken with his beautiful little cart but said he was so sorry he forgot to put his teeth in today. I said it really didn't matter and I'd send him a copy anyway.

It's time for the book launch so I push through the crowd back to the Sheep Heritage tent and catch sight of an elated and terrified Colin. Miss Needham has arrived, ninety-one this year, the president of the Whiteface Dartmoor Sheep Breeders' Association and, without doubt, one of the most knowledgeable sheep people on the planet: who better than she to introduce Colin's book. The tent is so crowded I can't hear a word and just thrust my camera rudely through the crowd. A professional photographer sees me and, thinking I'm one of his kind, helpfully makes a little space for me. I feel a fraud but take it! There are speeches and clapping and cheese and sweet wine and a moment when Colin brushes the back of his hand across his tear-stained face. Hazel looks so proud of him. The big pile of beautiful books goes down and down. Colin glows.

We struggle out into now pouring rain, gather up the anxious dogs waiting outside the tent, grab a pasty and a glass of cider and head home wondering if it will all happen once more next year on the second Tuesday of September.

Home from the fair and a quick supper is called for. I will just have time to put Sautéed Chicken with Garlic and Herbs into the oven before we go up to the yard to feed the animals. I have some chicken pieces in the fridge but a whole chicken cut into six works just as well.

Quickly, I chop some fresh herbs: at this time of year parsley, thyme, a little sage and a few wild garlic leaves. In spring and summer, the mix will be different, maybe tarragon and lemon zest or basil, chives and marjoram. The flavour of the dish will reflect the season.

I brown the chicken pieces, skin-side down, in butter with a little oil in a heavy-based saucepan that has a tight-fitting lid. Once nicely browned, I lower the heat and turn the meat once, cover and cook for 40–45 minutes.

That leaves me just time to feed dogs, dash up to the farmyard, chivvy the chickens, collect the eggs, check the sheep and donkeys and hurry home!

I take the cooked chicken from the pan and keep it warm. Now is the time to add the crushed garlic cloves and chopped shallot to the pan, then stir in the wine, scraping up all the residue with a wooden spoon. Letting it bubble, then adding lemon juice and half of the chopped herbs, tasting and adjusting the seasoning. Then back goes the chicken for a further 5 minutes. With more chopped herbs, a baked potato or crusty bread and a green winter salad, this is a really quick supper after a wonderful day! Phew!

AUTUMN INTO WINTER

Autumn is suddenly fading into winter. The wind blows, leaves fall like huge crispy golden snowflakes and colour vanishes from the valley. The smell of wet, fallen leaves takes me back, in a split second, to my London childhood, to Kensington Gardens, the Round Pond, the Broad Walk, Christopher Robin, Peter Pan. There I am walking home with 'Nanny' in my little tweed coat and gaiters, kicking leaves into the air.

All these years later I watch my own little grandchildren playing in the leaves on the farm just as I did along the pavements and under the plane trees. They help me to muck out the donkeys' stables too, which is a slow and hilarious affair. Flo-jo is too small just yet and may only look on, but Bee and Harry get right down to it. Bee, two and a half, shrieks that the chickens are pecking her bottom. She has to duck and weave to avoid being sprinkled with donkey poo as Harry man-handles a huge shovel into the wheelbarrow, all the while regaling us with a running commentary about his future life as a farmer or maybe a 'plane flyer'. He's four.

Autumn gradually became wetter and wetter. We lost so much of our wild harvest. Blackberries that looked so promising in the late summer sun turned to water in the constant autumn rain. They rotted on the brambles before I had a chance to pick them. Rosehips went the same way but sloes glistened in the hedgerows and the quince tree has produced its heaviest crop ever, the medlar too. Quince ratafia and medlar jelly are in the pipeline.

Quince Ratafia will be wonderful by Christmas. It will add a glow as we drink it with our Christmas pud and mince pies. It will cheer up vanilla ice cream and add a sparkle to the winter fruit salad. Added to the pork gravy or stirred into a pheasant and apple casserole, it will enrich and bring a sweet wintry depth to the sauce.

To prepare it I grate a really ripe quince into a litre jar, add a little sugar and fill the jar with vodka! Then I cover it with a tight-fitting lid and store for at least two months in a dark place. Occasionally I give the bottle a shake to help the sugar dissolve. The longer you keep it the better it gets!

Quince, Apple and Tangerine Compote is also really worth making too – so good!

I peel two quinces with a potato peeler and core and chop into even-size chunks. Even a ripe quince is very hard, so I watch my fingers! I peel and chop 1kg of apples too, then slice three or four tangerines depending on size, just taking out the pips. I put everything into a heavy-based pan, tip in 500g of sugar and heat through, gently at first, until the sugar melts, then I let it simmer for about an hour until I have a thick, rich purée.

It freezes brilliantly, so over the winter months we can eat it in so many ways: with yoghurt or ice cream, or make it into a winter fruit fool.

PIG!

Our new bullocks have arrived, two big Sussex boys, snugly housed in the big barn for the winter, munching their way through a great bale of sweet-smelling haylage. Rams are in with the ewes now, tupping almost completed. The ewes, round and fit after the summer grass, are in the peak of health to start the lambing cycle once again. We hope Junior will bring new blood to our flock and produce big strong Whiteface lambs next spring. The Jacob cross ewes and their handsome fellow will give us really good roast lamb too!

We have hoggets, year-old wethers, ready to go now. Their meat will be wonderful, more flavour than young lamb but without the fat of mutton. Our local small privately run abattoir is just fifteen miles away in Ashburton. We can load our animals ourselves early in the morning and have them there in time for immediate slaughter – no stressful long lorry journey or hours waiting to be dispatched on arrival.

Many years ago now a friend and I were invited to share some pork after the slaughter of a pig on a local farm nearby – a very rare occurrence now, I'm very glad to say.

It was a cold foggy morning. I crept along the lanes in my car trying to make out a gap in the hedgerows marking the farm entrance. The fog made me so late I was fortunate enough to miss the actual slaughter. Pig was already dead by the time

I arrived. I remember standing in deep mud in a desolate farmyard surrounded by beautiful, dilapidated old buildings. Everything seemed disembodied, surreal in the mist. My friend, Gay, introduced me to the farmer, his wife and his brother as we ducked out of the way of the slaughter man as he staggered past, pig on a shoulder, towards a shed.

Some days later Gay and I were asked back to participate in the butchering of the pig. With a saw in one hand and book in the other, we embarked on the task with the farmer's wife. My respect for our butcher's skill doubled and trebled as the morning progressed. Leave it to the professionals!

Once our attempts at butchery were complete the farmer's wife showed us how to make sausages. 'My boys don't like 'erbs and seasoning' was her ominous introduction. We were ushered into the dark back kitchen where a huge aluminium pot bubbled on the range. Plunging in a great spoon she fished out ears and jaw bones complete with teeth, all steaming in a greasy, grey broth. We were instructed to pick out the meat, stir in pounds of oatmeal and force the grey goo into sausage skins.

Loading our portions of pig in the car and declining offers of pounds of grey sausage, we determined to have a go ourselves. Back in Gay's kitchen we embarked on a most ambitious programme of pork charcuterie ably assisted by Jane Grigson's wonderful *Charcuterie and French Pork Cookery*. For days we minced and chopped, salted and cured. We filled sausage skins and fashioned salamis. We prepared our hams and persuaded the local smokehouse to smoke them for us. We talked nothing but pig products and dreamed pig recipes.

To my delight I recently found Gay's account of our efforts printed in 'Twelve Times a Year', the newsletter for the Carved Angel Restaurant, in Dartmouth, back in chef Joyce Molyneux's heyday. I read with disbelief that we made '12lbs of dried sausage, half of which was smoked, 18lbs of sausages in three different flavours, all with seasoning and herbs, 4lbs of Cyprus sausage, pig's cheese, hog's pudding, 4 hams in two different brines and cured pork belly'. An amazing quantity! She goes on to say we were a little overambitious. I think so too! We certainly produced some wonderful results even if I have to admit our success was less than 100 per cent – and we did have tremendous fun! We still laugh about it now.

I was thrilled to find her record of our endeavours. How things have changed since then the newsletter tells us. 'There is a divide in the world of cookery. On the one hand, the restaurants think, or have thought that home cooking is of little interest; on the other, the domestic cook has been loath to embark on food of a professional style. That dichotomy is ebbing as chefs and their like realise that the skills of Jane Grigson and Elizabeth David have a lot to offer them, and as people in their own homes become more adventurous and surer that their produce is as good if not better than that of the most skilled restaurant.'

With ready-prepared food available everywhere I fear that sadly things may have changed again. In fact, I think, rather than becoming more adventurous, culinary skills are disappearing fast, despite the many wonderful cookery books in print. No doubt Gay and I were a little extreme with our mountain of pork but many people now are no longer obliged to even cook a daily meal themselves, let alone pot and preserve for the future. Cooking has become a TV entertainment and the supermarkets are taking control of the national diet!

I wonder if Nicolas Appert knew what he had started when, in 1803, he found a way to fix the seasons at his establishment: spring, summer and autumn in little bottles, like those delicate plants protected by the gardener under glass domes against the intemperate seasons. Tinning and bottling on a commercial scale had begun.

Even as late as the 1980s we still did not suspect what would follow.

As supermarkets began to take over, they have gradually taken away our need to cook. In the developed world there are few food shortages, winter or summer. We can buy what we like when we like from anywhere in the world. All we have to do is warm it and eat it to stay alive and yet, at the same time, a huge part of the world's population is starving. What a strange world we live in.

BACON

Back to pigs and curing bacon. I become fussier and fussier about the bacon I buy. What is that awful, white, fishy smelling, sticky goo that emerges from each rasher as it fries, rendering the lot soggy and welded to the pan? Why doesn't it turn crisp and fill the air with that irresistible coffee mixed smell of breakfast as I struggle back, cold and hungry from the yard?

With Lesley and Richard having moved on to pastures new, I have just bought half a pig from the splendid 'state of the art' butchery where our lambs are now butchered. Together with excellent butchery skill, all mod cons and the necessary European Economic Community (EEC) Cutting license, it's a very satisfactory arrangement and their pork is wonderful too.

So, I put the pork belly into a dry cure: salt, bay leaves, crushed peppercorns, juniper berries and soft brown sugar. I rub the mixture into the meat and place it in a plastic tray, on no account metal. I then cover it with a tea towel and leave it in the fridge overnight. The next day, I pour off the liquid that has leached out of the meat and, if necessary, rub in a little more salt mixture. I repeat this for three or four days. The longer I leave it the saltier, but the more stable, it will become. Finally, I take it out of the cure, rinse it well and pat it dry. I wrap it in muslin or maybe greaseproof paper and make room in my fridge for it to hang from a shelf. It will keep for a month like this. Mild weather makes me feel the fridge is the safest option.

I would like to have it smoked but my local smokehouse is now too large a concern to take tiny pieces of home-cured affairs, so I'll enjoy it 'green'. Maybe one day I'll tackle home smoking…

Delicious meals start to fill my head, such as Petit Salé with Savoy Cabbage and Mashed Potatoes. I soak the bacon to remove the salt, rinse and bring it gently to the boil, then simmer for about 40 minutes. I chop a Savoy cabbage, blanch in boiling water and drain well. I drain the cooked bacon and keep warm and set the liquor aside for future soups. I then melt a piece of butter in a heavy pan, add a tablespoon of the bacon liquor and reheat the cabbage. We'll eat hot boiled bacon with cabbage and mashed potatoes.

Or, how about an anglicised Tartiflette? Fry some bacon until just beginning to crisp, add a couple of chopped onions and a leftover boiled potato or three. When the onion begins to caramelise, tip the lot into an ovenproof dish and pour over a little cream. No, this is not a light, slimming dish! Top with cheese, which, traditionally, should be Tomme de Savoie, but I use up whatever I have. Bake until the cheese melts and bubbles. Delicious!

For a really quick supper, I just fry bacon cubes, shallot and cooked, sliced potatoes and, maybe, some mushrooms all together and top with a fried egg. So simple and so nice after a cold day in the farmyard!

FLOOD

Rain continues to fall. The Devon sideways rain is usually steady and relentless, not a thunderstorm, not a summer storm. It simply fills the valley: a huge sideways moving curtain. But on Christmas Eve 1999 it took a different guise. At eleven o'clock that night we fell exhausted into bed, the last Christmas turkey dispatched and delivered, animals safely housed and fed. All last-minute preparations completed for guests and festivities in the morning. Sleep at last, then at 2 a.m. the phone rang, I put out a sleepy hand to the receiver. My ninety-year-old father in the little barn by our gate: 'We seem to be flooded'. The phone cut off.

'I'm coming, Dad.' We fell out of bed, pulled on clothes and raced into the garden only to be met by a raging torrent. Down the valley from the yard the water roared, carrying everything in its path. We struggled along the higher ground, hearts in mouths, towards the yard. Chickens floated on their straw; the goose house was so full of water old Humphrey bumped his head on the roof. Paul waded through the swirling water, grabbed the poor bird and threw him in with the donkeys whose stables, still dry, stand on slightly higher ground.

Then he jumped into the big old Lamborghini tractor and started off towards the Barn. Hopeless, the water was so deep in the lane that the great beast, dancing through the water, slewed sideways; he reversed nervously back into the yard. What now we thought. We ran back through the garden just above the torrent. I struggled recklessly, water waist high, across the bridge over the stream. Paul climbed into the Land Rover and drove through the crater appearing in the drive at our gate. The stream, usually piped underground here, had burst through. Down he went, then up and bounced out into the lane. As he turned up the hill to their front door, water was breaking over the bonnet. Soaked and frightened, I met him at the door. The Barn is upside down, bedrooms downstairs sitting room upstairs. Downstairs water poured in over the windowsills, upstairs the water seeped steadily under the door. There they sat, two tiny little old people, wet and confused. By now two and a half hours had passed since their phone call.

Dad stood in his vest and pants complaining his socks were wet. Mother, wearing only her little pink negligee and curlers, shivered. They were very, very cold. Together Paul and I lifted them into the soaked Land Rover. I fought my way back on foot through the water, over the bridge while he, holding his breath, risked the now huge crater that had been our drive. Down he went again, up he came again. We reached our front door above the water and helped them up the steps into our house, into a dry, safe bed. We fed them sweet tea and calmed their fears. The rain stopped; at 5 a.m. we went to bed. The next day they remembered nothing.

We faced the devastation. The neighbour's millpond outside our gate was gone; it was full of the tarmac from the lane. Even the white lines lay crumpled like tissue paper where the water had been. The trees had gone, the stone wall had gone, our drive had gone. And mud everywhere; thick red Devon mud filled the Barn and all that surrounded it.

Our friends arrived for Christmas. All celebration abandoned, they put on their boots and begun to dig with us through the rubble. Julia came up in rashes on her face from the chemicals washed down from neighbouring hills in the mud, as she worked to clear the mess. The weather turned; the ground froze. Dad fell on the ice trying to assess the damage to his home. And then a miracle: a neighbour wading by to assess the damage stopped at the gate and offered my parents his nearby empty cottage. A wave of relief; I knew my old parents would be quite unable to manage all the stairs in our funny tall old house.

The whole farmyard, with the amazing exception of the donkeys' stable, was under water. Miraculously, chickens subsided on their straw and survived. Just one little sheep got caught in the brambles in the worst part of the torrent and was lost. The others fled uphill.

We surveyed the damage. It took us twelve months to restore and repair. We were lucky we lost no one.

SHEEP, COWS AND DONKEYS!

'Get your boots on, find the dogs, Barbery sheep're in Jim's.' I groan, put down my coffee and climb back into my green waterproof wonder suit. It's Saturday morning and I've just finished my eighth day in a row in the farmyard alone as Paul languished in bed with really bad flu. Today he struggled out for the first time and drove over to check our wethers in a neighbour's field while I fed, watered and mucked out. I'd been dreaming about coffee for nearly an hour.

We jumped into the Land Rover and raced up the lane to find four of the seven small delinquents had crossed the stream, limboed under a broken bit of fence and reached pastures new: new and vertical. Paul looked pale.

The leader of the gang, a feisty Jacob cross boy, stamped his feet defiantly at the dog who, taking one look at him, said to herself, 'Me, a sheepdog? No, not today,' and vanished. She's a funny Yorkshire lass is Meg. Some days she's ready to star in *One Man and His Dog* and another day she completely forgets her 'coom' bye lass, Way, way, walk 'em on, walk'em on. Ey and that'll do'. On a good day, once the job is completed, she races across the field and hurls herself through the air into Paul's arms, completely consumed with pleasure at her own success. On other days she simply vanishes and leaves me to inadequately impersonate her.

Today was such a day: one look at the four wethers and she was over the hills and far away. That left just me and my lurcher, Wellie, a sweet obliging soul, but without her mother's training. She and I were just ready to start training together when, several years ago now, the foot-and-mouth curfew fell on us all.

So up and down the hill we went. 'Slowly, slowly, now, no, not so fast.' Ah, nearly at the gate, whoops they're gone again. All right then, we'll walk them up the lane. Car arrives, wants to pass, hoots, sheep gone. Move Land Rover, let car pass, feeling a touch uncharitable; race uphill again to cut them off. Big boy stamps feet and I swear he stuck his tongue out and made that rude sign children use. Well, OK, projection, but that's how I was beginning to feel running all over the field attempting to impersonate Meg.

All the while there was one poor old ewe trying hard to keep up with the youngsters. She wasn't one of ours and seemed to be all alone. She was so lame she kept falling on her knees and struggling along at half-mast, a pathetic sight.

'Leave them,' Paul called, collapsing with post-flu exhaustion. 'We'll get Stephen to help on Monday. I'll go and see Jim and tell him.' Our neighbour is famously tolerant of these incidents, saying: 'They be right if they got they mouths with 'em.' So tolerant indeed, that he gave us a long explanation as to why he'd abandoned the poor old ewe. Would cost money to cull her, he said. I hatched a plan. I knew Stephen would be my accomplice in my rescue mission.

Monday morning, raining of course, we set out to bring the wanderers home. Employing different tactics and with not only another pair of longer legs but also a fantastically efficient sheepdog, the job was done in under the hour! Back over fence, through stream, join others and all up the lane together to the waiting trailer. Our patient postman, seeing what we were doing, simply turned his van and went the other way – no hooting or trying to push past us.

Stephen and I manhandled old Mavis, my new name for the old lady, across the field and into the trailer with the youngsters. She sank down with relief and didn't move: my kidnapped sheep. We brought her home and put her in 'intensive care' next to the Whiteface ewe with a bad foot. Warm, dry, with plenty of food and no longer alone, she relaxed on the clean straw. I left Paul the embarrassing task of ringing Jim to tell him what his wife had done. 'Oh,' he said, laughing, 'tell 'er, keep 'er.' No fool, he! In time, when the weather improves, she will join my other old timers, Madge and Maisy, and live out the rest of her days in their gentle company. Sheep live in flocks and need one another, like us really.

ROAST BEEF

After a busy week it's time for a traditional Sunday lunch. It's not something we do very often but I'm already on the phone inviting friends! A piece of our own beef will cheer us on through these winter days! I'll cook a fillet maybe, a piece of sirloin or a rib: all will be caramelised on the outside and pink in the middle and served with good gravy, Yorkshire pudding, fresh horseradish from the garden (grated into clotted cream!) and seasonal vegetables.

Having counted my guests and selected my piece of beef I preheat my oven to 220°C. I rub the meat all over with olive oil and a sprinkle of salt and pepper before it goes into a very hot oven in a robust roasting tin for 20 minutes to seal the meat and give that dark rich coating to the meat. Then I reduce the heat to 180°C for the remaining cooking time. This will depend on how well cooked I want the meat to be. A rough guide to cooking times is: 10 minutes per 500g – rare (very pink), 15 minutes per 500g – medium (just pink) and 20 minutes per 500g – well done. But, of course, all cookers vary!

When I am satisfied that the beef is cooked to my liking, I remove it from the oven, take it out of the roasting tin and leave it in a warm place to rest for at least 30 minutes before carving. All roast meat benefits hugely by being rested after cooking. Resting allows the juices to settle evenly through the meat. It also gives me time to cook the Yorkshire pudding, finish off the vegetables and make the gravy.

To make the gravy, I first pour off excess fat from the roasting tin, then deglaze it with a little stock or vegetable water and, maybe, a dash of red wine. I mix a couple of generous teaspoons of cornflour with a little water and stir it into the gravy over the heat. I keep stirring until it thickens and clears, then add salt and pepper to taste and, if necessary, strain it through a sieve into a gravy jug.

Topside and silverside make very respectable roasting joints too, provided that the meat is well hung and the cooking is slower and gentler. I give the meat a quicker hot blast as above, then lower the heat to 195°C and cook the meat for 20 minutes per 500g. Slow roasting will become braising if I add some vegetables and liquid and cover the pot!

LAMBING AGAIN

How the years vary. Last year winter flew by amidst howling gales and driving rain, sleet and snow. This year the contrast has been striking. Up until the third week of March it was so very cold with unusually hard frosts, sun and not a drop of rain. The grass has only just begun to grow and the fields are unusually bare and brown for the time of year. We fretted and fretted that there wouldn't be enough fresh grass for the ewes with their new lambs. Then suddenly as we reached the end of the month the temperature went up and the rain came down. Warm sun followed and the whole valley burst into life.

Now daffodils, primroses and celandines suddenly carpet the hillside in yellow. Birds shout about nest building in the hedgerows and ducks quack on the stream. Bantams keep marching out of farm buildings with a clutch of tiny chicks. If they all survive, we'll be overrun with them this year.

The bullocks were beside themselves with joy as they blundered out of their winter quarters into the fields. They bucked and danced and rubbed their faces in the mud before skipping up the hill to pastures new and green.

This year's lambing is different too. No year is ever the same but I have never before had five fit little lambs to feed at regular intervals. The first lambs to be born were triplets to a Jacob cross old timer, a calm, quiet, experienced ewe. But she had no milk. I climbed into the pen to give her a hand, first with colostrum to get the babies started, then at four-hourly intervals, with bottles of milk. She checked the bottles and the lambs, sniffing and tasting, then, pushing her face into mine, seemed to say, 'That'll be OK, thanks'. Back in the field, she has some milk at last, but not enough for all three lambs, so they race towards me for a top-up every six hours now.

And the twins are also getting on wonderfully well at last. Their mother was too ill to produce any milk at all and I thought for a while we'd lose them all. But she has recovered and the lambs, slowly gathering strength, have learned to suck from the bottle. Now they too race across the field to me, pushing and shoving and competing with the others. I have mastered holding three bottles in two hands but still some ravenous youngsters have to wait.

Nearly all the ewes have finally lambed and we are beginning to look forward to our routine returning to normal and a good night's sleep. Although we have cut down our flock it is still a very busy time. We realised we were not alone when our neighbour said he'd fallen asleep on his feet during lambing this year!

Paul was taking a similar much-earned rest, deliberately this time, in the afternoon recently when I found a ewe in trouble. 'Don't interfere' is the rule, but after watching for some time I knew I must help her to deliver a large dead lamb. As I showed it to her, I thought *I wonder...* Gently I felt around and found another lamb. Poor girl, she was too exhausted to do any more. So very carefully I gave her a hand and out slid the second little chap full of life. Each year brings sad moments as well as success and over time I have learned to watch the ewes and trust their unfailing instinct about their newborn. They are so wise and caring and they know if all is not well.

This year I have had so many visitors, many more than in the past. Suddenly everyone wants to have a look at the lambs and help me feed them. In the daytime of course! I was pondering this as I was mucking out the donkeys' stables one morning and have come to the conclusion that we somehow represent an interface between farmers and non-farmers. We came to this way of life as a second career. Unlike our neighbours we are not from generations of farmers and our farm is very, very small, a large smallholding perhaps. Somehow this seems to make us more approachable to our non-farming friends and acquaintances. They are curious and puzzled. Why do we work so hard? Is it worth it? Do we just do it for 'fun'?

I try not to yawn and mutter, Fun? Getting up through the night to feed lambs?' But I restrain myself because, yes, it is our choice and we do enjoy it, even when we're very, very tired.

The knowledge of life on the land is trickling away from everyday awareness. I am at once both delighted to have all these visitors and deeply saddened by the lack of understanding from the increasing number of people who live in the country, among the farming community, and yet are quite unaware of how their lives are supported by farming and the production of their food around them.

Faces are all turned to the supermarkets without the slightest idea how or from where the shelves are filled. Lasagne was the dish chosen by the village for Harvest Supper last year even though we live in the heart of a farming community. I love Italian food but just this once wouldn't something traditional like cottage pie have been more appropriate, I wonder.

Soon it will be time to feed all the sheep and bring them down from the hill for the night. The lambs will need bottles and the donkeys their tea. New chicks must be made safe and chickens shut up for the night. We know there's a fox about. Poor Idi, my dear, funny goose, disappeared mid-afternoon recently. The donkeys eeyored but I was too late. I found her feathers in the hedge the next day. Humphrey is alone once more. The foxes have hungry cubs to feed, the badgers too. We all share the valley and must take our chance.

COTTAGE PIE

It will be a quick cottage pie for supper tonight – one I have prepared earlier! Traditionally both cottage pie and brother, shepherd's pie, were made from the leftovers of the Sunday roast. The cold meat was simply chopped up, mixed with the leftover gravy, put into a pie dish, topped with mashed potato and reheated in the oven – a bit dull!

But a Cottage Pie made with fresh minced beef is a different thing – quite delicious, so simple to prepare in advance and so useful at this busy time of year. First, I peel some potatoes, boil them, then mash with butter, a little milk and salt and pepper. Next, I chop a large onion or a couple of shallots and crush two or three peeled cloves of garlic. I soften them over a low heat in a little oil, then raise the heat and add minced beef, stirring until nicely browned. I sprinkle the meat with a tablespoon of flour and add stock, homemade if I have any in the deep freeze or made from a cube if I'm in a big hurry. In goes a little leftover red wine maybe and a large tablespoon of tomato purée. Another stir and I cover the pan and simmer gently for 25–30 minutes. I tip it all into a pie dish and cover it with the mashed potato. Now it can wait until all our work is done. When we're ready it will go back to the oven to heat through and crisp the potato topping – a warm comforting supper after a cold day on the farm.

A COLD SPRING

Lambing now finished, fat, sturdy little lambs graze on the higher fields with their mothers and I can turn my attention to the garden once more. How different from last year – I read with incredulity of a heatwave, of meals in the garden, seeds frying in the polytunnel and fruit and vegetables racing away. As I write the rain pours down. The Cairn looks out of the window and grizzles, the lurcher and the sheepdog are curled up on the blanket at my feet and the old Labrador, crammed into a too-small basket like a giant brown dormouse, paws over face, is dreaming, I'm sure, of those lovely 'delphiniums (blue) and geraniums (red)', oh and, of course, what's for tea!

I wonder whether to switch on the fire.

The hedgerows are only now bursting into flower, bluebells push through despite the cold, mixing blue with red campion and the still standing, white ramson. Apple blossom opens reluctantly in the cold air and little plants, recently taken from the safety of the polytunnel, stand still, shivering in the cold ground. How the years vary and yet the cycle is the same.

Despite the vagaries of the weather, I revel in the wonderful reassurance of the rotating seasons. The cold spring this year has put this in such sharp relief for me. Each day as I work in the garden I wonder if summer really will arrive and change the valley into a lush green bowl again. Will the twigs disappear behind fresh green leaves. Will vegetables grow in the cold bare soil? Will the roses flower. Will apple blossom really turn into fruit? Of course, it will and the momentum will gather as always, all be it, a little slower, maybe, this year. There will, I know, be the usual July-August crescendo followed by the gradual fading into autumn, then winter yet again.

As I dig the buttercup invasion from the asparagus bed, wondering crossly why I let it get so bad, I realise that I too will, God willing, be doing the same in the garden time and time again, for all the years of life and good health I have left ahead of me. It is an addiction, a relentless and yet life-fulfilling thrill to watch the bleakness of winter turn to the lush abundance of summer year after year.

And this year has seen such a huge reshaping of the garden. For the first time I have help, expert help, and two and two makes so much more than four. In just three hours a week Alison has helped me turn the garden round. We've re-landscaped here and enlarged beds there; we've done away with this and planted that. We've moved trees, dug up shrubs and replanted borders. We've pruned rigorously and hacked back undergrowth ruthlessly. The result is astonishing. Ali is a hard taskmaster, thorough and skilled with the drive of a perfectionist. She has taught me so much.

The vegetable garden is taking shape as I apply her standards there as well. The ground is so cold it is giving me time to clear and thoroughly clean each bed before planting out. Some time ago now I divided the whole area into fourteen, eight-foot squares. Some are filled with herbs; others I rotate with herbs and vegetables. Bindweed and buttercups are a recurring problem and a few years ago I made the mistake of tipping a packet of nasturtium seeds all over the place. They are now a menacing colourful curse, choking everything if I let them, a real example of the importance of the right plant in the right place.

Broad beans already fill one square. They are in flower but small and cold. Sweet peas and runner beans stand still in two others. I pray there won't be a late frost to wipe out the early potatoes in another. I will use potatoes once again to 'clean' the ground in the four central beds that surround the cherry tree. Actually, I think it's the harvesting that does the cleaning not the spuds, all that digging to find the crop. I will plant Charlotte, Pink Fir Apple, Rocket and Anya. And next year I promise myself these beds, at last weed free, will be filled with herbs and edged with the dwarf box, the traditional *Buxus sempervirens* 'Suffruticosa'.

Life is a little warmer in the polytunnel and the greenhouses. Geraniums wait nervously in one, wondering when they will have to face the elements. They will soon replace the tubs of tulips which have given us wave after wave of colour for weeks. I planted them in layers for the first time and watched in wonder as each colour pushed through to replace its fading predecessor.

The other little glasshouse is full of tomatoes and dwarf *Tagetes patula*, the latter to deter white fly, I hope. This year I lost seedlings inside the polytunnel for the first time; it was so cold. But Golden Sunrise, Pineapple, Green Zebra and San Marzano survived together with something mysterious called Marshalls' 'Experimental'. Big pots of tiny basil seedlings help me dream of warm days and tomato and basil salads drenched in unctuous, sweet-smelling, green, virgin olive oil...

The polytunnel is housing the strawberries this year. The fruit cage is full to bursting with raspberries, gooseberries and black-, white- and redcurrants so this is another experiment. Not only will it give us an earlier crop but will also protect the fruit from the birds. We'll see.

And, of course, we have had green salad all year round. Rocket and Chicory (*Cichorium intybus* and *Grumolo verde*) and rocket stood through the winter and now the new mixed salad leaf seedlings are ready to harvest. I will continue to sow small patches of seeds on fresh, peat-free compost all summer, cutting the young leaves with scissors rather than thinning and planting out. To the various lettuce leaves, I add mizuna, mustard leaves (*Brassica juncea* 'Red Giant'), rocket (*Eruca vesicaria* subsp. *sativa*), parsley (*Petroselinum crispum*) and land cress (*Barbarea verna*). Then, from the herb garden, I add the fern-like fennel leaves of *Foeniculum vulgare*, chives (*Allium schoenoprasum*), tips of marjoram (*Origanum vulgaris*), French sorrel or *Rumex scutatus* and at this time of year the wild garlic leaves, *Allium ursinum*. I always add a few flowers too, nasturtium (*Tropaeolum majus*), majoram, chive and the sweet-smelling rocket petals. Unwashed, chilled and sealed in a plastic bag in the fridge these salads last for several days, crisp and fresh.

The rain is still falling, washing petals from the *Ceanothus*, the forget-me-nots and my precious *Meconopsis*, their big blue faces sad against the grey sky. Sometimes I think I would like to turn my whole garden into a mass of just blue and white and green. Maybe the sun will shine tomorrow.

FILLING THE LARDER

As we reach the equinox once more the autumn sun drops from our heavens into the southern hemisphere. It joins us later and later each day creeping up over the hill. And, leaving earlier and earlier, it soon, all too soon, slides away, sinking like a huge red barley sugar. The golden autumn light seems to wrap itself around the whole valley, easing us towards winter. As the days get shorter the light becomes hard and sharp. Mimicking shadows, long, crisp, exaggerated, fall across the grass. The days are still warm but there is a chill in the misty morning air as we set off for the yard before breakfast. Donkeys loiter in their shed hoping for a little something extra, eyeing the remains of last year's hay with distaste. Days begin to shrink as we watch the clock at dusk. We hurry to reach the chickens ahead of the foxes and the badgers. Dimpsey is their favourite time to dine.

This year's lambs are big and fat now and away from their mothers. Bullocks are waiting in the wings to be butchered and sold as beef boxes. I felt sad to see the great dignified beasts leave on their last journey and had to remind myself that theirs could have been a far less happy lot had they not been here with us. Richard will butcher them on the farm in his butchery at Gara Barton. Lesley and I will pack and label and make up individual boxes for our customers. After nurturing the beautiful beasts through their short life, it is of huge importance to me that the butchery and presentation is of the highest quality and does them justice.

Junior is building up his strength once more in a lush neighbouring field preparing for the high spot of his year. He has grown into a fine Whiteface pedigree ram and we are very relieved that his good Scrapie score will spare him from the compulsory government cull next year, when he will still be in his prime. Young Scruff, last year's orphaned ram lamb, is now an almost respectable grown-up chap too. He has proved himself a useful and calming summer companion for Junior. Having nursed him from near death when he was so small, I begged for his reprieve and am so glad his life has found a purpose!

Everywhere I look there is a burgeoning, bursting, harvest. Sloes weigh down the hedgerows; blackberries snatch at me as I climb over styles and untie gates between fields. The runner beans need picking and freezing, potatoes need digging and storing, tomatoes fill the greenhouse, courgettes turn into marrows if I turn my back and tomatillos daintily fill the polytunnel.

This is the season to fill the larder and the deep freeze. I have turned the goose into confit, chicken livers into pâté and plums and cucumbers into pickles. Chutneys will follow. This year some of those beans will join the last green tomatoes and windfall apples into the chutney. A recipe with fresh ginger sounds delicious. Maybe I can add all those tomatillos too! I'll make piccalilli again and crush some crab apples to make old-fashioned verjuice. The cider apples will be collected in sacks beneath the trees. When all are gathered, we will take them to the local press. Well, I may give a sack or two to Richard's pigs.

TOMATILLOS

I have never grown tomatillos before. I was given a packet of seeds as a gift so I had a go. They germinated easily and, after pricking out, I planted them directly into the ground in the polytunnel. Tall graceful plants produced pretty little white flowers similar to a potato or tomato. These were followed by masses of green fruit each wrapped in a little paper jacket. Raw they reminded me of something between a crunchy tomato and an apple! I discovered that they are wonderful in salsa, with ripe tomatoes, garlic and chillies.

I made up a tomatillo recipe this summer: Sal's Salsa!

I prepared two red peppers, ten tomatillos, ten plum tomatoes and three large cloves of Elephant garlic, then put them on a roasting tray sprinkled with olive oil and into a very hot oven. I kept a check on them and removed each as they became soft. The peppers took the longest. I skinned the cooked tomatoes and garlic and put them into the food processor. Next, in went the softened tomatillos and the peeled peppers. I took the peel off a lemon with a potato peeler, making sure I left the pith behind. The peel and the juice of the lemon went into the processor too with a good handful of parsley, chervil, two hot chillies and freshly ground black pepper. Now a very quick blitz for just a few seconds, some more olive oil, maybe a dash of hot chilli sauce and it was done. I let it stand for an hour to allow the flavours to mellow. Delicious!

TUDOR KITCHEN

Last week I spent a day in the 'Tudor Kitchen' at the Weald and Downland Living Museum in Sussex. We salted and smoked, pickled and preserved all manner of things in the ways of the Tudors. The room was dark and smoky, lit only by candles. The windows were without glass, giving us some relief from the heavy smoke billowing from the open grate. Coppiced logs some three feet long lay across dog irons feeding the fire. Oak burns slowly we were told, giving the long-lasting background heat, but the smoke is acrid. Beech and ash give the main heat while a quick burst of flame is provided by the coppiced birch. Fat iron pots on little legs surrounded the fire, their contents bubbling away; a pig's head destined for brawn, apples on their way to becoming apple leather, vegetables for pickling. Often one pot would contain several different dishes each wrapped in its own cloth. Embers were pulled under the pots or pushed away to control the heat. Herrings, salted and strung up above the fire, smoked slowly to make early 'kippers' and pork and beef were preserved in various spices, salts, 'ale gars' and vinegars.

How strangely similar it all seemed to our methods today but how quickly these skills are being lost and forgotten in Britain now. Pigs' heads are hard to come by, but if you are lucky enough to find one and are not too squeamish to deal with it, the results are wonderful. With some refinements on Tudor methods, they can be transformed into brawn, fromage de tête or galantine de porc and make a delicious addition to a cold lunch. Bath chaps are equally rare and very few people bother to salt a leg or belly of pork for jambon de Paris or petit salé any more. Fortunately, in France the tradition continues. How could there be cassoulet or garbure without confit of duck, goose or pork? What would all we tourists do without our confit de canard et frites?

But do people have larders in Britain any more?

AUTUMN MELANCHOLY

Relentless wind and rain have battered October. Even today's crisp sunlight illuminating a transparent clear blue sky does little to lift my perennial autumn melancholy. It evokes memories of childhood solitariness and isolation, of boarding school at seven, of a strangely emptying world. I hate dark mornings, afternoon shopping by streetlight, grey foggy days and the knowledge that it will only get colder! Most people struggle with ice-cold January and February but for me November is the low spot of the year. I yearn for those first snowdrops on Boxing Day, dear mild Devon, to lift my spirits once more and carry me on towards spring.

And this week it is not helped by sick animals. How strange it is that days, weeks, months, years even, go by and everyone is in rude health, then suddenly a wave of misfortune. A recent visit from Richard, my vet, saw an orderly queue forming in the yard. First up was my little donkey, Friday, whose whole body is working overtime to reject the massive sarcoid on his throat. How fortunate I was that the Donkey Sanctuary agreed to take him, together with his mother, into the veterinary hospital for two months in the summer. He received the best possible state-of-the-art treatment while providing them with a useful research model. He was even fortunate enough to be examined by the guru of the equine veterinary world who visited the sanctuary to lecture to overseas vets – lucky little Friday. Now we wait to see the outcome of all that care and research.

Next, the oldest donkey, Sweep, had her teeth rasped, an undignified procedure for one of such advanced years but by allowing, all be it somewhat reluctantly, the equine dentist to file her teeth, it will help her manage her winter forage in the lean months ahead. It was ten years ago that Richard shook his head and advised me to get a companion for Dandy as Sweep was clearly reaching the end of her days. Now he just laughs in amazement as the old donkey wobbles off happily into the field to join the others.

And finally, it was Dog's turn; we discussed Wellie's fear of loud noises, which is making her so anxious she tries to chew her way out of everywhere and everything. What is going on in the doggy brain? Then a second look at dear old Truffle, my twelve-year-old Labrador, who had a stroke on Monday. So maybe it's not just my autumn sadness after all.

The garden cheers me up. If I'm not careful it begins to look like one huge fruit salad once more. Apples carpet the grass faster than I can gather them into sacks. Originally there were two orchards here. Many of the old trees in the east-facing cider orchard, planted so long ago, and in those bygone days such an important part of the farm economy, needed replacing. Extraordinary as it sounds to us today, farm workers were paid in part with cider.

A few years ago, with the help of a matching grant from the local Council, we renovated and extended it, replanting with old varieties. This year we have fruit for the first time, so exciting. Opposite, facing southwest is the remains of the culinary orchard, which, we're told, used to belong to our house. Now only rough woodland remains, with just a few remaining apple trees – one or two dessert varieties and a cooker or two. It's so wild and overgrown it is impossible to reach. Maybe one day we will be able to buy it back and restore it to its former glory.

Apple orchards are disappearing at a staggering rate everywhere. Ninety per cent of Devon orchards have vanished since 1945. Kent has lost eighty-five per cent in the last fifty years. In 1883 Herefordshire had approximately 27,000 acres of orchard, now the whole of England has a mere 44,000 altogether. And thanks to the new Single Payment Scheme even more are being grubbed up as I write.

Although the scheme purports to be 'designed to give extra protection to the environment, soil, wildlife habitats and landscape...' it goes on to say that 'land used for permanent crops including orchards cannot be used to support claims'. It may just be possible to get around this one if sheep graze beneath the trees but that's of little consolation to commercial growers. As land is not eligible for a subsidy its value plummets and it is difficult to sell. Out come the orchards.

Nothing changes. I am reminded of the words of Bernard Palissy, *c*.1510–*c*.1589, a natural philosopher and man of a wonderfully quick and acute mind: 'There is no art in the world to which a grand philosophy is more necessary than to agriculture, and to approach agriculture without philosophy is to degrade the land and its produce, and indeed I marvel that the land and its natural products do not cry out for vengeance against those ignorant and ungrateful folk who do nothing but spoil and squander trees and plants without consideration...the acts of ignorance I see daily in agriculture frequently torment my mind...'

These sentiments were bluntly reiterated by Swift in the eighteenth century: 'whoever could make two ears of corn or two blades of grass grow upon a spot of ground where only one grew before, would deserve better of mankind...than the whole race of politicians put together.' Only this morning I heard the Prince of Wales talking in a similar vein, lamenting the loss of family farms and century-old traditions, skill and husbandry thrown out for profit and mass production. *Toujours la même chose.*

How few old English apples are available in the shops now. It seems to be cheaper for supermarkets to import apples from all over the world all year round than source UK crops in September and October. Where have all the old varieties gone? And what has happened to ones we know and love? Where are the Cox's Orange Pippins of 1825, the Worcester Pearmain of my childhood? The modern versions seem to have lost their character completely and become a bland parody of their former selves. In fact, most apples seem to taste exactly the same as one another now, sort of apply flavoured water. It is so good to be able to pick some of the weird and wonderful old varieties still growing in our orchard. Beware the cider apples though. They look ruby red or goldenly enticing, but one big greedy bite is followed by a very dry mouth! Oh, how bitter and sour; perhaps it was a cider apple that Eve bit into all those millennia ago in that Garden.

So now it's time to take a trip to a local nursery to find some wonderful old Devon varieties; time to restock the old orchard. Devonshire Quarrenden maybe, a tiny red Tudor apple, or Pig's Snout or Paignton Marigold, Sour Bay, Spotted Dick or Sops in Wine. The very names cheer me up.

NORMANDY PHEASANT WITH APPLES, OF COURSE!

This, without doubt, is one of my favourite pheasant recipes and is ideal for oven-ready birds that have been commercially prepared. Pheasant like beef is better if it has been properly hung. If it is not it is inclined to be dry and dull when roasted. Apples and Calvados prevent the meat becoming dry and complement the flavour wonderfully.

I brown a brace of pheasants in melted butter in a heavy-based frying pan then set them aside on a plate. Then I melt more butter in the pan and fry 1kg of peeled and chopped apples until golden. A sweet apple is best, such as Cox or Renette. The two birds will go snugly into a casserole, breast-side-down, on a thick layer of the apple with the remaining apple packed all round. I pour on about 125ml of crème fraîche and cook gently for about an hour at 180°C checking after 40 minutes or so. After about an hour I take them from the oven, increase the heat to 230°C and pour over more crème fraîche with 4 tablespoons of Calvados. Back into the oven for 5 minutes, then I leave to rest while I finish the vegetables. As I say all meat rested for a while will be easier to carve.

APPLE, CABBAGE AND GINGER SOUP

Fresh, spicy and delicious this is another great way to use up a few windfalls and a bit of cabbage. But, a big but, it's essential to have some good strong chicken stock to back up the flavour.

I shred half a large white cabbage and chop two or three onions and a few green apples. I turn them over in melted butter, then put a lid on the pan and sweat for about 10 minutes until soft but not brown. Next, in goes a clove of garlic crushed with salt, a small piece of finely chopped fresh ginger and 1 litre of chicken stock (…made from that carcass I was about to throw away…). I simmer for a few more minutes until the cabbage is tender, then blend, reheat, taste, season and serve. Very quick and very nice!

NO MORE TURKEYS

No turkey chorus in the farmyard this year: all is eerily quiet. No turkeys or table birds for the first time in ten years. We finally made the decision to stop rearing both Christmas turkeys and year-round chickens. So, as a turkey-free Christmas approaches, I find my heart filled with so many mixed emotions.

Can I have forgotten already those December sleepless nights, tossing and turning at 2 a.m. wading through the orders again and again in my head, adrenalin rushing, hands aching: Will I have enough small ones? Will I have enough huge ones? If I give a fifteen pounder to the Smiths, I could give that monster bird to the Joneses. Would they notice it was bigger than their order? Oh, will everyone go home on Christmas Eve with the perfect turkey for their own very special family ritual. Finally, I would fall into a troubled sleep.

No ringing phone, no order book, no worries that Mrs So and So has forgotten to order, or worse still, thinks she doesn't have to because 'I always get my bird from you...' I'm not bad at mindreading but not that good! And Mrs X has already telephoned twice to see how her turkey is getting on. When I say it's doing fine, she's horrified to think it's actually alive!

Last year we closed the turkey shed forever on Christmas Eve. All killed, all drawn, all trussed, all packed and, hoorah, all delivered for the last time. Relief and regret filled my heart: I loved it, I hated it – the buzz of it, the being at the hub of it, the worry, the exhaustion, the relief as I saw the last smiling customer depart, the marvellous phone calls after Christmas. So many memories. Do I really miss all that? 'Where will we get our bird from this year?' I'm asked over and over again. It is so nice to be missed but it is so good to have a turkey-free holiday at last.

When our neighbour retired the supply of wonderful chickens dried up: free-range, fat ones raised without masses of chemicals. What was his secret I wondered. 'Well, let's have a go,' said Paul. 'Let's try a few turkeys first for Christmas and see how we get on.' So, we bought our first few turkey poults little knowing where it would take us. We raised them in one of the big sheds and processed them in another. We had no idea how or if we would sell them. We just offered them to our friends and enjoyed one for ourselves.

'Can we have a turkey next year too?' We bought more turkey poults, then some day-old chicks. We raised the table birds and fed them to our friends when they came to supper. Gradually people began to ask for them and the whole thing suddenly took off. Next thing I knew Paul was rebuilding the shed into a specialised unit and I was learning all the regulations. We had visits from Environmental Health, Trading Standards, MAFF then, DEFRA now, the Department for Environment, Food and Rural Affairs, and, of course, Meat Hygiene. Paul went on training courses to get his slaughterman licence and I delved into my culinary past to remember how to draw and truss birds. Our little old refrigerated van buzzed round the Devon lanes to all our wonderful loyal customers. I never dreamed that such a world existed.

ROAST LAMB

No turkey for us this Christmas!

Instead, we will have our own Whiteface Dartmoor hogget.

Traditionally most cookery books say to roast a leg, loin or shoulder of lamb for 20 minutes to 1lb, a little longer if you like it well done, but I prefer to sprinkle the joint with a little olive oil, coarse salt, crushed garlic and rosemary and start it in a very hot oven (230°C) for the first 20 minutes. Then I reduce the heat to 190°C, and finish the cooking at approximately 30 minutes to 1lb. I have a Range so I simply move it to the lower oven. This way the meat cooks more gently and stays succulent and slightly pink in the centre.

When it is cooked, I put it onto a serving dish and let it rest for 15 minutes; as I always say, this makes it so much easier to carve.

A shoulder is very good browned in oil then cooked in a slow oven for about 2 hours in a covered pot on a bed of peeled potatoes, a little stock, crushed garlic, chopped onion, salt and pepper. Sometimes I leave out the potatoes and halfway through cooking, I add chopped tomatoes, onion, aubergine, green olives, garlic, salt and pepper instead.

I love this little Victorian rhyme, 'Vicarage Mutton', for a week of suppers!

'Hot on Sunday
Cold on Monday
Hashed on Tuesday
Minced on Wednesday
Curried Thursday
Broth on Friday
Cottage Pie Saturday'

SNOW ON THE WAY!

It's beef stew and dumpling weather, Lancashire hotpot, chicken pie weather, comforting food weather. The week has been clear, sugary, crispy, crunchy and cold, cold, cold. As the sun appeared slowly over the hill the grass began to steam and boil. Gradually the land turned green again but now it's cold and damp and getting worse! Snow forecast for tomorrow, so unusual here, and freezing fog and dark, dank days. And now suddenly it's just a little warmer and the sky has taken on that certain ominous, pinkie yellowy tinge we so rarely see in South Devon: time to hunker down, fill the stables with straw, feed the sheep on the hill and prepare for the freeze.

Junior has done his job; ewes with bright pink tup marks on their backs graze contentedly, a sure prophecy of lambing in the spring. Scruffy has blossomed and, despite his early trauma and slightly strange looks, is being quite a gigolo among the older Jacob cross ladies up the hill.

Friday's sarcoid has come off at last and the wound is slowly healing, Sweep has been caught eating the new hay so her ordeal at the dentist was worthwhile. And Dandy's foot abscess has finally gone. Truffle shows no sign of her recent stroke and Wellie is calming down. Oh, and the ram lamb attacked by crows is out in the field again. What a bad animal month we have had.

And now the snow has arrived. Oh boy has it snowed! And the West Country, not used to these conditions, is in chaos. A trip across the Moor to collect food for our chickens turned into a slippery slidey six-hour nightmare. And we're the lucky ones; many people are still stuck in freezing conditions waiting for the helicopters to rescue them. Climate change and the reality of global warming is unfolding around us right here, right under our noses.

OLD-FASHIONED BEEF STEW AND DUMPLINGS

A warming supper is called for in this freezing weather, one that will cook slowly in the oven while we tend the animals. To make a quick beef stew with dumplings I first cut up 500g of braising beef, chuck steak or shin of beef, into large squares and dust it with flour. In a heavy-based frying pan, I heat olive oil and soften two large sliced onions. When they are just beginning to brown, I transfer them to a casserole dish and start to fry the meat quickly in batches, giving the pan time to heat up between each batch. The meat then goes into the casserole with the onions together with 500g carrots cut into sticks, salt and freshly ground black pepper and a bouquet garni made up of a bay leaf, and two or three sprigs of parsley and thyme.

I sprinkle a spoonful of flour into the frying pan and deglaze with 750ml of stock or 300ml of water and 450ml of stout. Once it has come to the boil, I pour it over the meat, put on the lid of the casserole pot and cook for about 2 hours in a preheated oven preheated to 170°C until the meat is tender.

To make the dumplings I sift 100g of self-raising flour and mix with ½ teaspoon baking powder, ½ teaspoon of salt, 50g of shredded suet and 2 tablespoons of chopped parsley. I add enough water to make a sticky dough. On a floured board, I roll the dough into small balls. When the meat is nearly cooked the dumplings go into the pot on top of the stew and cook for another 30 minutes until they are double the size and cooked right through. It helps to baste them a couple of times during cooking. When all in the farmyard are fed and safe for the night we will eat this warming stew with a crisp green salad.

This is the basic principle for all stews and ragouts. I ring the changes with my choice of vegetables, herbs and liquid. For example, if I add red wine, garlic, bacon, tomatoes and orange rind it will turn it into a French Daube. Juniper berries, peppercorns, Parma ham and white wine will make an Italian Stracotto. Kidneys, mushrooms and oysters will bring me back to Britain with Steak and Kidney and Oyster Pie or Pudding.

JANUARY AGAIN!

January days are so short, so grey, so cold. Well, not really so cold I suppose, after all this is South Devon, not the Highlands of Scotland! But sharp, dark and sad, frosty, wet, slow and oh, so heavy. It all seems such hard work in the deep sticky mud at this time of year. We climb out of bed and struggle reluctantly out of the house, tramping up to the yard in the dark dreaming of sunshine, lambs, fresh grass and spring. Not long to dream now, snowdrops are beginning to take hold, but it is much colder than usual this year, which means so much more feeding both morning and evening.

Eeyores fill the valley as hungry donkeys protest about the lack of grass. But not for long; I have a fine new system for moving hay and straw. An old bathtub, gifted by a friend, now acts as a trough, which is much easier for the donkeys to reach than the old hayrack. We have placed it in the big shed and now, with the aid of a large builders' dumpy bag, I can drag large quantities of hay and straw across the yard to them with ease. They are ecstatic, well I think so, but maybe enigmatic would be more accurate! Full, any way! I'm certainly happier; it's so much lighter than the wheelbarrow.

And there is another very strange new development: bantam hens are hiding away and sitting on eggs – most unusual in January! They keep appearing suddenly from some secret corner with a crocodile of tiny chicks rushing behind them desperately trying to keep warm. It is quite the wrong time of year for their arrival and many perish despite my best efforts. I have small crèches with lamps or heaters in all sorts of corners of sheds. Once hatched I cannot bear to see them die! Of course, I will shortly be overrun with a small black, feathered army, far too many cockerels and quantities of tiny unmarketable eggs! I cannot understand why hens are sitting in mid-winter.

As the dogs and I take our usual turn across the hill to check the sheep, ewes follow asking for more food. Some bold old timers even come right up to me nudgingly, saying, 'Come on, we're in lamb, you know how hungry we get.' Up we go again each evening to top up with haylage and beet shreds. Oh, when will the grass begin to grow again? Phil's sheep stare at me over the gate just the same. 'He's on his way,' I say to comfort myself!

There are visiting rams to feed too. As a result of the devastating foot-and-mouth outbreak that ravaged flocks and herds across the country a few years ago, the Rare Breeds Survival Trust has launched a regeneration appeal. The government's National Scrapie Plan has made this even more urgent. All rams are being compulsorily tested for scrapie and categorised. About 40 per cent of all rams in our breed fall into Groups 4 and 5 and must be slaughtered by next year in a bid to eradicate scrapie from the national flock, thus depleting the breeding stock even more dramatically. Scrapie, of course, has been in sheep since time began. It is only since the recent bovine spongiform encephalopathy (BSE) outbreak caused by the now illegal feeding of animal remains to herbivorous cattle that this anxiety has been aroused.

Our Junior is thankfully a Group 3 fellow so, although an old ram, he has been selected to donate his sperm for posterity. He, together with a beautiful ram from North Devon and a handsome chap from Dartmoor, will travel north on Friday to ensure the future of the breed. Both visiting rams have lodged here for a while because of the government six-day movement rule. Six days must pass between any movement of any animal on any farm. Another foot-and-mouth safeguard. Images of those awful days still haunt all of us who farm, so any precaution is welcome.

Gradually we work our way through the list of winter tasks: new fencing here, a hedge planted there. Plans for a pond are taking shape and, of course, the lambing shed is being prepared once again. Soon it will be spring.

Meanwhile, I paint the house and dream up comforting meals to shut out the biting north wind. Not for me the post-Christmas frugal fare; much too much physical work for that! Having said that, a high-fibre diet, low in fat with lots of our own fresh vegetables and fruit and plenty of protein keeps us pretty healthy all year round. A high-energy diet is what we need!

I am amazed, as I run through my large collection of old cookery books, how our eating habits have changed over the years. The menus of thirty, forty, fifty years ago sound so heavy now; even during those frugal years of rationing in the 1940s and 1950s and daunting childhood memories of school food! And then suddenly everything began to change with the food revolution of the 1960s and the indelible mark of Elizabeth David on our diet.

We have two hoggs coming back from the butcher on Monday. Maybe that is why my mind drifts back to those old books. Mutton is not on the menu very often now and has definitely fallen from grace until a very recent revival. I think of mutton chops and Lancashire Hotpot. How the methods vary. Years ago, Dorothy Hartley floured and browned her mutton chops before standing them on end in an earthenware pot. In went an onion per chop, large pieces of carrot, then some oysters. The lot was covered first with sliced potato, overlapping like tiles on the roof, then on went a thick, and to my taste, rather heavy gravy with flour, boiling water and the fat from the fried meat. To this we must add salt, pepper and a sprinkling of sugar. No, no, I say! Next in goes a dash of Yorkshire relish or anchovy essence. All this is poured over the meat and vegetables and the whole is covered with a lid and baked 'with a good fire' for 2 hours. Probably not entirely to our taste today!

Mrs Beeton fries nothing but simply layers meat and vegetables in a fireproof baking dish; no oysters here, just water, salt and pepper. The lid is removed 20 minutes before the end of cooking to crisp the potatoes. Constance Spry favours the oysters, mushrooms and a good stock. She covers the pot with greaseproof paper instead of a lid, removing it some 20 minutes before the end of cooking to crisp and brown the potatoes. No mention, of course, of such a dish from Elizabeth David. Her mission was to encourage us to look beyond our shores. I suspect a tour of Lancashire itself would bring as many, maybe more, variations. So, I'll steer a course through the middle, probably leaving out the oysters and cooking everything a day in advance, cooling overnight and removing the fat from the top before reheating.

FEBRUARY, THE CULLING FIELD...

No grass, no rain, just cold grey days; even the snowdrops are reluctant to show their little green petticoats. As I look back to this time last year, I find talk of camellias, daffodils and singing crocuses; no sign of any of them showing their face this cold, dark February. In fact, as I look out beyond my desk the cloud seems to be sitting over the whole valley, topping the trees with a thin grey veil. And still, we wait for rain.

My mind has been on chicken problems recently, not avian flu, I'll cross that bridge if I have to, if I must, when I have to; all necessary registration in place, etc. No, it's more to do with cockerels, cockerels, cockerels. They are taking over the yard! Fierce little men squaring up to one another ready to take on the world regardless of size. Sound familiar? They sidle up, fluff out their feathers to look as big as they can and launch themselves at one another in fiercesome battle. Their ferocity is appalling, injuries horrific, something has to be done.

So, with great reluctance and some sadness because they are all, without exception, such handsome birds, we must round them up for a cull. Not a pleasant job at all, but essential to avoid a blood and feather bath. The two big Maran boys are reprieved as are the two Araucana fellows. I couldn't let Mr White go either or that little Maran bantam boy and, oh, perhaps we should keep just one of the Minorcas. Of course, that means creating separate dwelling places, international boundaries, for them all!

The Maran boys live with the regular chickens, some two hundred and fifty little free-range 'orange egg machines'. Both cockerels seem to have a code in their house by night and in the fields by day, enabling them to pretend the other simply doesn't exist – enough space I suppose. Mr Lavender lives with the few Araucana ladies who survived last year's badger attack. Miss Winedott lives there too. She's happier away from those huge bossy Maran women who push her about and stop her feeding. Those same big women can stay with old Mr Araucana, together with the Light Sussex lady and that sort of Wellsommer hen. That leaves the Arucauana bantams and their cockerel in the Ark, Mr White and his Minorcan girls in the stable, Mr Minorca and his ladies in the sheep shed and, oh dear, still too many, Mr Bantam Maran in the field shed with his really beautiful harem of mixed up Minorca bantams. And I thought I'd rationalised and simplified by sending some fourteen cockerels to their heavenly maker and cock au vin!

So, of course, that inevitably takes my mind to the culinary end of the scale. What to do with all those eggs again? More pickling, I suppose. It's funny how each year our retail outlets cry out for eggs in November, December and at Christmas time, when the tourist trade lurches briefly into gear again before the winter hibernation. Chickens say, 'No thanks, give us a break, it's dark out there.' No eggs, many visitors. Then the light creeps back, the evenings begin to draw out just a little, the chickens perk up and start laying. 'Oh, no, not now,' say our customers, 'really quiet at this time of year, no visitors.' Hotels close for a breather; pubs rely on the locals. No one wants an egg! So pickled eggs it is again. Eggy gifts to friends, donations to anyone; anything rather than waste. Then suddenly it's spring, Easter, the new season and everyone is clamouring for free-range eggs once more.

I confit'ed an old cockerel a while back; delicious he was too! Others turned up in a terrine de campagne for guests at Christmas. No one knew, just said 'what delicious pâté', well it was! But these chaps will, I think, be the classic Coq au Vin.

Hmm, but what on earth is 'Classic Coq au Vin'? *Larousse Gastronomique* dispatches it in one brief paragraph. Constance Spry doesn't give it a mention; only Hugh Fearnley-Whittingstall does it proud, of course. But I, as usual, return to my dog-eared ancient copy of Elizabeth David's *French Provincial Cooking* where she reiterates once more that however apparently simple this classic appears, to get the balance right is a real skill: sauce just the right consistency and chicken perfectly cooked. Maybe this is why it has fallen from grace for far too long: too many nasty stringy chickens in thick pink goo...and where on earth do you get a cockerel? Well you know that now! But, oh, how delicious it is if you can get the balance right.

COQ AU VIN

This is my version. First, I warm about three-quarters of a bottle of red wine in a saucepan together with a crushed garlic clove, a bay leaf and a pinch of dried herbs before adding a little really good chicken stock. In another heavy-based pan, I soften a handful of peeled button onions in the fat, which gently flows from some chopped streaky bacon. I cut the cockerel or chicken into four pieces and add them to the pan to brown gently. Next, I set alight a ladle of brandy and pour, flaming, over the chicken. The wine and stock go in next as the brandy flames die down. I simmer gently for about 40 minutes depending on the age of the chicken. When I'm confident the cooking is almost complete, I add button mushrooms and simmer for a further 5 minutes.

I carefully remove the chicken, onions and mushrooms into a large serving dish and keep warm while I thicken the sauce with a beurre manié, that is to say, 1 tablespoon of flour worked into 1 dessertspoon of butter. I stir it gently into the sauce until it is thick and shiny, and continue to stir for a minute or two until the flour is cooked. We eat it with a salad and maybe some fried bread, so unfashionable, and oh, so wonderful!

JUST DONKEYS

'Sal, she's gone, you don't have to ring the vet.' A rush of grief and relief flooded through me. I knew it was inevitable. I had hoped so fervently that she would leave without help. How could I have doubted her; such a wise, self-contained, private old donkey – she knew her time was up. The change in her was so subtle just two days before she died. I was planning to ring my friend and donkey companion, Briony, and say, 'Come and see old Sweep; I think it's time for her to go.' But Briony has a sixth sense about animals and just appeared on Wednesday evening. She took one look at the little figure in the stable and said goodbye, her eyes brimming with tears.

All donkeys went into the stables as usual for tea. Sweep ate two helpings then quietly lay down and left us in the night. Dear old donkey, she must have been well over forty. When she came to live with us twelve years ago my vet shook his head and suggested I look for another donkey to keep Dandy company.

I took his advice and soon two donkeys became six! Why? Well, it was like this…

Way back my grandmother let her two meadows near Reading to a Miss Green who looked after donkeys for an elderly lady called Miss Philpin. There were six in all. Bill, charming to your face but quite prepared to bite any bottom as soon as a back was turned and Bluebell, a gentle grey and others whose names I don't remember. But, then of course, there was Treacle.

Many years ago, when our children were small, we lived in Granny's converted stables at the bottom of her drive. One night when I was alone with two small children – Paul was away sailing to Ireland – the doorbell rang. It was 2 a.m. I ran down stairs in my nightdress and spotted the blue and white hatband through the glass front door. My stomach lurched, a storm, a shipwreck, a young widow, alone to bring up the children; my mind raced. I opened the door to a grinning young policeman. 'Can you identify this donkey, madam?' Tears of relief, laughter all mixed up, I looked past him at a very small scruffy hunchbacked donkey, so like old Sweep. 'Yes,' I said, 'that's Treacle. He used to live here but recently went to live with a pony up the road.'

'Well, we found him coming home,' said the copper. Treacle had brought his new companion back to his old home, to his old friends. I fell in love with donkeys.

When Miss Philpin died Treacle, and some 203 other donkeys she had rescued, went west to Sidmouth: a huge donkey legacy left to Dr Elisabeth Svendsen, founder of the now famous Donkey Sanctuary. In her book *For Love of Donkeys* Dr Svendsen mentions Treacle who, despite his diminutive size, became known as 'The Boss' of the 'Big Boys' Group' at Brookfield Farm.

It wasn't until many years later, by now living in Devon, that my turn came. One day I saw a small ad in *Smallholders News* asking for a home for two donkeys. We drove east with our new sheep trailer and loaded up two sad little creatures. Feeling at once anxious and not a little foolhardy, I remember wondering about future vets' bills as we trundled home. Dandy, we were told, was about twenty-two and had been with the same family since he was two. Sweep, much older, came free with Dan, a sort of early 'buy one, get one free'. She was thought to have been an unlicensed beach donkey from North Devon at some time, but no one knew for sure. Both donkeys looked so thin, lice ridden and dejected.

We hurriedly converted an old bullock shed into a stable, bought fresh hay and shampooed frequently to kill all bugs and clear the mange. Spring came, the grass grew, tatty winter coats vanished and suddenly they were transformed into sleek round little donkeys.

Sweep had a strange groove in her neck and never managed to lift her head properly. My vet thought that at some time she had been tightly tethered and the groove was the scar of a rope burn. But as she grew fitter and more cheerful it caused her no problem. We just remembered to put the hay on the ground for her. She was incredibly greedy and would shove us all in the back of the knees if she felt we were a little slow at teatime.

The addiction had taken hold by now and in no time I found the terrible naughty Nutmeg up the road at a local leisure park. She is a beautiful dark brown mare. She simply knows she's beautiful and has all the diva qualities to go with her good looks. Dandy, a gelding fortunately, fell slightly in love with her. Sweep simply pretended he didn't exist.

Some months later I noticed Nutmeg was 'bagging up'. I rang the previous owner and learned that she had indeed been running with a stallion: unfortunately, her own sire, hardly ideal. Another stable was quickly built and on Good Friday, 'Friday' was born. His night-time arrival was as silent as Sweep's departure.

Despite being a small, frail, interbred little chap, he grew into a fine-looking donkey like his mother, but with a much gentler temperament. However, I am absolutely indebted to the Donkey Sanctuary for his continued survival. They have taken mother and child into their wonderful veterinary clinic three times in the last eight years. My vet says he has a very poor immune system due to that interbreeding; he has one problem after another. I doubt he'll reach Sweep's extreme old age but right now he's fit and happy.

Bunty and Luke arrived next and are known here as the Lodgers or more accurately foster donkeys from the Donkey Sanctuary, my only way to thank the Sanctuary for all their care and kindness. Luke, a large gentle, obese grey, comes from Skegness. His previous owners send him a Christmas card every year, which he eats if given a chance. He sends one back with news of his life in Devon and companion donkeys. Bunty is a strawberry roan with Eire on her notes. Even after all these years she still hates having her ears touched; I guess they were cruelly twisted sometime in the past. She too has a rather strange figure, covered in lumps and bumps of hardened fat, making her less than streamlined; but she is a quiet, gentle, sweet-natured little mare.

So now there are six!

Dandy, the most sociable of all the donkeys, went for his Equity card recently. He has starred patiently in Nativity plays, standing for an hour or so, while minute angels sat on his back and diminutive shepherds stroked his head and stuck their fingers up his nose. He processed to church on Easter Sunday with a gloomy looking Sweep in tow. He adores children and, when younger, was happiest when he was giving rides on the 'Ham', our village green, on Village Day. Even now he nuzzles grandchildren and stands quite still as they sit on his back and stroke his long, soft ears.

Right now, I have a close eye on him to make sure he is not grieving for Sweep. Donkeys often go into shock when they lose a companion and fall victim to the fatal hyperlipaemia. Dan was in the stable with her when she died and next morning we made sure all the donkeys had a chance to see her. They came one by one into the stable, sniffed her, stood for a while and then went off to eat some hay. They needed to know that Sweep had left them. In the wild they live in small social groups and look out for one another. I won't forget the day Sweep trapped her leg in a rat hole and the others shouted and shouted until I arrived to dig her free.

Dear little donkey: I miss her.

TORTILLA

After a sad day a quick comforting supper was needed. I looked in the fridge.

There I found three cooked new potatoes, six tiny tomatoes, a couple of rashers of streaky bacon, a wrinkly red pepper, two shallots, a scrap of good Cheddar, a Jerusalem artichoke and a small bag of last summer's frozen spinach from the garden! The chickens are laying well again as the light increases, so eggs are plentiful once more. It had to be tortilla.

I soften the chopped shallots in a little olive oil in my big old cast-iron frying pan that goes safely into the oven. Then I add the bacon and the rest of the chopped vegetables, stirring over a gentle heat until they just began to soften. I take the pan off the heat while I beat six eggs with a splash of water and a good pinch of salt and black pepper. Then, putting the pan back on the heat, I melt a knob of butter and pour in the eggs. I grate the cheese on top and put the pan into a moderate oven until the eggs set and the cheese melted. It rose magically like a soufflé. We ate quickly with crusty bread and watercress; just what was needed, comforting and delicious.

Comfort food is what is needed on occasions like this. Dear friends to supper on the next freezing March evening helped to lift my spirits. Old-fashioned Steak and Kidney Pie and a Hazelnut Meringue Cake seemed to fit the bill, as well as keep me occupied.

I always cook the steak and kidney filling first, then make up the pie. For this I brown 500g of diced beef skirt or chuck steak in hot oil, then remove from the pan into a heavy casserole pot. I brown the chopped ox kidney, having made sure all sinew has been removed. The kidney goes in with the beef. Next, I heat a little more oil and soften three fat finely chopped shallots, add a piece of celery, a few chopped parsley stalks and a couple of rashers of streaky bacon. All these add to the depth of flavour of the finished pie. I sprinkle 1 tablespoon of flour into the pan, give it a stir and add a spoonful of tomato purée, red wine and homemade stock. As it comes to the boil, stirring briskly, I deglaze the pan, then simmer for a few minutes, pour over the meat, add a bay leaf, cover the pot and place in a moderate oven. I let it cook gently, stirring once or twice, for two and a half hours. Cooking time will vary according to the quality of the beef. Don't be tempted to boil hard; this will only toughen the meat. While it's cooking, I slice 350g of flat mushrooms and fry quickly in oil and a little butter.

When it has cooled a little, I put the steak and kidney and the mushrooms into a pie dish, filling to the brim. I have a little old pie funnel that I put into the centre to let out the steam. Meanwhile, you can, if you like, make the flaky pastry if you're really dedicated. I don't! I buy ready-made and enhance it with some extra butter; cheating I know, but so much quicker and really very effective. Simply roll out the pastry into a long strip, butter the centre section, fold one-third to the centre, butter again and fold again. Now roll out for the pie topping and as you do so, the extra butter will be spread throughout making a lighter flakier texture.

Next, I wet the edge of the pie dish and cut a strip of pastry to go around the edge of the dish, then I wet that too. I roll out the remainder to a little larger than the dish; make a cut in the centre of the pastry for the funnel and, using the back of the rolling pin, gently lift the pastry onto the pie, lower it carefully onto the damp edging strip, being careful not to stretch it.

I press down round the edge and, holding a knife at ninety degrees, trim off the excess. Next, I seal the edges with the tines of a fork, or crimp with my finger and thumb. I decorate the pie with traditional pastry flowers and leaves and brush with beaten egg. In days gone by, when baking was done once a week, the savoury pies were identified in the larder by their decoration. I put the pie into the fridge until I need it. I will bake it in a hot oven until the pastry is crisp and golden, about 30–40 minutes, and serve it with boiled or mashed potatoes, buttery vegetables or a green salad.

RAIN AT LAST!

Rain at last; a sweet veil of soft weather glides sideways past my window enfolding the valley. The wind has suddenly swung round to the welcome familiar southwest, so much kinder than the swingeing north-easterly we've suffered for months. It brings with it the soft, salty, earthy smell of spring. I had forgotten how much I love it. Suddenly the daffodils, in limbo for so long, glow in the dampness, drinking in the welcome wetness softly landing on their upturned petals. Raindrops hang like skeins of tiny pearls on the rose bushes by the back door. At last, at last the air is damp, the earth turns dark chocolate again and the birds shout out for joy.

Fat ewes stand expectantly in Sunday Orchard, wool glistening as water dances on lanolin. Emerging insects flee marauding chickens. Like magic the fields turn green as grass begins to grow. The rain brings life back to the valley. It's been the bleakest, driest winter I can remember, day after day of icy, drying wind, black skies, dark days. How I love this returning sideways rain!

And then suddenly, as if celebrating the changing weather, lambing begins; fine Jacob triplets to an old timer, twins to a big strong Whiteface. More and more are born, night and morning. Tiny 'Fly' is not so lucky; his mother collapsed with exhaustion; his twin did not survive. So once again I am surrogate ewe, feeding him every four hours. He's a sturdy little fighter with a terrific will to live despite his minute size. I'm cautiously optimistic.

Lack of sleep dominates our lives as usual now; each day is dictated by the same rigid routine. At 6 a.m. it's up to the yard, check all ewes, pen new mothers with their lambs, spray umbilical cords, make sure lambs are feeding, feed ewes with shreds, hay and water. Feed Fly, tend to his mother, feed any ewes in the nursery. Let all remaining ewes into the field. Scrape yard, feed donkeys, let them out too for a while, rationing their intake of sugar-rich grass. Clean stables.

As the sun comes over the hill, open up the chickens, making sure all foxes and badgers have turned in for the day. Grade, stamp and box the eggs, then label and date each box ready for delivery. Wash all equipment. Wash the 'Clean Room' floor. Walk home across the top fields, over the hill to check the ewes and lambs gently grazing the new sweet grass. Home for breakfast.

Phone calls and paperwork follow, then back to the yard to feed Fly again. If it's not raining too hard, cup of coffee and into the garden digging and planting for the new season. If it's pouring with rain, then it's into the polytunnel. And so, it goes on until evening, when the ewes come in for tea, donkeys are fed and stabled and chickens shut up for the night. Relax briefly, a glass of wine, cook supper, eat quickly then back to feed Fly. Sit down until midnight then back to see who has started to lamb…eventually to bed. Life continues like this until the last lamb is born. I find it hard to remember that once I had another life in the city; feels like a bad dream disturbing brief sleep!

FLAMING JUNE

It's been the busiest of springs, no time to turn. We don't seem to have caught our breath since lambing. Three ewes slipped through the net and, just when we'd taken our eye off the ball, decided to give us five more lambs, thus successfully throwing all post-lambing plans into the air. Paul went for a wonderful sail on the beautiful old pilot cutter, *Jolie Brise*. Late lambs meant I stayed behind to man the fort. I prayed that I wouldn't need complicated midwifery skills in his absence. He had a wonderful time, ten knots in a force nine but, alas, returned in agony with a strained back and was unable to move for days! I remained in charge of the flock!

And then the badger made another unwanted visit. He gorged himself and, no doubt, fed his family too, on my Araucana chickens and numerous bantams. Handsome Mr Lavender and all his pretty girls became the banquet. I can only hope he ate so much he was sick! He secretly tore a huge hole in the back of the chicken house. Poor little birds were all trapped inside. I sat on the grass and cried. Then I remembered all the really dreadful things going on in the world and got on with my life... Some Araucana eggs hatched in the incubator. I pushed the remaining blue eggs under a broody Maran and then a Maroque lady appeared from some secret nest with six tiny children. So, on we go once more.

The very same day I learned I must relinquish my two dear donkeys, Friday and Nutmeg, to the Donkey Sanctuary where they will get the ongoing veterinary treatment they need for recurring sarcoids. I'm so fortunate to be able to hand them over to such expertise, but it's tough after nine years. Nutmeg was such a Prima Donna, such a beautiful Diva, when she arrived here. Within months she surprised herself, and me, by giving birth to the dear little Friday. A wayward teenager, she always looked to me like the one with the handbag and the white high heels who would go to the pub, or was it a rave, leaving the child neglected and alone. But I was wrong; despite being so young and beautiful and quite unready for maternal responsibility, she gradually adjusted to her role and mother and son became inseparable. I miss them both so very, very much.

And now the sun burns down on the valley as it explodes into colour. The borders are packed like a beach on Bank Holiday, everyone pushing and shoving to find room to turn their faces to the sun. The roses are wonderful; they seem to have thrived in the dry, cold winter and even survived the constant downpour that was called May. I've never had such a profusion of colour.

Sheep are shorn, thank goodness, and graze coolly with fat lambs on the top fields. Fly has grown but he's a lonely little chap still wanting bottles and company. Phil says hand-reared ram lambs turn into the most dangerous rams. 'Knock you down and get you in the kidneys,' he says. Phil would know, so young Fly is a testosterone-free wether now for our safety. I guess he won't care as long as he still gets attention.

The blackbird snuck into the polytunnel when my back was turned and feasted on strawberries but raspberries look promisingly out of his reach. Broad beans are covered in flowers and peas just romping away. Runners follow and sweet peas scent the whole vegetable garden. Tomatoes, of course, are out of control already – oh, lovely summer.

PICNICS

Picnics have been on my mind for some time recently, which surprises me because I usually hate them, rather in the same way that I hate barbecues, well, usually anyway. Rain, feel cold, uncomfortable, food full of grit, stodgy, burned sausages, charred raw chicken, beer, no wine, all bon amie, please can I go home now, oh so antisocial, me!

But it was my father's ninety-seventh birthday on Friday! Paul had the great idea of taking him a picnic. Dad was thrilled. Aunty Molly, ninety-nine in August, was invited. She and my father, first cousins, friends and playmates since childhood, are companions now, both still razor-sharp despite failing sight and hearing. Dad started planning the menu two weeks ago; each time I phoned he checked I had it right… 'Scottish smoked salmon with lemon and black pepper, not that River Dart stuff' and him a Devon boy! So sorry Dart salmon fisherman, we have now established some misinformation on his part! 'Avocados too, organic; they tend to taste less like soap I think, with good olive oil.'

'Ah, not that stuff from Boots then, Dad, you put in your ears?' I asked wickedly, thinking of my very unfoodie mother. 'Don't you remember, I lived in France, Lyon, 1927…' Ah yes, Dad, so you did, whoops, sorry.

Main course: Rare Roast Beef, our own Sussex boys raised on the farm. I'll probably be in trouble here too; it's not Aberdeen

Angus, but I'll risk it. Must have mustard. 'Horseradish?' 'No, and potato salad, Jersey Royals of course and a tomato salad, get English tomatoes, more flavour.'

'Yes, Dad.'

'And a nice green salad with a really good French dressing. Can you do that? And, if you can, make a big bottle and leave it with me.'

'Yes, Dad, yes, Dad.'

'Now, really crispy rolls, never get them here. I'll probably eat two. Molly likes them. Got all her own teeth, you know.' All her own teeth at ninety-nine, good heavens. 'And French Brie: must be French.'

Yes, yes, French Brie, Brie de Meaux, ripe and delicious from Simon's deli in Dartmouth. 'I know it's wrong, got into terrible trouble from a Frenchman once, but I do like butter and bread with my brie.'

'Yes, Dad.'

'Oh, and then we'll have strawberries. Can we have yours?'

'Um, no, sorry, that blackbird…'

'And Devonshire clotted cream.' Big hint here: Dad is a Devon boy and my husband, a Cornishman; ah, the ongoing clotted cream debate. I'll leave it there, I think.

The day came, the sun shone, we filed into the tiny, side dining room of their residential home. Oh joy, not on the lawn. I served the whole from my old ice box onto an elegantly laid table. They live in a beautiful place. Why is it that older people so often have to put up with dreary, depressing surroundings and yet here at the Old Vicarage at Otterton, all is uplifting? But that is a whole other story. I digress.

'Delicious,' said Dad, tucking in. 'I just wish I could see what it is I'm eating a little better though.'

'Yes,' agreed Molly, 'so annoying not knowing what's on your fork,' as all before her vanished.

'Hmm,' said Dad, ever the actor: RADA 1935! 'It's lovely, darling, but I'm reminded of Shakespeare's *Seven Ages of Man*: sans teeth, sans eyes, sans taste, sans everything.'

Later we sat together in the sun and drank coffee and I wondered if I had inherited the family gene. Would I be doing the same in nearly forty years' time?

RABBITS!

Rabbits have been on my mind rather a lot recently too: grey furry rabbits, large and fat, small and sweet. Peter Rabbit, Benjamin Bunny and my childhood favourite, Alison Uttley's Little Grey Rabbit: all of them, sisters and brothers, children and cousins, aunties, uncles, old ones, young ones, suddenly here they are invading this valley. Like night-time travellers, they have silently appeared. And now I watch them on the back lawn strutting across the grass in broad daylight. They take a rest, sit down fatly and stare boldly back at me. How long it will be, I wonder nervously, before they find the salad in the polytunnel and munch their way through the fattening pods of peas and beans. There are rabbits in the garden, in the orchard, in the quarry, in the fields, up and down the whole valley, rabbits everywhere. Where have they all suddenly come from, I wonder.

Rabbits, whole or dismembered, turn up in my kitchen. A crunching beneath the table reveals Fred, the big ginger cat, supplementing his already enormous diet with fresh meat. Dogs compete for leftovers, guests pale in distress. Mini, the ageing Cairn, so incensed to have a warm morsel removed from her jaws, took off past me yesterday, rabbit on her mind, and disappeared up the valley in seconds. It was only a message from a very irritated Parcelforce driver that led us eventually to find her, tired and confused and rabbitless way up in the old quarry. Oh rabbits!

Naturally my mind floats towards the culinary virtues of *Oryctolagus cuniculus*, the coney introduced to the UK in the twelfth century by the Normans, even then, to supplement our diet.

We all know that a rabbit is a furry animal that lives on plants and burrows in the ground, that it has its varieties as well as other animals, and that it is an especial favourite with children. Among its varieties, the short-legged, with width and substance of loin, is the hardiest, and fattens the most expeditiously. It has, besides, the soundest liver, rabbits generally being subject to defects of that part... Rabbits are divided into four kinds, distinguished as warreners, parkers, hedgehogs and sweethearts. The warrener, as his name implies, is a member of a subterranean community, and is less effeminate than his kindred who dwell upon the earth and have the world at their will, and his fur is the most esteemed. After him, comes the parker, whose favourite resort is a gentleman's pleasure-ground...the 'hedgehog' is a sort of vagabond rabbit, tinker-like he roams about the country and would have a much better coat on his back if he were more settled in his habits and remained more at home. The sweetheart is a tame rabbit, with its fur so soft, sleek and silky that it is also used to some extent in the important branch of hat making...the fruitfulness of this animal has been the subject of wonder to all naturalists...in the time of the Roman power, they once infested the Balearic Islands to such an extent that the inhabitants were obliged to implore the assistance of a military force from Augustus to exterminate them... And so on!

As I searched for recipes for cooking rabbit, stewed or baked, the example below took my eye and reminded me once more, to my relief, of how our eating habits have changed! This is probably *NOT* one to try!

No:1013 – Rabbit a la Minute

Ingredients – 1 rabbit, ¾ lb of butter, salt and pepper to taste, 2 blades of pounded mace, 3 dried mushrooms, 2 tablespoonsful of minced parsley, 2 teaspoonfuls of flour, 2 glasses of sherry, 1 pint of water.

Mode – Empty, skin, and wash the rabbit thoroughly, and cut it into joints. Put the butter into a stew pan with the pieces of rabbit; add salt, pepper and pounded mace, and let it cook until three-parts done; then put in the remaining ingredients, and *boil* for about 10 minutes; it will then be ready to serve. Fowls or hares may be dressed in the same manner.

Time – Altogether 35 minutes. Average cost, from 1s. to 1s 6d. each. Sufficient for 4 or 5 persons. Seasonable form September to February.

All my old cookery books list endless, to my mind, rather unappealing ways to cook rabbit.

For example: Number 34: Roast Rabbit, Braised turnips or carrots, baked potatoes followed by Apple Charlotte.

Regulo Setting 7. Time 1 Hour: The whole dinner is placed in the hot oven. It is cooked without any attention and is withdrawn at the end of the specified time, ready for serving.

Here are just two slightly more enticing ways in which I cook the occasional rabbit now!

Rillettes de Lapin: This is my version of a traditional rillettes recipe with rabbit replacing some of the pork. I cook the rabbit slowly with garlic, herbs and pork belly, then drain off the fat, first pound, then pull apart the meat with two forks, pile into an earthenware dish and completely cover with the carefully strained fat. I cover it all with foil and store in the fridge. We eat it with toast or crusty bread.

Sauce au Vin du Médoc: Rabbit stewed so slowly in red wine with beef and pork that it almost becomes a sauce. I chop six shallots and brown them in dripping, add three large carrots, cut into big pieces. Then in goes the meat, a jointed rabbit and 1½lb each of stewing beef and pork. I add garlic and herbs, sprinkle with flour, stir and pour over a bottle of red wine. I add a little water and a square of plain chocolate. I let it simmer for 3 hours, then let it cool completely and leave it in the fridge overnight. I simmer it once again the following day for a further 2 hours. We eat it with plenty of bread and maybe a mousseline of potatoes.

It is 'la grosse cuisine de la campagne' and is the perfect dish for cold winter days not – I stress, in the heatwave of today! *Bon appetite!*

FOOD, FAMILY, FRIENDS

Summer seems to have tumbled over itself in a hurly-burly holiday extravaganza. We revelled in a July heatwave and sailed in Bahamian sunshine to the white sand of Bryher on the Isles of Scilly. We walked on deserted beaches, sat silently on hilltops gazing out to sea. We were buffeted by wind and tide, spray soaked, searching for puffins and seals. We followed the sensational Island Gig race, shouting encouragement, egged on by the locals. We swam in crystal clear water watching tiny fishes scud beneath our toes. All was relaxation, warmth, wine, wonderful.

Then home and the tone was firmly set for the weeks to come – regattas, large and small, Red Arrows, fireworks, friends and family, birthdays, wedding anniversary, parties, sun, music, laughter, love and happiness. All quite exhausting actually!

After Bryher, the family arrived from Bath and Tokyo! Suddenly the house was humming with squeals and shrieks of laughter; five little children from three to eight raced round the garden playing happily despite language barriers. Funny, isn't it, how language doesn't matter when you're small.

We crabbed on the jetty, had picnics on the beach, paddled in streams and played cricket on Dartmoor, had supper at Dartington and suddenly they were gone. A deafening silence gripped the house. We sat down gloomily and stared at the emptiness.

Then the Bath brigade returned, hurrah; more lunches at the café, boat trips, beach and suppers in the evening sun. At last we celebrated forty years of marriage with, oh, so many of our dearest friends and family and suddenly autumn had arrived!

As summer fun drifts away behind us, it's back to business now. Sheep to sort out – who will stay and who must go. Old ewes that have had their day must be moved on. Difficult decisions, ones I always find so hard. Some of last year's wethers must go too and sadly the dreadful Scruff. He produced nice enough lambs but, alas, his temper is not all it might be. It bears out Farmer Phil's warning on the dangers of keeping rescued lambs entire. Hand-raised rams are not a good idea.

One young Whiteface ram, yet to be named, has already started work in the orchard with a harem of mature Jacob cross ladies and Junior is due home soon for his last season with us. He has been on loan to some Shropshire lasses up the road.

Hoggs must be booked into the abattoir, customers contacted and chickens 'rationalised'. Bantams are still running riot despite the badger's best efforts! Fields are being topped again, gates mended, fences repaired, hay and straw bought in. All the preparations for winter have suddenly begun.

Donkeys are coming in for tea now as the days shorten. Poor old Dan walks sadly into his stable alone after the death of his long-time companion, Sweep. Bunty and Luke have taken very quickly to Nutmeg and Friday's quarters while they are away at the Donkey Sanctuary veterinary hospital. I have a feeling the boys are fighting with just one female in their midst. But I do have a plan to find Dandy a new companion in the coming weeks. I still can't get used to just three donks instead of six. Oh, how I miss the naughty Nutmeg and Friday and the dear funny old Sweep.

And then of course there's 'Harvest'. Garden and fields are bursting with goodies again just waiting to be gathered. I have never seen such a year for wild bullace; the bushes are bent double, simply glistening with blue black fruit. I shall pick loads and treat them like hard, tart little damsons and make jam. The result is rich and dark but somewhat irksome to make because of all the tiny stones. Finally, I gave up with the mouli and simply rubbed them laboriously through a sieve – worth it though for the velvety, unctuous result.

Others, I will prick with a darning needle, pack into jars with sugar and cover with gin or vodka, to warm future Christmas guests.

Huge blackberries wink at me as I pass by yet again without a bowl. Hazelnuts hit me on the head in the farmyard reminding me of scrumptious praline and hazelnut meringue cake! Even the pear tree dying by the kitchen window is performing a spectacular swan song laden with jewel-like pears. The vegetable garden is beginning to look weather beaten and tatty but it still holds plenty of treats in store. Spinach, chard, late peas and potatoes are still to come. Quince ripen, beans still need picking, beetroots bulge from the soil. I've grown my best-ever sweetcorn this year too, great fat yellow batons so sweet and tender, delicious with butter or green, virgin olive oil.

Cucumbers have been amazingly prolific too but alas, tomatoes a complete disaster. No more 'Heritage' seeds for me! Back to my dear old gardening book *The Vegetable Garden Displayed* first published circa 1941, and old-fashioned 'trusty cultivars'. I love those little black-and-white photos!

Our 'Dittisham Plums' were brief but in abundance. Mildew sprang up on the fruit as it ripened, which turned harvesting them into something of a race. But I did manage a plum flan on quince custard, which was nice. The plum, orange and walnut jam is wonderful – a great alternative to marmalade. The orange and walnut seem to cut through the strong plum flavour and really lift it.

My fig tree has suddenly gone into overdrive producing more figs than even I can consume. I found a delicious recipe for Fig Conserve hidden away in my beloved Jane Grigson's *Fruit Book*. Simply cover the halved figs in half their weight of sugar and leave overnight. By morning the sugar has drawn the juice from the figs. Bring everything gently to the boil and immediately scoop out the figs into sterilised jars and boil down the syrup. A few walnuts and some lemon zest, added now, make it even more delicious! Pour the syrup, thick and sticky, over the fruit and cover in the normal way. I have a feeling a dollop of this figgy bliss on a warm croissant with a large cup of strong black coffee will cheer cold winter breakfasts!

FLOATING IN A MIST OF TIME...

This year really is a season of 'mist and mellow fruitfulness'. Early morning mist shrouds the valley, spider's webs glint in the sharp early morning light. The whole landscape has an ethereal, floaty-ness. Trees and shrubs seem to drift, disembodied down the hills. The dovecote has no earthly anchor.

I walk slowly up to the yard with Wellie, Meg and Min and wonder if old Truffy will make it all the way today. Sometimes she does, sometimes she doesn't. I let her choose these days. Occasionally she still manages a walk across the hills but I trail her on a long piece of baler twine; she is easily disorientated, wandering off and sitting patiently at the wrong gate, gazing in the wrong direction. Dear old dog, deaf and a bit wobbly too, she's still so happy and just as greedy as ever!

The morning mist suddenly clears as I clean the stables and chat to the donkeys. The sun burns through, revealing the world and reconnecting land and sky. Another day of warm autumn sun and showers begins. The grass is growing again at last, 'spring' grass full of sugar. For months the fields have been sad and brown and we've fretted about grazing. We've wondered just how soon we would have to start using up the winter feed to supplement the sheep's diet.

But October brought with it rain and we cheered to see the wet veil blowing sideways through the valley once more. We stood in the farmyard looking to the heavens and letting the welcome water soak our upturned faces. Everything seemed refreshed; chickens pecked through puddles, sheep shook the dust from their shorn bodies, donkeys let the water soak into their oil-free coats. Even old Humphrey the goose came out for a short swim, with a little help.

And then the sun returned: beautiful golden autumn days, unseasonably warm taking us gently towards winter. The final crops are harvested, preserved and stored for the cold empty months ahead. Apples must be sacked up, leaves raked away, tender plants housed safely before that first unexpected frost. And all the while the blue sky and sunshine seem to say 'no, not yet, you've still some time'.

I sit at my desk gazing out of my window at the huge monkey puzzle tree framed in blue sky and my mind begins to drift away. Harvest now, harvest then, the years roll round and round. Everything changes and nothing changes. My mind is full of images of the Holbein exhibition I visited this week at Tate Britain – of sixteenth-century faces that I still seem to meet every day in town even now.

As I re-read Thomas Tusser's *A Hundredth Good Points of Husbandrie*, I realised that while Holbein was doing his exquisite drawings for his portraits of King Henry's Court, while he ducked and weaved, recording all around him and managing to keep his head, Tusser was giving his good counsel to all and sundry, working through the seasons much as we do in the countryside today. City life is quite unrecognisable but country life still has many parallels. Man still hasn't yet managed to change the rhythm of the seasons although global warming is an ugly threat.

In September Tusser urges us to 'Geue winter corne leaue, for to haue full his lust: sowe wheate as thou mayst, but sowe rye in the dust'.

As I look across the valley, I see our neighbour's great tractor, traversing the chocolate soil and sowing winter corn on the hill. He is mobbed by a great cloud of seagulls shrieking harshly overhead.

Tusser tells me the 'sede being sowne' I must 'waterforow thy ground: that the rain that cometh may runne away round. The ditches kept skowered, the hedge clad with thorne: doth well to drain water, and saveth thy corne.'

Well, I can't argue with that either as, so often, I have watched the water flow down the hills into stream, river and sea, taking all before it. 'Then furth with thy slinges, and thine arowes & bowes: till ridges be grene, kepe the corne from the crowes Good boye abrode, by the day starre appeare: Shall skare good man crow, that he dares not come near.'

How Wellie and I hate our neighbour's automatic bird scarer! The shots ring out every twenty minutes ricocheting around the valley, echoing an ear-ripping crack as the sound waves bounce off the hills all around. And all because those crows are eating his twenty-first century winter corn!

In October Tusser urges us to gather fruit from the tree when the 'mone in the wane. The riper the better for grasse and for thee'. We must gather the firewood for the winter ahead, feed up our 'swine', and make sure we 'have done sowing wheate before halowmas eue'; not much change there either, good counsel indeed.

In this world of uncertainty and terrifying headlines, it feels increasingly important to hold on to a sense of connectedness with the natural world and an awareness of our tiny place in history. Very unfashionable, I know!

Which of course brings me to food, what else! Comfort eating as autumn closes round us and food for thought... Pigs, what is it about pigs? How I would love to keep pigs but I dare not. They're just so charming; I feel sure I'd have to give up eating bacon. But would I? Surely not; I eat my lambs, chickens too! Ducks are a dilemma though. But I digress!

LADIES-IN-WAITING

We seem to have tumbled into the New Year; it arrived with a great whoosh in every way, drama on all sides. As I sit here looking out of my window I'm wondering if the room will be blown clean off the side of the house. Such a storm is raging; trees are bending over at ninety degrees lashed from side to side. The monkey puzzle tree is doing an extraordinary swirling dance, all seventy feet of it. Oh, I do hope it stays rooted to the ground! The noise is amazing as the howling wind funnels its way down the valley. Gusts of ninety miles an hour were recorded off the south coast this morning, so shouts my radio.

And January usually cheers me up after the dark dank days of November and December. But this year, so wet and wild, even the carpet of snowdrops, early camellias and smiling hellebores fail to give my spirits the usual lift. I hope things improve before lambing begins. We're starting earlier this year in anticipation of another long, hot summer! Fat ladies-in-waiting graze the hillside and race rudely, pushing and shoving, into the yard for afternoon tea.

The village pantomime added a certain frizzon to the weeks before Christmas. Chaotic rehearsals spiked my anxiety as I asked myself over and over again why I had agreed to play a rather fading old fairy godmother in our version of *Cinderella*. The whole village pitched in to help one way or another. But nevertheless I was racked with fear for all three performances to a packed village hall.

Of course, it was a resounding success with a marvellous troupe of small villagers and minute fairies. So many children took part. Cinderella was beautiful and Prince Charming did remember her lines. The Ugly Sisters looked out of this world, one even retaining his greying beard. The Baron conquered his nerves, a minute Dandini nearly stole the show and this old fairy godmother exploded onto the stage among appalling bangs and bursts of confetti; she turned pumpkin into carriage, mice into fairies and Cinders into a Princess... 'You shall go to the Ball.' The barracking and laughter from the audience nearly lifted the roof of the hall. New Year came in with a bang!

But, then down to earth with a bump: a sad donkey time. Last year saw the not unexpected demise of old Sweep, dear old friend of nearly fifty. But then just before Christmas I had a call from the veterinary department at the Donkey Sanctuary saying no more could be done for my beloved, little Friday. He and Nutmeg had been at the Sanctuary since last summer for yet more treatment for sarcoids. At first things seemed to improve a bit as they joined the 'Sarcoid Group' for groundbreaking research into this horrible equine condition.

But then everything flared up again for little Friday and a decision had to be made. He was only eight. Poor mother Nutmeg was distraught, they said, having never been separated from him since he was born. To my huge relief the vets decided I could have her back on condition they continued to monitor her regularly.

She arrived home last week after six months. She stepped straight out of the horsebox, marched to her stable, kicked the other amazed donkeys, refused to come near me and sniffed her way round every inch of every stable. Was she looking for Friday, I wonder? When her search was complete, she walked quietly up to me, gave me a gentle shove and went into the big barn to eat hay. She has been sweet and quiet ever since. So now the little group is complete – two geldings and two jennies, a perfect balance.

I foolishly thought everything seemed to be settling back to normal as I set off with the dogs to check the sheep yesterday. A rash thought indeed. We trudged up the slippy, slidey hill feeling unpressured and relaxed. Old Truffy decided to come too so I knew it would be a slow expedition. She'll be fourteen in March. Wobbly, deaf, greedy and happy, she must stop to sniff every blade of grass in old Labrador fashion. We walked through the top field and last year's lambs looked up at us enquiringly as I opened the gate; I should have guessed. Three dogs ran through, I turned to wait for Truff and before I could think, blink, turn around, quick as a flash all those fat little yearlings flew past me, in one bound into the next field. Bother, I thought, still without concern, thinking the field was still empty. Just then I spotted the ram. Alas, I didn't know it, but Paul had moved everyone around the day before.

Anxiety began to creep over me. Oh no, had I, had I really? Surely, we didn't have that many wethers, did we? Had I let all the ewe lambs through too? I tore down the hill to look to see if the ewe lambs were still with the ladies-in-waiting. Then I realised I must wait for old Truff. Panic was rising inside me. Hurry Truffy, do try to hurry, old girl.

Into Sunday Orchard and the panic took hold. Only fat ladies grazed quietly on the hill. No yearling girls to be seen. I knew without a doubt what I had done.

Heart pounding, I slid across the muddy field chivvying Truff and gathering a reluctant Cairn under my arm, yelling at sheepdogs to follow. Once in the house I grabbed the phone to ask Paul what to do. 'It has not been possible to connect your call…' I nearly hurled my handset across the room. Calm,

calm, calm I thought, I'll ring the farm shop landline. Shaking, I explained what a foolish thing I had let happen. 'Don't worry, just go back, move them back into the first field, shut the gate and then push them through into the little top yard and shut them in.' Ah, fine, so simple, of course... why hadn't I thought of that?

Back we trudged up the hill again, Labrador and Cairn-free this time. Sheepdog, lurcher and I moved the ragged little flock into the next field as per instruction. Dog helped, 'thank you, dog'. Then sheepdog decided, as sheepdog does, that that was quite enough for sheepdog and, anyway, what on earth was I expecting her to do about it. She sat down. Once again, I did my, by now quite impressive, sheepdog impersonation. 'Come by, come by, walk'em on,' I said to myself. 'Oh God, why on earth do we have sheep anyway? Stupid things. Any minute now the ram will spot the yearlings and be with us, hurry, hurry...'

Finally, on the third attempt they funnelled into the tiny space outside the top tumbledown old barn. I slammed the gate behind them and, grabbing a hurdle, thrust it against it for double security. Breathless, heart pounding, I glowered at them, daring them to move. Motionless, we stared at each other, waiting for the farmer to arrive home. I had kept them all so busy the ram hadn't had time to realise his luck. Phew!

Farmer arrived, fortunately, irritatingly calm. We penned them up, turned each one over again and sent them on their way to separate fields, girls this way, boys that way. No harm done but most of the day wasted, and, oh how furious I was with myself! The only sensible thing to do was to go home for tea. Good thing I don't sheep farm in Australia...

A COMFORTING TEATIME CAKE!

I turned, for comfort, to my beloved *The Constance Spry Cookery Book*, first published in 1956. 'In those days the disposition of a woman's time made teatime possible, and the taste for, shall I say, the cosier figure gave no cause for apprehension.' She goes on to discuss the merits and, indeed, politeness of teatime entertaining, going into the tricky business of whether one puts one's milk into the tea before or after pouring. There follows a delightfully trivial debate of what was and was not *de rigueur* at afternoon tea! Suddenly I was that child again having tea with that scary granny!

An absolute must, she tells us, is an Old-fashioned Sponge Cake with a Crust. Here are instructions learned from my granny's cook: 'take five eggs and their weight in caster sugar, and the weight of three of the eggs in flour, plus 1 tablespoon of orange flower water…' The latter is difficult to find now so I will substitute a little orange zest in mine; not the same I know, but something rather than nothing.

'Separate yolks from whites. Take 1 tablespoon of sugar away from the total quantity for every egg white. Put the remaining sugar into a bowl with the egg yolks. Whisk over a gentle heat until white and mousse-like. Add the orange flower water. Whisk the whites stiffly, incorporate the remaining sugar and fold into the mixture with sifted flour. Turn at once into a greased and sugared cake tin, bake in a slow to moderate oven 40 minutes to 1 hour.'

She gave me no more instructions, so you're on your own! I just turn it onto a wire rack cool and eat! *Bon appetites*, sit down, relax, enjoy your afternoon tea!

MARCH LAMBS

Farming's fun, yes, it is, I repeat to myself as dogs and I trudge up to the yard yet again in the relentless rain. Bother, welly stuck, wet sock, whoops, squelch. 'Remember,' I repeat my mantra, 'you could be in that traffic jam on the M6'. The driving sideways rain rides roughshod across the valley on the south wind. It clears for a few seconds only to taunt me briefly with a snatch of blue, then returning, soakingly triumphant, trickles down my neck. And still the great monkey puzzle tree dances dangerously; it's been dancing all winter. Wind and rain, rain and wind, icy wind, stinging rain. I dream of curling up by the fire with a book. It's the mildest winter since records began apparently, and surely the wettest…mud, mud, mud. Snowdrops fade and daffodils riot wetly across the orchard in their place. Camellias explode into flower, ducks start shouting again, mewing buzzards ride the thermals, nests are built noisily, chicks hatch, lambs are born. Despite the rain's best efforts, the valley is waking up to spring; grass is already growing.

It's 1 March and suddenly the rain stops. Sun at last, I jump into my boots and rush outside into the warm brightness. All plans are suspended to take advantage of this glorious respite. I sweep the yard, clean stables, feed the latest clutch of chicks; all this without getting soaked, how wonderful! As usual, of course, I have far too many cockerels. Little bantam hens appear from nowhere, busying into the sunshine, followed by yet another posse of tiny feathered ping-pong balls.

It's too good a day to stop; time to turn my attention to the neglected winter garden. I find it so hard to enthuse about summer when all plant life seems suspended in muddy hibernation. But as the early sun warms down on me, spring hope takes hold within. Out come the last of the beetroot, in go the broad bean seeds, and out too come all those rampant Jerusalem artichokes that have been marching stealthily across the vegetable garden with their stinging nettle accomplice.

In my enthusiasm raspberry canes are thinned and tied, the fruit cage weeded and donkey manure applied. Oh, I'm on a roll now! The strawberry bed is cleaned up too; even tomato and lettuce seeds find their way out of the packet and into the propagator. The fig tree is pruned and the lower bows taken from the cherry tree. So much more to do but at last winter is behind us and the new season begins.

Back to the yard and I poultice Dandy's foot. At last I have found a little canvas boot small enough for him to wear. Now, bandaged and booted, he can join the other donkeys in the sun. Fortunately, Martin, the farrier, was due to trim all donkey's feet last week just as Dandy went lame. We caught the problem quickly this time. Poor old donkey, he's had so many problems with his foot. As he walks through the mud up to the field, his feet soften and grit works its way up the fault in his hoof. Despite regular manicures it happens all too often. As Martin cuts away to relieve the pressure Dan just stands patiently seeming to trust that we will somehow stop the pain.

Meanwhile, the dreadful Nutmeg gives me a shove and gently bites my bottom. Luke rests his head on Dandy's back and lumpy Bunty just looks on. It's so nice to have naughty Nutmeg back from the Donkey Sanctuary. She seems to have settled down again and forgotten about the loss of her poor little Friday. I still miss him though, and dear old Sweep too, even though it's a whole year since she died.

The ladies are no longer in waiting; in fact lambs are arriving thick and fast, one after another – the fastest lambing I can remember and we seemed to get off to such a slow start this year. Better by far this way though. A slow lambing means weeks without a proper night's sleep – down from the yard after midnight and back again at 6 a.m. You can always recognise sheep farmers in spring by their yawns and the way they fall asleep, dormouse-style, in their soup – or is it the teapot?

It is some years now since I started to write about my everyday life on our little Devon farm. As I look back to the beginning, I do see some sort of pattern emerging across the years and yet I never cease to be surprised at the variations in the seasons. Each year's lambing, for example, is the same and yet so entirely different. Last year we only had one little orphan lamb; the year before I was feeding in shifts. Last year we fretted about the lack of rain. The ground was hard and brown. Grass was so scarce we were buying in hay and feed for months. Oh, how different this year as I squelch across Sunday Orchard, a huge, steep, east-facing field, in search of new lambs. Ah, there's the next one, an experienced Whiteface ewe who's done all this before. She's right at the top, clever girl, sheltered by the hedge from the biting wind.

I approach her quietly as she cleans her new baby. I don't want to startle an old timer who knows just what she's doing, but I do want to keep the crows at bay. They are our daytime predators; foxes do their worst at night. Paul catches me up and picks up the slippery little ewe lamb and, trying not to slide down the hill, walks slowly backwards towards the yard. Mother follows, baaing gently to her lamb. Once in the dry shed, we spray the lamb's navel and put mother and child in a dry pen.

In this very wet weather, we keep the ewes and lambs in for a few days until we are confident that the lambs are thriving and feeding well. After two days in individual pens, we move them on into the nursery where lambs begin to play together leaping over straw bales and spinning in the air. I can waste hours just watching them tumbling and bouncing on top of one another. The ewes seem to take it in turns to be in charge of the playgroup, giving the other mothers a chance to feed and rest.

If ever I doubted that each ewe could recognise the baa of her own lamb it was Fly who dismissed those doubts. He was that solitary orphan lamb last year. After his mother died, he relied entirely on me for his survival. Even now, almost a year later, I can recognise his baa in a field full of other wethers. And a very imperious baa it is too.

'Never buy a sheep with a name!' says my sheep farming neighbour; Phil's words ring in my ears. 'Never keep a hand-reared ram lamb entire,' I listen to Phil. Having watched Scruff, another poor little fellow I nursed through thick and thin several years ago, turn into a very aggressive ram, I agreed that Fly must be neutered. Even the charming Junior, handsome sire to this year's Whiteface lambs, had turned into a grumpy old man by the time he left for pastures new last autumn. So, yes, because I do listen to Phil, our new ram, Junior's prodigy and sire to this year's Jacob cross ewes, has no name! Seems rude somehow after those early ladies, Hazel and Phyllis and Madge and old Maisey…but fortunately we have far too many sheep now to name them all. Not enough sheep, though, to make a living any more: we are very, very small now and must supplement our income in other ways. We are not alone. All farmers, large and small, are facing a tough time as the huge food distributors call the tune and control prices. Since the devastation of foot-and-mouth much has changed. We were lucky; many of our neighbours on the Moor were not. Even so we will never forget the fear that in turn helped us to decide to cut right back, give up rented pasture and reduce our flock to a number sustainable to our own land even though it would not be commercially viable.

But enough of that; now it's time to turn my attention to all those Jerusalem artichokes and the large bucket of muddy beetroot that have made way for next summer's broad beans.

As I look through old cookery books, I remember why so many people wrinkle their noses in distaste at the mere mention of beetroot despite its recent media renaissance. Remember those insipid pinkish, soggy, malt vinegar, soaked balls trapped in plastic or bleeding into fierce salad cream?

It doesn't have to be like that. Think of fresh glistening borsch made with a really good home-made stock, grated raw beetroot, shallots, tomatoes, a few new potatoes and a sliced courgette or two, all cooked quickly and served bright and glistening with sour cream and chopped spring onions. Beetroot is wonderful hot too, baked in its skin in the oven like a potato and served with marmalade…yes really, or warm in a salad of apple, goat's cheese and walnuts with a rich, green virgin olive oil. We'll enjoy our bumper crop and it will keep us going until next summer's fare. I shall gently wash my bucketful, being careful not to puncture the skins. Then they'll go into the oven to cook long and gently in a large tin, covered with foil. When they are cool enough to handle, I'll peel them all, eat some now and freeze the rest.

I love Jerusalem artichokes too. Though as my old nanny said to my horrified and terrifyingly austere grandmother, 'No thank you, madam, rather windy things…' She was right of course; a little goes a long way. Nevertheless, I shall make soups. I'll fry crispy artichoke chips and 'stove' some too, cooking them in butter and olive oil, oh so slowly in a sauté pan with a few sliced potatoes. They'll be topped with Parmesan or, better still, served with a Béarnaise sauce, delicious with grilled meat. I will roast some in the oven round a leg of lamb or a piece of beef.

But whatever I plan to do with them, first they will be carefully peeled before cooking and plunged into acidulated water to stop them turning grey, which they do almost immediately their peel is removed. Oh, and just a very few will go back into the soil for next year and grace the garden with their sunny, yellow autumn flowers.

RUBBISH, LOSS
AND COMFORTING FOOD

Lambs are all born now. The playgroup, monitored by a rota of ovine mothers, has moved up the valley to a warm south-facing field. Every day dogs and I walk over the hill to count heads and watch the latest games.

Today giant, gentle raindrops plop onto shiny young ramson leaves and softly soak the primrose faces. Daffodils waver in the breeze; a soft wind dances on my wet cheeks. The raindrops mix with the steady stream of sharp, salty tears trickling down my face. I have forgotten again and turn to make sure she is still keeping up, trudging behind her younger companions, as they race up the track with me to the top fields. The sharp reality returns; abruptly I remember, old Truffy is dead. I stand and stare unseeing at the empty wonder that is the yellowness of spring. My fat, gentle, beloved, fridge raider, foodaholic, dishwasher prewasher, my dear, dear friend and companion of fourteen years, my old chocolate lab is gone.

She left us as happily and peacefully as she lived. She even gobbled up her supper with gusto moments before a massive stroke shook her body leaving it limp. She looked quietly up at us and said goodbye. As I hugged her, she made me smile again through the tears. Funny old friend; eating was her favourite thing so we've planted a crab apple tree over her grave, and cowslips to aid her journey to eternity.

Min, the ageing, delinquent Cairn, looks even smaller than usual as we climb the steep hill. Half-drowned, shrunk even, in the recent torrent, her usual enthusiasm is for once abashed. Despite being the smallest of the four dogs, very little usually dampens her spirit but today something's wrong. She sits quietly with Meg the sheepdog and the lurcher-cross, Wellie, watching as we bury Truff and plant a tree for her. Min's companion of thirteen years has left.

Inevitably my mind drifts back over those years. Truffle joined us as a tubby, little brown pup with a wrinkled brow in May 1993 some eighteen months after our lives had changed dramatically. Min arrived next. I had no idea that so small a terrier would turn into the leader of the gang. To her enormous annoyance, Min still spends too much time on a lead these days; despite her age, she is still quite unable to give up on a scent, rabbit, rat, squirrel or badger, once sniffed. Her tail goes up in the air and, nose twitching, she's off across hill and vale. Selective deafness prevails.

Even now in her 'twilight' years the warming sun puts a spring back in the old paw. At home she returns once more into the sweetest, gentlest little dog, adored and adoring. But she, like us, is missing Truff.

As the sheep population exploded Paul declared he needed the skill and assistance of a trained sheepdog. He'd always been a fan of *One Man and His Dog* so I was not entirely surprised. Off he went to Yorkshire where he spent a week being trained by Meg and her skilled owner. They returned utterly inseparable with all the 'coom'by, lass', 'way, way', 'that'll do, that'll dooo'. And, as usual, when she finishes the task, she still races across the field and hurls herself, delightedly, into Paul's arms. Occasionally she forgets completely her mission in life, looks with disdain at the sheep and skulks off leaving me, yet again, to do what has now become a fine imitation of her duties, without so much as a bark: exhausting.

And then there's Wellie, the lurcher-collie puppy, daughter of Meg and Buck, the village beau. Thinking I was being responsible, I carefully tied Meg up in the yard as I let out the chickens one morning. Alas, I discovered I could not run as fast as a healthy young lurcher. Meg had nine puppies. I found homes for them all but could not resist the small black-and-white puppy who spent her days burrowing into our Wellington boots. I kept the 'welly puppy' and so we had four.

Now that lambing is finished, down in the farmyard it's time for spring cleaning. Rubbish, rubbish, rubbish! One man's rubbish is another man's treasure! Our farming predecessor was probably the most ingenious recycler of all time, long before the word existed. Old gas cookers became garden fences. Corrugated tin divided fields; roofed hen houses supported banks and sheltered cattle. Greenhouses, collapsing on all sides, became chicken runs; cardboard boxes were transformed into a baby's play pen. Nothing was wasted.

What treasures will we find this time, hidden deep underground or lurking at the back of some dark shed? Once as I dug the vegetable garden, I unearthed the body of a motorbike, rusty but complete! Jars, bottles, iron bars, old hand tools, shards of pottery have all emerged over the years. We have a great collection of horse-drawn farm implements too: a seed spreader, plough, harrow, cutter, rescued from corners of fields or buried in undergrowth.

We too seem to have been recycling for ever. I think it's a farming thing

Old sheds become chicken houses; bathtubs turn into hayracks and water butts. Even an old gun cupboard becomes a nesting box. A rickety garden table is wired up to become a run for tiny chicks. Fence posts are recycled in the fields or turned on their side and made into steps. Old tractors are dismantled and rebuilt or used for spares. All timber is carefully stacked away to wait its turn again. Old muck spreader chassis take on a new life supporting a 'new' trailer built from those bits and pieces. Telegraph poles become gate posts; railway sleepers hold back the banks of the stream. Very little is wasted. I do draw the line, though, on aesthetic grounds, at carpet on the vegetable garden, labour-saving though it may be! Or the old kitchen cookers, galvanised tin and all the other eccentric 'building materials' we have had to remove from the garden over time!

I wonder what I would have said all those years ago if I had known I would still be ordering skips some twenty-five years later! Another skip arrives today and the rain returns. Did we really think this and this and even this would one day come in handy? Oh, thank goodness for recycling and freedom from junk!

COOKING FOR FRIENDS

When I'm feeling sad or very tired, I find cooking strangely soothing, therapeutic – a great displacement activity. It is sufficiently creative to hold my attention and gently lift my spirits as I see a meal emerge from my labour. That's exactly what I needed now as I mourned old Truffy. So, I was delighted to be suddenly asked by very special friends to cook a large dinner for their wedding anniversary. As the numbers kept rising at the last minute the challenge held my concentration!

Antipasta, Orvieto Chicken and Tarte aux Pommes was the agreed menu.

I rushed out to buy the Antipasta, a simple and delicious mix of smoked meat and fish, salami, hard-boiled eggs with anchovies and lumpfish roe, cherry tomatoes, avocado and various pickled fish. I arranged everything on two large plates – one meat, one fish – each with a bowl of homemade aioli, strong garlic mayonnaise, and accompanied with warm freshly baked rolls.

Next, we had Orvieto Chicken. I poached chicken breasts lightly in stock in the oven while I quickly blanched diced new potatoes. I sweated shallots, sliced fennel and whole cloves of garlic in olive oil until just soft, stirred in fresh rosemary and added the drained potatoes and pitted black olives. All this joined the chicken in its large tin. I returned it to a hot oven for 30 minutes. Once cooked, I set it aside, covered with foil, until the evening. With the remaining stock I made a velouté sauce, which would be handed round with the gently reheated chicken and served with a green salad.

TARTE AUX POMMES

I love making these traditional French apple tarts. There's a comforting symmetry in the arrangement of the apple slices and a sticky deliciousness to the shiny glaze: just the thing to keep my mind off dear old Truff.

I used to make the pâte sucrée by hand on a marble slab gradually drawing all the ingredients together but now I have a food processor!

I whizz 200g of plain flour, 100g of soft butter, 75g of caster sugar and three egg yolks in the processor, wrap the paste in clingfilm and chill for at least an hour before I use it. Even well chilled it is hard to roll out, so I find it easier to dip my knuckles in icing sugar and press it carefully into a loose-bottomed flan ring. I chill it again.

I often make a double quantity of pastry and line two fluted flan rings. One goes into the freezer; the other I bake blind. Then I make the crème pâtissière with 50g of butter, icing sugar, ground almonds and an egg. I spread it over the base of the cool flan case, sprinkling it with 1 teaspoon of dry semolina.

Next, working fast, I cut red dessert apples into thin slices and arrange them in circles on top of the crème pâtissière. Every few minutes I squeeze lemon juice on the slices to stop them browning. Then another sprinkling, this time of caster sugar, and back into a hot oven just long enough to soften the apple. Finally, I warm some redcurrant jelly and carefully 'paint' the flan with a pastry brush to give a dark red, sticky glaze. We eat it warm with Devonshire clotted cream or a really good local ice cream.

We had a wonderfully uplifting and happy evening.

THE VALLEY IN JUNE

As we march into June the valley puts on its thick summer coat. The skeleton shapes of winter, clothed, oh, so gingerly in spring, are suddenly engulfed in furry foliage. Shapes merge and disappear; hillsides take on different contours, swathed in green lushness. Strong winds blow huge billowing cumulus across the transparent sky. Giant shadows come and go, playing tricks with the light. Sparse pastures are replaced by shimmering grass and the hedgerows are littered with wildflowers.

Bluebells have faded and gone to seed; red campion linger on. Sorrel springs up casting its own red tinge over the grass, clover and buttercups push through among hawkbit and daisies, tiny specks of brilliant blue speedwell and shining yellow spiky crosswort. Herb-Robert and cranesbill, hoary plantains, foxgloves, toadflax and alkanet all grow beneath a canopy of huge plate-like elderflowers. It's nearly time to make cordial again. Pink and white briar roses sprinkle the hedges with their delicate petals.

Lambs, fat now, are pigging out on the sugary sward. Donkeys must be strictly rationed. Like erstwhile Labradors, they have no stop button and laminitis is always a lurking danger. Min, is getting used to life without Truffles now and bounces once more through fields of uncut hay, follows rabbit scent and baths lingeringly in the sheep trough; old dog, happy once more.

June is a wonderful month in the garden. The herbaceous borders are a mass of colour this year. I'm not sure if it is the result of such a warm spring heating up the soil early, followed by plenty of gentle rain. Maybe it is simply that plants are getting established now and bursting into celebratory bloom. Huge cerise peonies jostle with big blousy poppies among great clusters of astrantia. Blue and yellow iris stand tall beside billowing clumps of *Libertia grandiflora* and, oh joy, my beloved *Meconopsis* survived the winter and is exploding into huge, fragile, luminous blue flowers once more.

Tiny *Dicentra* peep out beneath floribunda roses. 'Gertrude Jekyll' fills the border with her luscious scent. 'Seagull' and 'Kiftsgate' climb wildly by the pond. What was I thinking when I planted two such thugs side by side, I wonder. But their huge combined cascade of simple white flowers is breathtaking.

A nameless pink rose, a star every year, smothers the pergola. I bought it as a tiny plant years ago from the wonderful Hill House Nursery near Ashburton. Of course, I lost the label almost immediately. The messy little pink flowers tumble over one another for weeks and weeks tangling through honeysuckle.

The pond glistens with water lilies, a gift from a dear friend who died two years ago. I look at the huge waxy cream flowers and remember him with love and laughter.

Buddleja alternifolia drips blue branches onto the water's edge. Dark delphiniums spike up between David Austin's 'Sweet Juliet' and 'Abraham Darby' roses. I love the English roses. Foxgloves are on the march everywhere and the *Embothrium*, scarlet against the blue sky, positively hums with working bees.

This year I'm trying to turn my vegetable garden into a true potager. It's beginning to take shape as I dedicate more squares to herbs and promise myself some box hedging in the autumn. I like the layout of small square beds in a formal pattern. Somehow, I find it less overwhelming to dig and plant one at a time. The sight of a vast solid stretch of weeds defeats me before I begin!

I love to mix the herbs and cutting flowers among the vegetables; sweet peas climb up bamboo poles in the middle of purple-headed chives and blue sage. Thyme and marjoram form a border for sweetcorn and leeks. Sorrel and fennel guard beetroot and chard seedlings.

Purple peas, runner beans and climbing French beans are all accompanied by courgette, parsley, potatoes and rhubarb. Broad beans stand stiffly to attention between supports, their regimented white and black flowers promising wonderful summer salads and winter soups.

Reluctantly I take the last leaves from last year's spinach and chard before they collapse in the wind. I hate to throw them on the compost until the last leaves are eaten or frozen. Once they are gone, I must wait patiently for this year's harvest. Then the usual cycle starts again; eat some now, freeze some for the winter.

The little greenhouse is doing a fine job with the tomato plants. For once I'm remembering to pick out the side shoots. No fancy varieties this year after last year's disappointment. 'Trustworthy cultivars' as my dear old book says: 'Tigerella', 'Golden Sunrise', 'Gardeners Delight' and little tiny 'Floridity'.

The garden fills me with joy at this time of year. I cannot think of a more pleasurable day than one spent working in the sun among herbs, vegetables and flowers. Digging and planting, weeding and pruning, helping the valley transform itself into colour and shape. I come in finally, as the light fades in the evening, covered in mud, my limbs singing with the tingle of stinging nettles. I climb in the shower, watch the dirt slither away, put on clean clothes and pour a glass of wine. I flop delightedly into a chair – that wonderful feeling of exhilarating physical tiredness suffusing my body. Minutes later I'm on my feet again cooking supper for friends. Perfect!

I will cook them chicken with fresh tarragon cut from the herb garden. We'll have tiny early potatoes too and the last of that spinach and, maybe, some asparagus too – a bottle of Chablis to help it down. For pudding we'll have pears in sticky red wine syrup with ice cream, then a runny French Brie, grapes and coffee...

TARRAGON CHICKEN

I gently poach two large chicken breasts in stock, add a little white wine and a few sprigs of fresh French tarragon and let them cook for about 20 more minutes. Once cooked, I keep them warm while I make the sauce.

To do this I strain the cooking juices through a sieve, melt 1oz of butter in a little pan, stir in 1 tablespoon of flour off the heat and gradually add the strained juice, stirring all the time to make a smooth mixture. I return it to the heat and continue to stir until the sauce thickens and cook a couple more minutes. Finally, in goes a large spoonful of crème fraîche or cream. I warm it again gently without boiling and spoon over the chicken. The new potatoes, spinach and asparagus will go so well with it.

PEARS IN RED WINE

First, I heat 300ml of water, 125g of caster sugar and about 50ml of red wine in a pan large enough to take four pears. As this comes gently to the boil, I peel the pears and slice a small piece off the bottom of each one so that they will stand up in the pan. I cook them gently until soft, pink and shiny. I stand them on a serving dish. I boil the syrup quickly for a few minutes to reduce a little, making sure I don't make toffee by mistake, and spoon the syrup over the pears. They can be prepared a little while in advance but not the day before because the juice slowly runs out of the pears and spoils the syrup.

OLD TRADITIONS, NEW SKILLS

I wake abruptly at three o'clock to the sound of more rain beating on the windowpanes – more rain and still more rain. Will it never stop? Nervously I look out of the window into the first shards of dawn light and watch a veil of water drifting sideways past the window. The wind howls. I watch the trees bending their knees in the half-light. It's July.

Floods are swamping Britain. The biggest rescue operation since the Second World War, shouts the radio. Television pictures show towns and cities under water, houses destroyed, people staring uncomprehending at the wreckage of their homes, crops submerged, fields turned to lakes, herons fishing among the corn. Pea crops rot before harvesters' eyes as they wait for the deluge to ease. In the South West gentle rivers on the Moor are transformed into raging brown rapids. Sheep, shorn for summer sun, shudder coldly in the relentless tropical downpour. I climb anxiously back to bed and await morning.

Refusing to rest, my mind, racing now, flicks here and there. Memories of waking in the night several years ago as flood waters engulfed us. When will the rain stop this time? I cannot sleep. I think of all the people out there facing that right now. Will it happen again here? I turn over and pull the bedclothes over my head.

It's been a bad enough few weeks in this valley, one way and another, one thing after another, but no floods here yet; instead, an impressive black eye and a sprained ankle for me. The wind, rewarding me for sweeping the donkey's yard, caught the stable door, knocking me senseless as I waited for the vet. Dogs and donkeys stared at me as I staggered to the gate. I greeted an astonished Richard speechlessly, seeing stars, amazed my glasses were still in one piece!

Cars broke down too and the dear old Dexta tractor, restored at last, decided to try going it alone. A terrible rushing sound reached my ears as I sat in front of the computer. 'Are you OK?' I yelled, hobbling up the steps. I found a slightly stunned Stephen, still in one piece, staring bewilderedly ahead. I followed his gaze. 'It's under the tree, went there on its own,' he said. As he lifted the last paving slab from the link box, off it went, flying through the garden all by its own. Unable to stop, it hurtled off, missing people, dogs and the beech tree until it finally came to rest in a pile of grass cuttings just before the banks of the stream. Restoration not so entirely complete perhaps, but no one hurt.

Then real disaster struck. We visited my father for tea on his ninety-eighth birthday, only to return home to find all but nine of our huge flock of chickens gone, simply gone. Apart from a few feathers and the remains of two of my dear old Maran ladies and a Light Sussex hen I've had for years, we found nothing else. The terrified Araucana cockerel cowered in his empty shed alone. He let me pick him up in my arms and carry him to safety with the nine orange survivors.

The wonderful Warren egg machines had simply vanished. The elderly Maran boy eventually came screeching out of the stream but in such poor shape he didn't survive. One or two bantams flew down from the trees. We are still asking each other what happened. Did a very bold band of foxes, cubs big now, come down in a pack from the hills and strike in broad daylight? We will never know but our lives were changed in an afternoon.

I really miss my old feathered friends. In the autumn I will get a few more pretty hens just for us. Meanwhile, we nurture the survivors back to health, try to keep them safe and ring our customers to say no more eggs. In an afternoon we found ourselves without our egg business. Farming's hard from every angle.

PHIL'S FARM

I visited Phil Bond on his farm one evening last week. Phil is a local sheep farmer with a big commercial flock. He shears our Whiteface Dartmoors for us; he's done it for years.

We walked together across his beautiful land six hundred feet above sea level, talking sheep in the rain. High on his top field the view stretches from Princetown far away in the Dartmoor distance across a huge sweeping patchwork right round to Torbay. 'When we make hay and stand on the hay wane, we can see Salcombe too, and the sea towards Plymouth.' I couldn't help but stand there and think what tiny specks we make in this majestic natural world.

Phil's family have farmed this land for generations. There is very little he doesn't know about sheep breeding. Before he took over the farm, he spent nine months on a sheep farm in New Zealand. He spent a further four months in Australia honing his skills and adding more strings to his bow. Now he runs the farm with his father and hopes, maybe, one day his daughter will join him when she finishes college.

Phil's ewes are so big compared to our local Whiteface Dartmoor girls. Every year he travels to Cumbria to buy new stock and inject fresh blood into his flock. He buys the progeny of Swaledale ewes put to a Bluefaced Leicester ram: the strapping great North of England Mule. Once back in Devon he puts Texel rams to these ewes and he has his fast-maturing, stocky little meat machines.

Although they only came to England in the 1970s Texel sheep can be traced back to Roman times on the Island of Texel off Holland. Despite their late arrival to our shores, Britain has the largest registry of Texel sheep anywhere in the world. They are predominantly a meat breed and exceptionally thrifty, giving lambs with tremendous get up and go. Stocky Texel rams are famous for transmitting their hardy qualities to their progeny.

When these tough fellows are mixed with the big, Roman-nosed, long-eared Bluefaced Leicesters with Swaledale blood running in their veins, they produce outstanding lambs. With their big-boned frames and broad deep hindquarters, the ewes are strong, efficient mothers with plenty of milk. Last year Phil had fifty sets of triplets. This can put a lot of strain on a ewe, leaving her out of condition once the lambs are weaned and at constant risk of mastitis. So, Phil takes away one of the triplets and raises them on milk substitute. I have to smile here, because it was Phil who told me firmly, 'Never buy a sheep with a name.' How come then, all his hand-reared triplets have names running through the alphabet? 'Purely practical,' says Phil briskly, 'helps Gale and I know who's who and who's had what.' Ah, yes Phil, such a hard man! No, not at all, he just really loves his sheep.

The Swaledale can be traced back to a genetic group including Bluefaced and Rough Fell sheep. The Swaledale Sheep Breeders Society was formed just after the First World War in the 1920s. The Bluefaced Leicester sheep were bred by Robert Bakewell in the 1700s and were originally called Dishly Leicesters. Over the years they evolved into the Hexham Leicester eventually becoming the Bluefaces of today.

Bluefaced Leicesters provide length in the cross-bred lambs, which enables the ewes to carry multiple births with ease and the wether lambs to be taken to a wide range of carcase weights. Crossbred lambs are blessed with vigour at birth and eagerness to foot and suckle. They are also well protected to withstand harsh conditions. Pure Bluefaced Leicesters are capable of obtaining lambing percentages in excess of 250 per cent, given good management. This trait is in turn passed on to their progeny and it is not uncommon for Mule Flocks to produce 'Prime Lamb Crops' exceeding 200 per cent. Small wonder Phil reaches these percentages with his thriving mix.

Farming in this country is changing radically; some say it's in decline. There is no doubt that times are hard for farmers everywhere. Open the local paper on a Saturday morning and you will find farm after farm up for sale. Beautiful old houses hived off from their land and sold as 'des-reses' with a couple of acres, a stable, maybe, and a paddock for the pony. 'Buying the lifestyle' Phil calls it.

Then, if you walk into the new shiny supermarket in our local town in the heart of this farming county you will find fruit and vegetables double, treble wrapped, flown in from across the world, chickens all the way from Norfolk and the north of England, beef that has travelled down from Scotland. Turn on the radio and learn how the multinationals buy local vegetables in Wales, truck them to East Anglia to be packed, truck them back again and sell them as, now, not so fresh local produce. The world has gone mad. I could go on. It makes me sad and furious living in the midst of this struggling farming community.

Farmers need new talents now. Their generations of traditional skills, years and years of experience adapted and passed from father to son, are no longer sufficient. In a changing world, farmers must take control to survive. They cannot simply stay on the farm anymore and lose control of their product once it leaves their land. They have to keep in touch from farm to the consumer.

Market prices fluctuate so dramatically; one week a lamb can fetch £70, the next £40. Wool prices have plummeted from

48p last year to a staggering 31p this year. A glossy leaflet saying 'Wool Clip: Why is it so low' arrives with our tiny cheque. 'World markets', it shouts. 'Rubbish.' I reply, hopelessly. 'Monopoly!'

The economy of England was built on wool in the Middle Ages. It fed the people and gave our kings and princes power across the world. The huge wool churches of East Anglia, built on the profits of wool, bear witness to the importance of sheep to our history. Now the value of the wool doesn't even cover the cost of shearing.

There is little chance for farmers to budget or embrace some sort of forward planning now. Too many middlemen between farmer and consumer skim off the profit and force up the price. But just a few entrepreneurs are beginning to see a way forward in all this gloom – to see a way to free themselves from this tyranny. And Phil is one of them.

Phil sells directly to his customers just as we used to sell our chickens and turkeys in the past. He breeds his sheep with years of knowledge and expertise. He finishes his lambs with skill to give himself a supply of meat across the year. After slaughter he oversees the butchering and packing. He organises sales, generates customers, delivers his meat across the county. He stands behind the counter at countless farmers' markets across South Devon: Totnes, Kingsbridge, Dartmouth, Ivybridge. His skills stretch way beyond the gates of his farm. He's in control of every aspect of his product. He is shepherd, quality controller, marketing manager and salesman all rolled up together. And it's paying off.

He says direct selling motivates him to improve his flock year by year, but some of his peers are watching him closely. 'It's OK for you, Phil, you've got the gift of the gab.' Oh, if only it were that simple! A few are still puzzled at what he's doing, but they are slowly becoming the minority. As time goes on my guess is that more and more farmers out there, with Phil's vision and tenacity, will follow his lead and take control of their destiny. Maybe they will even organise themselves into powerful cooperatives like the wine cooperatives in Europe and finally be able to stand up to the might of the supermarkets and get a fair deal. Pie in the sky, I hear you say? I wonder. Watch Phil…

Oh, and just to illustrate Phil's marketing skills, when I left the farm, I found myself the new owner of two small kittens that he placed in my arms and effortlessly persuaded me I wanted. Some salesman indeed!

At last, the rain has finally stopped, but only briefly, I fear. Now I need to cook comforting food to restore my equilibrium, but it must be light delicious summer food. Somehow, I think it better be lamb!

I'll roast a shoulder of our own spring lamb with garlic and rosemary. We'll eat it with young vegetables from the garden. I'll dig up some potatoes and pick mangetout peas. Or perhaps I'll take a little more time and pleasure to prepare a traditional Navarin Printanier.

This is not a dish for stewing lamb. It calls for tender, lean meat that will cook gently but quite quickly. I prefer to cut up a shoulder or even use a boned-out loin taking a little time to trim off any fat and sinew before cutting the meat into fairly small pieces.

I melt a large piece of butter and a little oil in a heavy pot and quickly brown the meat, turning it gently until it is sealed. Once nicely browned I set it aside while I add a chopped shallot and a clove or two of crushed garlic to the buttery juices in the pan and, heating gently, allow them to soften slightly. I stir in a spoonful or two of flour, scraping up the meat juices, and mix to a thin paste. Gradually, I add some stock and a little tomato purée.

Back goes the browned meat. I heat it all gently, adjust the consistency, which should be creamy, by adding more stock if necessary, bring it all slowly to the boil, cover the pan with its lid and place in a moderate oven for about an hour. I test the meat with a skewer to see if it is tender. If not, back it goes into the oven for a little longer but I don't want to overdo it.

Meanwhile I prepare some young, fresh, root vegetables: new potatoes, very young turnips and whole baby carrots. Once the meat is tender, I add these and cook for a scant half an hour without the lid. I top and tail some mangetout or shell some peas and broad beans, slice my first runner beans or harvest the early French beans. I use whatever I have in the garden or what I can find in my local farmers' market.

Once I have blanched the vegetables very briefly in plenty of boiling water, I drain them well and add to the lamb. I skim off absolutely any remaining fat, make sure it is heated through, taste, add salt and freshly ground black pepper and serve on warmed plates with hot, crusty bread.

Next, come fresh raspberries with really good ice cream; despite the rain I have a bumper crop this year.

AUTUMN

The relentless summer rain has finally given way to a little golden autumn sunshine. A chocolate box blue sky is decorated with perfect puffy flat-bottomed little clouds gliding majestically across the valley. But golden stubble fields, striped green, are evidence of the meagre harvest gathered at last after the summer floods that devastated livestock and crops alike. Feed and hay prices are rising; vegetables will be in short supply this winter. Even my own little harvest is the worst I've ever had. Potato blight destroyed my vegetable garden this year, caused, I suppose by wet, waterlogged soil. It swept through potatoes, beans, tomatoes. And then the badgers had a midnight feast, disco in fact, in my little patch of sweetcorn. They trashed the plants and munched on every cob, leaving their debris for me to clear up. Maddening as it is, I rather wish I'd seen them having such fun!

Until yesterday things were looking up and then the news broke of another foot-and-mouth outbreak in Surrey. Down came all the movement restrictions again only days after we had been given the all clear. Next week we had hoped to put the old ram in with the ewes but have decided against it now. We had planned to buy a new chap too but the Whiteface sale is postponed with all the rest. Once more the farmers are in crisis and, to make matters worse, at this, the most critical time in the farming calendar. It is truly heartbreaking. And again, this outbreak appears so far to come from the laboratory fractured pipe leakage of the last outbreak. Oh dear.

I will collect some new chickens soon and hope the foxes will find sustenance elsewhere for a while! I will clear the blighted beds and plant winter cabbage and winter salad. I will dig borders and divide herbaceous plants.

We will pick ourselves up, dust ourselves down and start all over again!

DIFFICULT TIMES

As I walk the dogs a lazy wind blows across the fields. Too lazy to make its way around, it goes straight through me with an icy lick. The sky has turned slate grey. The valley seems suddenly to be hunkering down and preparing for the swift descent into winter.

Wellie and Meg bound on ahead, but little old Min is getting slower now, fourteen next month. The new kittens, gifted to me by Farmer Phil, have taken to cross-country walking too, which is a little unnerving as they're still so small. They race along behind me meowing every few yards to make sure I'm still with them. Once home they lick tiny paws and collapse exhausted, for just a little while! I had forgotten just what fun kittens can be! Thank you, Phil!

On the other side of the valley, I spot a neighbour cutting maize; a huge spume of green pours from the funnel of the forager. As the wind blows, it tries to find its way into the following trailers. All is being gathered in. The hills are alive with the sound of tractors.

While Whiteface ewes graze quietly on our hillside as usual, the recent foot-and-mouth problems have prevented us buying a new ram this year to introduce fresh blood into our flock. There will be very few lambs for us next spring. The two young Whiteface boys, progeny of our ewes, are in with the cross-bred girls to give us just a few cross-bred lambs to sell next year.

The repercussions of the recent outbreak are nationwide and the gloom at the recent annual sheep sale was tangible. Old friends gave a cheerful, warm greeting to one another on the day but, caught in repose, worry and sadness was etched across so many faces – how to get through the winter with the low stock prices, soaring feed costs and unsold stock to feed for the cold months ahead. 'If I don't sell my sheep today, the twenty day standstill will prevent me getting my cattle to the next sale,' and so on and so on

Our spirits lifted briefly as we won first prize for the best pen of shearling lambs.

This pushed the price up a bit for us but was short-lived when we came to sell, or rather almost give away, a ram. Our only consolation was that we knew he'd gone to a good home – not much help to our bank balance though. At least we didn't have to bring unsold animals home, and our trailer was empty to hose down before we were allowed to leave the livestock market.

On a happier note, we visited the rare breed poultry sale a couple of weeks ago where prices were higher and faces happier. We replaced the old friends lost in the great 'Midsummer Murder' in June, with three fine large Light Sussex hens with huge white petticoats, three pretty, speckled Welsummers and two handsome Rhode Island Reds. Last night as I shut them safely into their foxproof (I hope!) shed for the night, a loud cheeping led me to an old crate high up in the implement shed where a black bantam was fiercely guarding ten tiny newly hatched chicks. We don't sell eggs any more since the massacre, but nevertheless nature is replenishing our chicken population for us. The foxes, fat and full, must surely still have a very well-stocked larder. I hope they stay away for a while.

The apple harvest has been wonderful again, so this year we've bought our own little press just for fun; but, oh, such hard work! For two days Paul gathered apples in a wheelbarrow, chopped them, crushed them and then pressed out the juice.

A five-gallon plastic drum sits in the warm kitchen. Each time he passes it he peers at the airlock trying to detect a sign of fermentation as he dreams of delicate, gently sparkling cider! Meanwhile, I rack off juice into old screw-top bottles and pasteurise the apple juice in a giant saucepan.

This is the time for pickles and preserves – a comforting way to fill the larder for the cold months ahead. Tomatoes in spiced vinegar to add a summer zing to winter meals and green tomato and apple chutney to cut through the richness of cold pork. The unctuous, velvety smooth jam made from those wild plums growing near the top barn, will add luxury to toast and coffee. Pickled eggs come around again, so does apple and quince cheese and huge piles of apple purée to freeze for pies and puds.

TOMATOES IN SPICED VINEGAR

I have never preserved cherry tomatoes in spiced vinegar before so this year is a bit of an experiment. I filled sterilised Kilner jars with tiny, freshly picked tomatoes that I pricked with a wooden cocktail stick. I added basil leaves, lemon zest and black peppercorns, then I covered them with hot spiced vinegar. I pushed the tomatoes down with the handle of a wooden spoon to get rid of air pockets and made sure the top ones were well covered with vinegar. Then I covered them with a wax disc and sealed the jars at once. I was careful to use new seals on the old Kilner jars.

To spice the vinegar, I brought distilled, clear white vinegar and a little clear apple juice to the boil, took it off the heat and infused it with a bag of mixed spice: cloves, black peppercorns, dried chilli, coriander seeds and allspice berries; I make my own mix. Importantly, I have discovered that if I boil the vinegar with the spices, it will go cloudy and spoil the tomatoes. So, once the cooled vinegar is infused with the spice mix, I remove the bag, reheat the vinegar and pour it over the tomatoes.

TURKEY TIME AGAIN

Repetition, repetition, repetition…grey sky, east wind, bare branches, clipped hedgerows, empty fields, a grey veil floating across the valley, it's winter again, December. Everything the same, year in year out, or is it? No, not quite; no more waiting for a slow old Labrador as we cross the fields to check the sheep. Instead, we wait for Min. It's her turn to slow down now; little fourteen-year-old Cairn terrier legs don't travel as fast as they did. Kittens still join us and play rough games while we dawdle on the hilltop gazing at Dartmoor in the misty distance. Four donkeys graze quietly instead of six, chickens are scarce in the yard, even old Humphrey, the goose, has gone.

In the quiet farmyard my mind drifts back to turkeys, the hustle, the bustle, the frantic pre-Christmas rush of previous years. But why turkey, I wonder, as I feed animals. Where do they come from? I wander thoughtfully home and, happy to be warm again, begin a trawl through old cookbooks and histories of food. After all, we know from countless records that chicken and pheasant, pigeon and snipe, swans and geese adorned medieval tables; but no mention of turkeys. I wonder why: gradually a strange story unfolds.

It seems turkeys begin to be mentioned in English manuscripts in about 1523 after the Spanish conquest of Mexico. Their exact route from Mexico to Europe is uncertain. There is not only confusion about how they got here but how they became known as 'turkeys' when they reached our shores.

These large birds, long domesticated by the Aztecs, were probably brought back to Spain by the Conquistadors. They quickly became popular on Spanish tables, enjoyed for their flavour and meaty carcass: a welcome change to goose. Soon merchants from Turkey and the Levant, en route from the Eastern Mediterranean, picked up birds in Seville and brought them to Britain and other parts of Europe.

The Mexican name of *uexolotl* was a little difficult to roll around the English tongue so 'turkey–cock' was used to describe the new fowl. This may have been after these Turkish merchants or the bird's preferred food, Turkish maize, which had also just arrived here. Birds ate the new grain voraciously.

History is full of contradictions but one thing is certain: when in 1530 the smaller and slightly similar guinea fowl or *numida* arrived in Portugal from West Africa, it was confused for some time with the turkey-cock. Despite the efforts of Archbishop Cranmer, whose sumptuary laws intended to discourage 'over-elaborate banqueting', the birds were classed with cranes and swans while guinea fowl remained with capon and pheasant.

The confusion continued into the eighteenth century with Linnaeus, the Swedish botanist. In his efforts to classify everything in nature with a Latin name, the turkey gained the generic name 'meleagris', the classical Roman name for guinea fowl familiar to Pliny and Aristotle.

By 1555 we are told flocks of fowl were being driven from Norfolk and Suffolk to London wearing little boots to protect their feet! Records show that the price of turkey was now officially fixed. The birds became popular on large estates and parks where the gentlemen are said to have delighted in their flying behaviour. They were often watched over by a boy who would whistle to call them to feed. Farmers, on the other hand, were not so keen; not only were they hard work to raise, but they ate all the corn!

And on top of that, the young birds were very frail, hated the wet and were constantly at risk to hawks, polecats and even stinging nettles, which would kill the little poults. It all sounds horribly familiar! For polecats read foxes and badgers and, on one dreadful occasion a few years ago, we lost a major part of our turkey flock to a pair of minks.

By 1586 Thomas Dawson was giving instructions on boning the turkey-cock for banquets. Gervase Markham's *The English Huswife* of 1615 contained many turkey recipes. So, when the starving Pilgrim Fathers landed in Massachusetts in 1620 and feasted, famously on that third Thursday in November, on turkey, they were eating familiar food!

My battered 1880 Mrs Beeton has no less than six pages dedicated to the turkey fowl. As well as recipes, she gives a great deal of information about the history and breeding of the birds. Her version of their arrival to our shores is a little different again. She thinks there is little doubt that turkeys appeared generally in Europe about the end of the seventeenth century: that they first appeared in France, brought by Jesuits who had been sent out missionaries to the West. From France the birds gradually spread across Europe. She goes on to say that the bird's mortality rate was very high indeed in the eighteenth century but was improving by her time of writing as the birds gradually became acclimatised to our wetter climate. She quotes Thomas Tusser as evidence of the popularity of Turkey at Christmas dating back to his *Five Hundred Points of Good Husbandry* in 1585:

Beefe mutton and pork, shred pies of the best,
Pig, veal, goose, and capon, and turkey well drest;
Cheese apples and nuts, jolly carols to hear,
As then in the country is counted good cheer.

Turkey meat has a reputation of being heavy and dry but this is entirely dependent on the cooking. Elaborate old recipes suggest boning and stuffing the turkey with a succession of smaller birds, ending with a tiny snipe or woodcock, itself filled with truffles. The whole is roasted in beef dripping and served with thick floury gravy; a tad heavy indeed to our modern taste!

Mrs Beeton's recipes do little to dismiss this myth even though she forgoes the bird within a bird and introduces sausages and forcemeat and chestnut stuffing, all of which we would recognise today. Interestingly she reproduces two of Miss Acton's recipes, lifted, no doubt, from Eliza Acton's delightful *Modern Cookery for Private Families* published in 1845. These too give instructions on boning a bird without breaking the skin. However, Miss Acton suggests one should draw the legs and wings into the body of the bird to reduce the large amount of forcemeat required to fill such a cavity and 'thus diminish the expense of this'.

It is not until I reach for the *Gentle Art of Cookery* by Mrs Leyel and Olga Hartley that my spirits begin to rise. Prunes and the chopped liver appear in the stuffing with chestnuts and bacon and Marsala. The bird is first braised with rosemary, carrot, cloves and garlic before being finished in the oven and served with a sauce made from the braising liquor. No wonder Elizabeth David found Mrs Leyel, she of Culpeper House fame, such an inspiration, such a breath of fresh air! Gone at last were the endless bland *réchauffés* and fricassees.

And as for me, a child of Constance Spry's Winkfield Place, a cook at London's Nick's Diner, (no women chefs in those days!), a disciple of Elizabeth David and Jane Grigson and, later, a turkey and chicken producer myself, raising these frail little chicks to poults to mature table birds, I could not let them go to the Christmas table without a few of my own hints on their cooking!

ROAST TURKEY

The first thing I do is to preheat the oven to 200°C/400F/gas mark 6. Then I set about making the stuffing. Stuffing not only tastes delicious but also helps to keep the bird moist as it bastes from within. The old cookery books often suggest stuffing the turkey at each end – traditionally forcemeat one end and chestnut the other.

I like to use prunes soaked in red wine, grated rind of half a lemon, peeled and cooked chestnuts, some chopped celery and onion, mixed herbs, butter, salt and pepper and a small beaten egg.

I simmer the prunes in the wine until tender, then cool, stone and cut them into four. Next, I soften the celery and onion in butter over a low heat, add the prunes with their wine, herbs, salt and pepper, lemon rind and the chestnuts, broken into pieces. I stir lightly with a fork, allow it all to cool thoroughly before binding it together with the beaten egg. I sometimes add a spoonful or two of breadcrumbs to stiffen the mixture if it seems a little soft.

I ring the changes with my version of an Italian stuffing. First, I sweat a few medium potatoes in olive oil. As they begin to soften, I add a bulb of fennel, finely sliced, and some chopped onions. Then, in go the giblets and a couple of cloves of crushed garlic. I continue cooking, stirring occasionally, over a gentle heat until all are just soft. Next, I stir in some twenty or more whole unpeeled garlic cloves, yes really, that's the Italian bit! Then, in go plenty of black olives, fresh chopped rosemary, grated zest and juice of lemon, salt and pepper, a glass of white wine and a good splash of olive oil. It makes a delicious stuffing!

Or I simply melt the potatoes, fennel and onions in the olive oil until just soft. I add the giblets and a couple of cloves of crushed garlic then stir in the rest of the whole garlic cloves (I don't bother to peel!), then in go the olives, fresh chopped rosemary, grated zest and juice of a lemon, salt and pepper and the white wine.

Once I have filled the turkey with a stuffing or two, I weigh it again.

To calculate cooking time, I allow 15 minutes per 1lb for a bird up to 14lb and 20–25 minutes for a larger bird.

I melt a little butter and oil in the roasting tin and place the bird on its side on a rack in the tin and spread it with more butter. If I haven't used them in the stuffing, I add the giblets and a pint of water to the roasting tin and cover the whole thing in foil. I keep the liver to fry and add to the gravy later. The bird goes into the centre of the hot oven.

A little before half time I take the turkey out of the oven, turn it on to its other side, baste well and re-cover carefully. Twenty minutes before the end of the cooking time, I turn the bird again, this time the right way up. I baste again and sprinkle with salt and pepper and return to the hot oven uncovered to brown the breast.

I test that the bird is cooked by sticking a long skewer into the thickest part of the thigh: if the juice is clear the turkey is cooked. If there are still traces of blood, back it goes into the oven. Once cooked, I allow it to rest covered in a warm place for about 20 minutes. This will make it much easier to carve and give me time to make the gravy and finish cooking the vegetables. I remove a little of the melted butter from the roasting tin, mix it with 1 dessertspoon of cornflour and return to the roasting tin. In goes a little red wine, maybe a little more water or stock and redcurrant jelly. I stir the gravy over a brisk heat until it is a rich syrupy consistency, strain it and add the sliced and lightly fried liver.

LA GOUGÈRE

However delicious cold turkey is, sometimes I want to ring the changes.

La Gougère is really delicious and a favourite way of mine to use up the leftovers, and simple too. I bake a ring of cheese choux pastry and fill it with the turkey, warmed in a rich cream and sherry sauce.

For the pastry I put 150ml of water into a small pan with 50g of butter, bring it to the boil and quickly shoot in 75g of sifted plain flour. I beat like mad with a wooden spoon off the heat, leave it to cool then beat in two eggs. Then I stir in 80g of tiny cubes of Gruyère cheese or Cheddar if I haven't any Gruyère, a pinch of salt and some freshly ground black pepper. I grease an ovenproof dish and pile the rich yellow paste around the edges to make a ring, leaving a space in the middle for the turkey filling later. I bake the choux ring at 220°C for about 40 minutes. The secret with choux pastry is to cook it longer than you think you should! It smells wonderfully tempting after 20 minutes but it must have a chance to dry out inside.

Meanwhile, I make a sauce in the usual way: 25g of butter and 25g of flour melted and mixed to form a roux, whisk in 300ml of milk, stock or leftover gravy. If I use gravy I cut down on the flour in the roux. I bring it to the boil stirring all the time and continue to cook for a couple of minutes to thoroughly cook the flour. Sometimes I cheer it up with a dash of sherry, a spoonful of that cream at the back of the fridge or a dollop of crème fraîche. In goes the cold turkey. I may even add a few mushrooms, a little blanched broccoli, leftover stuffing – whatever I have. I season it well, heat it through and pile it up into the crispy ring of choux pastry.

All we need now is a green salad and a glass of wine.

Turkey Pudding is a good one for the leftovers too. It's an old English recipe that still survives in Sussex. I just line a deep pudding basin with suet crust pastry, pack tightly with pieces of turkey, stuffing, cranberry sauce, gravy, whatever I have left, cover it with a lid of the suet crust and steam it just as I would a steak and kidney pudding.

RIVER WALK

Black storm clouds, driving rain and the gargantuan gales of the last two weeks have suddenly given way to a blue streaked, watery white sky, punctuated with little bursts of sunlight. Not only do I feel my spirits rise with renewed belief that spring will indeed return again, but I have proof of it every time I walk to the farmyard.

Morning and evening I find more evidence at last; we will not, after all, be in darkness for ever. Suddenly snowdrops cascade once more down the orchard slopes, a few primroses catch the light and crocuses, planted so long ago by our son, send up defiant little yellow daggers towards the sun. Hellebores nod nonchalantly and the first shaggy, wild double daffodil has burst into life. Today I spotted a white camellia.

Birds are singing again. Siskin and sparrow bustle through the hedgerows bossed around by robins, fiercely guarding their territory. A skylark calls across the top field and the occasional hobby swoops over the gate down the lane. Buzzards wheel high overhead calling as they swirl on the thermals. Wood pigeon land clumsily on the bird table frightening the blue tits and a large cock pheasant strides by regularly, to clean up under the table. January is marching us towards spring!

The old hens, newly feathered, are laying again and bantam chicks grow into sturdy little birds, too many cockerels as usual, of course. The few ewes in lamb this year grow fatter by the day. They no longer rush in from the storms forming an orderly supper queue by 3.30 p.m., but potter along as dusk falls. Donkeys eeyore joyously, thrilled to be out of their big barn after weeks of confinement; they find a warm spot to sunbathe. Dear, funny desert animals, they do not appreciate the wet but love the great outdoors.

I too have been feeling all cooped up inside during the storms. So desperate was I to be outside despite the weather that I foolishly set out with dogs in the rain along the riverbank on a rising tide. As we slid around on shale and seaweed wondering if we'd be cut off on the rocks before we reached the village, I was awestruck once more at the wild beauty of the river.

Water lapped over our feet. Meg hates paddling, fat old sheepdog; I wondered how I'd carry her home. Wind and rain lashed my face; boats rocked on their moorings; birds took cover squawking across the creek. The water, whisked into froth by the wind and driven in by the tide, broke in tiny waves on the shore. Huge storm clouds tumbled over one another menacingly above my head, putting an anxious spring in my step. Discretion being the better part of valour, we turned on our heels for home.

The next day, I returned but found a different world. The tide was out, the air quite still apart from the sound of the birds. Flocks of noisy gulls stood out on shiny riverbed. I spotted oystercatchers, curlews, a little egret, ducks of all sizes, pintails, mallards, shelducks. No roaring tide or howling wind – just the sweet sound of their calls as they fed on the slippery mud.

Rotting hulks poked their slimy spines above the water, reminder of days when the coal boats came up the creek. On the shore I could just make out the remains of the little depot where the coal was unloaded before being delivered by horse and cart. I read in our local library that apparently that is why our house has coal grates instead of log fires. We were the first stop on the delivery round for this eighteenth-century Georgian mod con.

As we round the end of the creek I can see right up the river to Dartmoor, a huge sweep of water then dark moorland hanging in the distance. The Dart rises 550 metres above sea level on the acidic peat bogs high up on the Moor. It tumbles down, fed by numerous little rivulets and streams until it becomes a respectable river flowing through grassland and heath, farmland and pasture and the old market town of Totnes.

Here it becomes an estuary, flooding a ria valley formed in the last Ice Age by rising sea levels and sinking land. It becomes tidal, freshwater mixing with salt from the sea. Oak trees dominate the shore. Dart is a Celtic word for 'many oaks'; some trees are thought to be more than three hundred years old. I even read of a cave on the edge of the Moor at Buckfastleigh formed before the Ice Age, where remains of hippopotamus, straight-tusked elephant, bison and lion have been found! I wonder. Now it is the home of horseshoe bats and rare blind shrimp.

The river is a spawning ground for Atlantic salmon, a resting place for migratory trout and a 'nursery' for sea bass. Strict fishing restrictions, often sadly broken, go somewhere to try to ensure their survival. Grey mullet are plentiful and flat fish and flounders are found near the mouth. Dolphins and porpoises occasionally swim into the lower estuary and grey seals have been seen as far up river as Totnes trapping fish against the weir. Otter numbers are increasing, hares too, I'm told, although I have never been lucky enough to see either. Water voles, on the other hand, have almost disappeared largely at the mercy of mink but dormice somehow survive in fields and woodland along the shore.

Squelching through the river mud, dogs and I reach the oyster beds – rows and rows of cushion-shaped crates lining the bank, visible only at low tide. Under my feet I try not to step on those who are free from the restaurant destiny of their crated kin. Oysters, mussels, cockles, winkles and clams have been gathered from the river's shoreline for hundreds of years. Then suddenly along came tributyltin anti-fouling and sewage pollution and the shellfish on the river were destroyed. Then in 1999 the river was designated by government to have 'shellfish potential'. By 2003 the Clean Sweep™ programme was completed and the shellfish is once again safe and thriving.

On we go, trudging over soft springy swathes of oak leaves, seaweed, mud, lichen-covered rocks, our boots and paws sliding this way and that. 'DANGER PRIVATE. KEEP OUT. NO RIGHT OF WAY' shouts a new sign on a locked gate. Times are indeed changing.

Rounding the next little headland, the village comes into sight, cottages singing in their Tobermory colours, those on the waterfront mostly holiday homes now. But despite this, the village boasts a thriving permanent population that, thankfully, has grown in the last few years. We have two pubs, a village shop, a village hall, a magnificent church and, of course the river drifting serenely by as it always has, on towards Dartmouth and the sea, flowing through hundreds and thousands of years of history.

Dogs and I turn inland up the hill and make our way home, pace slowed, along lanes away from the water's edge, tired and glowing, longing for supper.

FISH SUPPER

I find it difficult to imagine anything but a fishy supper after our watery walk. Maybe we'll have a traditional fish pie made with a mixture of wild salmon, white fish, smoked haddock and hard-boiled eggs in parsley sauce, topped with creamy mashed potato and grated cheese. The important thing is to buy whatever fish is available on the day and that, of course, is dictated by the weather at sea. Fresh and local are my rules.

My favourite quick pie is a Fish Gratin, which often gets me by when I'm short of time. First, I skin some white fish and maybe, a little smoked haddock, carefully taking out the bones, using tweezers if necessary. I put the skin and bones into a small pan with about 300ml of milk, a bay leaf, parsley stalks, a slice of onion, salt and pepper and infuse by heating gently. Next, I peel and dice a couple of potatoes and slice half a bulb of fennel and blanch them quickly until just tender. I dice the fish and heat a little butter and oil in a large frying pan or wok and quickly turn the fish around until nearly cooked, being careful not to break it up. I pile fish, potato and fennel into a well-buttered pie dish. Then I strain the infused milk and use it to make a creamy béchamel sauce: sometimes I add cheese depending on the fish I'm using. I pour the sauce over the fish and top with a mixture of bread, parsley, garlic, lemon rind and butter, all blitzed together to a slightly sticky crumb consistency. I bake for 10 minutes in a hot oven until the topping is crisp. We eat it with a crunchy, well-dressed green salad.

Fishy leftovers can be quickly transformed into delicious Fishcakes. With the addition of mashed potato and a dash of anchovy essence, the mixture can be shaped into cakes, dusted with seasoned flour and fried in a light olive oil.

Dart salmon is a luxury of summer not to be missed and anticipated with pleasure. And line-caught sea bass baked with fennel and Pernod is, dare I say it, even better! But that is many months away. As spring creeps nearer, now is the time to prepare for the long days and short nights of lambing.

GARDEN TIME

Bluebells march through Devon in May with such reassuring relentless energy it makes my heart sing. Like the pink waves of *Sakura* unfurling across Japan in spring, Devon turns blue. As the clouds of cherry blossom petals drift northwards from Okinawa to the northern tip on Hokkaido, the Japanese Meteorological Agency issues regular news bulletins tracking the progress of the blossom as it travels upwards across the country. Hanami festivals bring crowds to parks to celebrate the brief pink, fragile beauty that represents the fragility of life itself.

No parties in the park here to celebrate the blueness of May, no sake or beer festivals, no news bulletins or public holidays for the bluebell – just the overwhelming private joy of an intoxicating blueness pursuing me through lanes and woodlands wherever I go.

I wonder what it is that I find so irresistible about blue flowers. Forget-me-nots smother great swathes of the garden, *Ceanothus* drips heady scented blueness across the lawn. One small, stalwart, *Meconopsis* stares out at me from the border, iridescent and fragile, its petals falling all too soon. Lobelia springs darkly from beneath geraniums and sage and rosemary are bursting into flower in the herb garden. I cannot bring myself to pull up wild alkanet peeping out beneath every tree and around every corner, vying for position among marching pink campion. *Centaurea montana* threatens to smother everything in the border and yet I love its fluffy thistle-like flowers. I wait in anticipation for great clumps of geranium, 'Johnson's Blue', to erupt on the banks, for *Salvia patens* and glowing, majestic agapanthus. And, of course, for now there is the bluebell. I do so love blue flowers!

We may not have a Hanami festival here, but all is a frenzy of activity in this garden, in this corner of Devon, this week. We had a call from the vicar's wife asking if we would open to the public for Macmillan nurses on 1 June. 'Don't worry,' she said, 'I will organise everything: publicity, tea ladies, urns, tables, chairs, cakes, parking signs…' Maybe, I mused looking out at the nourishing summer rain, maybe, she'd even ask her husband to have a word with God about the weather.

She tells me I need do nothing but garden. What luxury is that – all energy and attention funnelled into the soil! The sun burns down on my back between showers, as, hat crammed on head, mud smudged across face, hands stained brown with compost, I dig, manure, weed, sow, plant out, plot and plan. Since the devastation left by the terrible flood in the valley several years ago, I have been struggling to restore the garden. Here is an amazing incentive to try to bring it back to its former glory. What happier life could there be?

Geraniums, wintered inside, are finally allowed out. Repotted and titivated, they line the steps by the back door. The olive tree, now so large in its huge pot, is dragged from winter protection. Others must stay inside but have space and air around to spread themselves at last. The lemon tree and abutilon are both already in flower. The avocado is nearly six feet tall and stands majestically like some beautiful elegant goddess arms outstretched. Oleanders are in bud, and the plumbago, another blue beauty, is bursting into leaf once more. All my treasures have made it through the winter; too tender for this frosty valley, they must be protected until all signs of frost are past. Now at last I dare to open their door.

This year's tomatoes are starting a new life in the greenhouse, while beans and peas are taking a chance with the bantams in the vegetable garden. And as usual broad beans already stand in robust rows held to attention by baler twine. Courgettes vie for space among last year's missed potatoes. Sweet peas are taking off at last after a terrible chilling by a late freak frost. And joy of joy, my new box hedge is sprouting greenly round the herb beds.

Strawberries sprout out of black plastic in the polytunnel, my new attempt to beat the nasturtium infestation. Salad leaves are ready to cut and aubergine and basil must be planted out this week. Brassicas are coming along nicely while beetroot seedlings, leeks and parsnips begin to germinate at last. French beans stare at me imploringly, bursting out of their seed trays. I wonder how I can possibly sit here writing with so many plants shouting for attention.

Ali weeds the herbaceous borders; Paul mends the pump in the pond, all the while gazing lovingly at his newly constructed pergola. Roger cuts the grass and Stephen fixes broken gates, clears the farmyard and dags the sheep.

Donkeys must be groomed, coats brushed, hooves oiled. Chickens will be put on parade, bantams, no doubt, allowed to wreak havoc as usual. Chicks will be on display with mother in the yard, ewes and lambs will decorate the hillside and old rams will doubtless gaze grumpily from the orchard. Oh, please may the sun shine!

Maybe I will share some of my Elderflower Cordial. This year the lemony scent of elderflowers filled the farmyard as never before. Even after I had harvested so many flower heads the bushes looked untouched. I was given a traditional recipe by a friend who was given it, in turn, by her grandmother years and years ago. My kitchen was filled with bowls covered with cloths for days and days and already I wish I had made more.

It is so simple: first soak sixty flower heads, eight lemons, 8lb of granulated sugar and 6oz of citric acid in 5 pints of water for five days. Then strain through muslin into sterilised bottles and store in the fridge. It can be pasteurised or frozen in plastic containers.

ALLOTMENTS

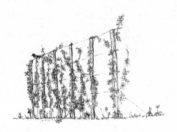

Meanwhile, as we prepare for our day in June, there is another pocket of frenzied gardening activity taking place in a corner of Swansea Bay! Tucked away behind tall trees on the edge of the park, under the battlements of Oystermouth Castle my dear childhood friend, Julia and husband Bill, together with their old friend, Ken, beaver away restoring their allotment to championship standards.

Julia had become increasingly frustrated at the lack of space in her exquisite little gem of a town garden. Every corner had been used to maximum effect but space was at a premium. She decided to put their names on a waiting list for a plot in the Mumbles. One day they reached the top of the list and were 'allotted' their quarter-acre site. It was a scene of dereliction; the weeds were simply winning. Digging began. Now, hours and hours, months and months of work later, perfect raised beds are host to a myriad of vegetables and flowers, standing to attention in perfect rows. Julia likes order!

Tea must be taken regularly to restore strength, so umbrella and chairs are stored along with tools in the recycled shed. Recycling is the allotment mantra. Community spirit binds the gardeners together. They share tools, salvaged treasures of all sorts, plants, skills and laughter, and, hmm, sometimes grumpiness and competition. All human life is here!

I wonder if Julia ponders the coincidences of history as she cycles along the seafront to her little paradise. Oystermouth Castle in the Mumbles is considered by historians as the finest castle in the Gower Peninsular. It was founded by William de Londres in the twelfth century but burned down twice by the Welsh in 1116 and 1215. Who were these Norman incomers? In the thirteenth century it subsequently fell into the hands of de Braose, Lords of Gower, who made the castle their permanent residence. Edward I is said to have been a guest in 1284.

As I read on about the emergence and decline of this majestic castle, my mind flicks back to those allotments so close by. Have they too been there since Norman times? Certainly, there is evidence in parts of Britain, of Saxon 'field' clearings in the woods to be held for common use. The invading Normans began to claim land both for themselves and for the church. Did Julia's allotment beneath the castle walls escape such a fate? Was the land confiscated from the church during the reformation?

In the late sixteenth century during Elizabeth's reign, common land began to be 'enclosed' and 'allotted' to tenanted cottages. The seventeenth and eighteenth centuries saw the beginning of a huge migration of people to the cities and common land continued to disappear. As life became more and more urbanised, the 1845 Inclosure Act tried to enforce field gardens of ten rods, that is gardens of 302 square yards or 253 square metres or, quarter of an acre to us now, for the poor. This was in line with the Victorian belief that allotments provided a productive use of time, keeping the poor from the evils of drink and providing wholesome food for a workforce housed in tenements and high-density terracing without gardens... In 1887 another act, largely ignored, obliged local authorities to provide allotments. It was not until 1908 that parishes and urban and borough councils had this responsibility forced upon them. Then, of course, the 1914–18 war brought food shortages and the threat of starvation to thousands of working people. It was the railway companies who came to the rescue this time, giving their workers plots of land beside the tracks on which to grow much needed food. Hence the rows and rows of allotments that whizz past us, as we gaze out of the train window.

The Second World War gave birth to the Dig for Victory campaign and once again allotments flourished. After the war and when rationing finally ended land prices began to climb. Allotments disappeared under urban redevelopment. There was a brief resurgence in the 1970 with the TV programme *The Good Life* but, as supermarkets took hold and land prices continued an upward spiral, vegetable gardening dwindled in the urban landscape and lost its thrill.

Now suddenly there is a great reawakening, a new awareness of the chemical content of our food, of air miles and insecticides. And people don't like what they read. They worry about their diet in this sea of plenty. They worry about the wholesomeness of the food that they are feeding their children. Allotments once abandoned and neglected, are suddenly sought after and desirable. Waiting lists are appearing. Young and old alike are turning up. Families, children in tow, armed with spades and cultivators, packets of seeds and a huge amount of enthusiasm are digging their way back to growing their own food. A gardening army is on the march again, a quiet revolution!

Oh, and then of course there is that other underground movement: the urban guerrilla gardeners causing havoc in the cites by clandestinely clearing litter, planting trees and flowers, vegetables and shrubs, turning barren urban wasteland into beauty, bringing fun and companionship back into communities. How bad is that!

So, hurrah to Julia, Bill and Ken, and all valiant allotment gardeners, who are helping us to revalue and preserve vital skills in such serious danger of extinction. Let's dig for the victory of the preservation of our environment this time.

MIDSUMMER DREAMING

The sun is shining down in that funny, crystal clear, watery-July sort of way. The sky glows an infinitive iridescent turquoise, crowded with outrageously unreal puffy clouds. Great blobs of soft white meringue race across blue emptiness. Dragonflies and glimmering damsels hover over the crispy white cups of water lilies on the pond. The wind stirs up the scent of roses hurling their petals into the air. Sheep and cows stand out like little plastic farmyard toys dotted across the hillside and the trees, silhouetted on the hilltops, surely all belong to Hornby. Of course, it is all too good to be true. Perfect visibility means rain, more rain, horizontal rain, sideways rain, rain, rain, rain.

It rained on midsummer evening as Titania and Oberon railed at each other over possession of the Changeling child, as Lysander and Demetrius, Helena and Hermia fell under Puck's impish spell. It continued to rain as the lover's confusion grew. It rained as the men drew their swords and Hermia and Helena ranted wildly exchanging insults.

It rained as the Mechanicals planned the performance of their 'Lamentable Comedy' of Pyramus and Thisbe for the Duke and Duchess. Alas, as they rehearsed with damp gusto, hoping nervously for riches rather than the gallows, Puck was still up to no good. Bottom found himself rudely 'translated' into an Ass. Titania, drugged too, by a magic potion, slept wetly in her bower, only to wake and fall hopelessly in love with this slightly soggy Ass. Fairies danced lightly in the raindrops and fairy lights twinkled through the trees glistening on the pond. Puck glowed greenly from his secret tree watching his mischief unfold. And still it rained.

It continued to rain as Oberon stepped in and made Puck undo his mischief and restore order and love. It rained as the grand Duke Theseus and his Duchess arrived for their wedding feast. It rained as the Mechanicals clumsily unfolded their impossible farce.

And, despite the rain, we had a huge audience in the beautiful terraced garden overlooking the river below. In they came with umbrellas, oilskins, tarpaulins, damp smoked salmon sandwiches, slippery bottles of watery wine, laughter and love!

'Surly they'll go home in the interval', we waterlogged thespians asked as we tipped toed from our polytunnel dressing room. 'They won't stay to the end, will they?'

We looked at each other astonished…they did. They gave us a standing ovation after both performances, and we, the cast, applauded them for their steadfastness. It was truly magical!

Fireworks cracked through the wet night air; music filled the dripping sky. Only in Britain, we laughed; only in Britain could we be so triumphantly daft and carry on with such huge success, in the pouring rain. Somehow the adrenaline cut in even more than usual!

Phone calls and emails followed. How had we done it? How come it was so professional? Were all the actors really just amateurs? 'I saw a production in Regents Park and yours was better!' 'Really?' 'Yes, really!'

But then of course, we live in this funny corner of the world where people appear from nowhere to lend their professional technical skill. 'Oh, by the way, I do/did that for a living. Can I help?' It happened over and over again until we had the most extraordinary team to bring this dream of the Dream to life. It really was one of the happiest and most fun things I have done for a very long time. Extraordinary!

Oh, and it's still raining!

CABBAGES AND SUMMER RAIN

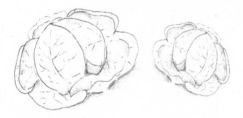

It's three in the morning and the storm that woke me from a restless sleep, is easing a little. Exceptional rain, the worst since records began, has dominated most of July. A few glorious days seduced us briefly into believing summer had finally arrived. Balmy heat haze across the fields brought the farmers out in a brief frenzy of activity racing to get in hay and cut corn while it was dry. But, alas, the rain is back with a vengeance.

The kittens greeted me wetly as I walked out of the backdoor in the middle of the night. They raced downstairs eagerly to my basement study hoping for a midnight feast. Min and Meg looked up from their baskets for a second and wearily shut their eyes tight. Wellie didn't stir. Ginger Fred is, I suppose, out hunting and picking fights.

Kittens, fully grown now, have left for more wet nocturnal adventures. Actually, they're not kittens any more. I've had them a whole year. A whole year since I visited Phil's farm and learned all about his sheep; a whole year since he and Gail pressed two tiny furry boys into my hands and said, 'Here you are, take these home with you!' They still bounce round my study when I'm writing, climbing across the computer keys, adding interesting punctuation and even weirder spelling than my very own. I am constantly amazed at the pleasure they give me – funny, happy affectionate little animals. Such a contrast to the grumpy

Fred, who only speaks about food, then says he wants a chat and rewards with a sharp bite. Funny old boy, he either growls grumpily at the newcomers or tries to pretend they don't exist; I guess he feels a bit displaced.

All the other animals are getting old. Little Min, the feisty Cairn, will be fifteen in September. She still potters off and gets lost but has finally given up ratting for a quieter life. Her great love is Boris, the boy next door, who is singularly disinterested in an old girl like her, having a bright new collie companion of his own. Deaf and a bit dotty she pursues him undeterred.

Meg at eleven is getting less enthusiastic about climbing hills to bring down the sheep but then, she's always been keen on me giving her a hand! Even her daft daughter, Wellie, is eight. Can it really be more than eight years ago that the wayward Buck, (pronounced in the village as BOOK) passed by, leaving me a legacy of nine collie lurcher-cross puppies? I ran fast but not as fast as him and, alas, I was too late. I remember wondering how I was going to tell Paul his beloved sheepdog was in pup! And now I have her daughter, the incredibly intelligent, loving, anxious Wellie whose terror knows no limit at the sound of thunder, gunshots or, indeed, even the odd champagne cork.

Dandy is thirty-five now by my reckoning – a dear old donkey, gentle and safe with my grandchildren. He's plagued once more with an abscess in his foot. A fault line right through one hoof makes him so susceptible to infection in this muddy wet weather. He's improving now and today we were able to put the little boot on his bad foot once more and let him out with the other donkeys, which cheered him up. He climbed to the top of his field for the best grass so I think he's feeling better.

A new generation of chickens is appearing in the yard as hen after hen appears leading another procession of those fluffy ping-pong balls. We rush around gathering up each new family and finding them safe, rat-free quarters to raise their young.

Some of the chicks have hatched from blue eggs so the old Araucana fellow has left his legacy.

Lambs graze wetly on the hill, fat now on sweet summer grass. Ewes are getting into shape for autumn and the arrival of a new tup. The last of the hoggs are heading for customers' deep freezes. Round go the seasons again. Maybe it's time to try for sleep once more and dream about what I can do with a truly enormous cabbage I have just been gifted!

I had a call from a friend recently, asking if she could bring someone to see me to learn about donkeys with a view to buying her own. My donkey advice was rewarded with the vast brassica – what on earth to do with it. It is a huge quantity for the two of us and the vegetable garden is at its most abundant now, despite rain and potato blight. Although I have broad beans and runner beans, French ones on the way, pea-beans and courgettes, carrots and turnips, lettuce and chicory, aubergines and tomatoes, but I have no cabbage. My own brassica, cavolo nero, purple-sprouting, and a new one this year, pink Brussels sprouts will not be ready for some time yet.

Restless and grounded by asthma and rain, I turned to Jane Grigson for some enlightenment on cabbage and, true to her great self, she told me that cabbage has been eaten here since the time of the Celts and Romans, that it has 'original sin' and needs improvement and has a nasty history of being good for you! I love it! Read Pliny, she says, if you don't believe me.

Cabbage still gets such a bad press! But it can be wonderful as long as it isn't boiled for so long that an awful rotten egg smell pervades the kitchen and it is reduced to a yellow mess reminiscent of my school dinners!

Well that was it, I tipped out all my cookery books from their shelves yet again and, intrigued now by this humble veg, indulged myself in hours of reading! I was on a roll! The Greeks and Romans believed cabbage would stop them getting drunk.

Some think this is indeed borne out by recent research at a Texan university where cabbage is said to be 'hostile' to the vine. And some Mediterranean farmers never plant brassicas near vines or beehives believing bees transfer the odour to both grapes and honey, tainting both.

Horace apparently liked it with pickled pork. Diogenes is said to have lived, astonishingly, on only cabbage and water. And I did indeed find out a little of Pliny's views on the subject too; he wrote recipes for cabbage with leeks, olives, semolina, pine kernels, raisins and pepper, while extolling the healing properties of this humble brassica. But, alas, from Roman times to Medieval banquets it was renowned for causing wind, inciting Lucullus to declare it had no place at a gentleman's table. Indeed, it was forbidden in sixth century BC in China and in India four hundred years later. And years later Dr Johnson mentions it in his rule of etiquette as the 'ill wind behind'!

The earliest cabbage was a wild tough derivative of the mustard plant and sea cabbage, *Brassica oleracea*, unpalatable to us now. It was grown as a herb and allowed to bolt, by northern European peasants, who stewed it with onions and the occasional belly of salt pork. It supplemented their meagre winter diet of bread, grain, porridge and ale.

In the Middle Ages cabbage plasters were used for sciatica and varicose ulcers. In the eighteenth century Captain Cook took crates of cabbage on board ship to prevent scurvy and cabbage compresses were used to prevent gangrene.

It was not until the sixteenth century the word legume, for vegetables, replaced the term herb and the Savoy cabbage arrived. It continued as the staple of northern Europe throughout the eighteenth century, appearing salted and fermented as early sauerkraut accompanying sausages. Over the border into France it was *choucroute*, with the newly arrived potatoes, and with veal cooked in fermented milk.

My splendid 1880 Mrs Beeton tells me to boil cabbage in half a 'galleon' of water, 1 tablespoon of salt and a small piece of soda. Cook in plenty of fast boiling water till tender… Savoy ½–¾ of an hour and summer cabbage 10–15 minutes; cost 2d in season. Oh dear, original sin indeed and a strong smell of sulphur to boot! Memories of 1950s school dinners fill my head once more! I always wondered how the cooks achieved the soggy, smelly yellow mess swimming around an enormous aluminium dish!

But cabbage *can* be delicious, yes, really! Red cabbage, cooked long and slow with apples, smoked bacon and juniper berries, is a delicious accompaniment to game birds, sausages and venison.

Spring cabbage fried quickly with a chopped shallot in butter and a little oil, to stop the butter burning, is a fresh and crunchy companion to grilled chops or bacon. Stir in some crème fraîche, pine nuts or a spoonful of pesto together with some chopped deseeded tomatoes and you have a quick pasta sauce; not a classic, I admit, but very good, nevertheless.

I stripped the outside leaves from my gargantuan gift and carefully blanched them for a couple of minutes in boiling water. Carefully dried on kitchen paper, then wrapped separately in layers, they went into the deep freeze. They will re-emerge in time to be stuffed with various spicy fillings of chicken or pork, rice or couscous. Placed in an ovenproof dish and covered with a cheesy sauce they will provide comforting warming suppers as an autumn chill descends on the valley.

I'm so glad to have received my cabbage gift!

DARK DAYS OF AUTUMN

Golden autumn sunshine briefly floods the rain-soaked valley. Geese are arriving once more for the winter. Sheep glisten on the hillside, their fleece still wet from the relentless summer rain. The dry interlude has brought yet another frenzy of activity across the county as farmers race to save the remains of their sodden crops. Tractors, combines, ploughs and harvesters growl their way over the fields cutting brown overripe corn, ploughing through mud, lifting overdue potatoes, saving whatever they can as fast as they can. More rain is on its way. Suddenly the dark sky is back, and there is a sharp chill in the wind. An air of gloom hangs over us all as we realise winter approaches following the summer that never arrived.

We are told August was the worst month since records began in 1929. Acres of crops have been lost across the whole country. Flooding has been widespread and hundreds of lambs have been lost in floods – 800 in Northumberland alone. For some farmers this is the second time they have been flooded in two years. It bodes badly for the winter months ahead. Wheat is sprouting in the fields as rain prevents harvest and crops must be written off as drying costs soar with the world hike in oil prices. Potatoes rot in waterlogged soil; other root crops simply fail to mature in the cold wet weather. Salad crops are not germinating and the cold spring and late frost devastated most of the fruit crop. Although cider makers say that they have a bumper crop of apples.

I worry about feeding sheep and donkeys as the winter months draw near. Hay and straw will be expensive and scarce and, although we have plenty of grass at the moment, it is poor quality and lacks sugar. We'll have to supplement everyone's winter feed, particularly the ewes, if we are to have sturdy lambs next year. This year's lambs have suffered everywhere from the lack of sun on their backs and are finishing more slowly than ever.

And then, of course, there is the world stage to bring us even more despair as financial markets crash around our ears. Our own political climate is no better with media feeding us a steady daily flow of doom and gloom – little to lift our hearts in these grey September days. Indeed, a creeping feeling of helplessness is threatening to take hold and must be resisted at all costs.

So, I turn once more to my garden for solace. I harvest what crops I can and enjoy the fading blooms of autumn. Gentians glow bright blue by the back door. Blousy pink cosmos, scarlet dahlias and pale anemones clash wildly by the pond.

Huge water lily leaves glisten in the evening light and the clerodendron tree fills the air with sweet scent. The last roses and geraniums flower bravely on despite rain and wind. Autumn leaves change colour and glow briefly in fleeting sunlight. The little Katsura tree, golden now, smells of burned toffee as I pass by on my way to the yard to feed chickens and donkeys and check sheep. Late broods of new chicks crowd the farmyard, miraculously surviving storms and predators.

Vegetables of all sorts go into the deep freeze, with more urgency than ever as food prices rise across the board. I managed to pick a good crop of beans before disease ruined the plants.

Courgettes exploding into marrows in the wet weather will feed all those chickens in the barren winter months. Chard stalks glow pink, yellow and scarlet beneath their glossy green leaves. Turnips, carrots and swedes swelled in the wet ground and have been rescued before they rot. Potato blight devastated the tops of the plants but, by cutting them down quickly, I still have a reasonable crop. Tomato plants turned brown and crisp, suffering, I suppose, from the same blight as the spuds but the fruit is still ripening on its dying host. In the polytunnel I have had a few small feeble aubergines and three fine pumpkins, huge, shiny and dark orange, but yet another blight has withered and whitened the leaves. Meanwhile a marauding army of cabbage white caterpillars marches relentlessly through the salad crop, stripping bare every leaf.

It has indeed been a very strange year in the vegetable garden but I have a great new arrival in my kitchen...every cloud, even one as big as this year's summer, has a silver lining! The terrifying rise in oil prices forced me to sit down and look long and hard at my oil bill and my poor inefficient old cooker. It had to go. It dried the clothes and heated the water but the minute I lifted its lid or put something in the oven to cook, it threw up its metaphorical hands and the temperature plummeted. We twiddled our fingers wondering when it would allow us to eat. And all the while it gobbled more and more oil.

So now we have a shiny new electric range with a separate heat source to the two hot plates, two ovens and, oh wonder, even a grill! This means they all independently hold their heat. If I use the simmering plate, the hot oven remains hot; if I bake bread in the top oven the simmering plate still holds its temperature! Obvious really, but I didn't realise how used I had become to limping along with my grumpy old fellow. Best of all the new girl has an 'eco' button, which turns the temperature of the whole cooker down all night, bringing it up again in time for breakfast. How clever is that!

Cooking has become a real pleasure and relaxation once more. I no longer think, 'Oh I can't cook that; poor old fellow won't manage it.' Potatoes roast, vegetables too. Pastry crisps, soufflés rise, gratins brown, bread bakes crisp and golden, meat roasts succulently and briskly. Stews and ragouts mellow gently in the cooler oven. Herbs and tomatoes dry in the third little warming oven and I am making wonderful real yoghurt once more. Cooking is fun again!

The last of the broad beans are blanched and added to a béchamel sauce that is enriched with cream and ham and accompanied by a baked potato.

Chard makes a delicious Flan. The leaves are blanched quickly too, before they are added to their colourful chopped stems, which have been softened in a little butter and oil, with garlic and chopped shallots. Mixed with a couple of fresh eggs from the farmyard and a dollop of cream I turn the mixture into a pastry case, sprinkle the top with grated cheese and bake in the top oven until the pastry is crisp and the filling quiveringly set.

Root vegetables are sliced and sprinkled with salt, then roasted in the hottest part of the oven in olive oil to make a light supper with couscous or rice.

Any of the garden vegetables are dragooned into use for a quick lunchtime soup; sweated in oil until just soft they are added to a tub of defrosted chicken stock, simmered gently, seasoned and served with crusty homemade bread.

And now I am even able to cook our own lamb chops, pink and succulent, under my fierce new grill. I blanch some of the last runner beans, before cooking them in olive oil with my own chopped tomatoes and a clove of garlic until the tomatoes melt. Add some Pink Fir Apple potatoes that have escaped the blight and we have a small delicious feast all harvested from our little piece of Devon.

I daresay I will even make a cake one day and maybe, at last, even manage exploding, crunchy, golden Yorkshire puds!

HOLDING ON THIS CHRISTMAS

My tipsy little Christmas tree sits jauntily in the dining room, sporting the same dear old decorations its predecessors have worn for years. I love the sameness of it, the reassuring repetition. Same old well-worn, slightly shabby decorations, presents piling up on the floor, excited grandchildren trying to guess the contents. The cats bouncing at the baubles, dogs sniffing out the chocolates, fairy lights winking in the dusk, crackers on the table, fire crackling in the grate, yummy cooking smells from the stove – same old rituals, same old timetable, all so reassuring.

And this year, as the very bedrock of our society wobbles precariously about us, as people are caught up in war around the world, the struggle to find enough to eat, to get medical help, keep homes and jobs, survive one way or another, that shabby sameness seems even more important than ever before.

Christmas and New Year are for family and friends, for loving and sharing. We have a chance to give each one another the free gifts of life – time, space, companionship, fun, laughter and love.

It's hard though, as we hear the news, read papers, watch television, look at the Internet; it's hard to hold the faith and believe that we do get through hard times just as we get through the good times. Time passes.

The sheep are getting fat on the hill. They'll be lambing in a few weeks without a clue about interest rates; hedge funds have quite another meaning for them. Sheepdogs aren't interested in subprime problems either; no mortgage on their kennels. Donkeys are just so pleased with their new hay and mineral derivative that they don't care about the credit crunch either. And the chickens don't waste a thought on politicians. Lucky them, I wish I could say the same! Instead I find myself wondering where on earth we're going and fretting pointlessly about what the New Year will bring.

So, unable to change the world, I turn once more to cooking a Christmas feast for family and friends. It's time for delicious traditional roast turkey, ham, sausages, stuffing, roast potatoes, Brussels sprouts and chestnuts, bread sauce, cranberries. I could go on and on. Oh, and I will. Next, comes Christmas pudding, mince pies, brandy butter, Stilton, port. Then before you know it, it's teatime: scones and cream, Christmas cake, all far too much, of course but, oh, so comforting and familiar in turbulent times.

We had nineteen for lunch last Sunday, which concentrated my mind wonderfully! We had a glazed ham and a beautiful piece of cold rare beef with fresh herbs, olive oil and wasabi. I cooked a Galantine of Chicken stuffed with marinated pork, juniper berries and spinach. A guest looked at it in surprise. 'Why is that chicken so flat? Is it road kill?' How I laughed and thought serves me right for showing off; but it did taste good!

I grilled polenta and boiled Pink Fir Apple potatoes to go with a salad of peas and broad beans with bacon and artichoke hearts. We had a green salad of leaves from the polytunnel, another of shredded raw root vegetables and grilled red peppers with plenty of garlic and olive oil.

I made tiny chocolate mousse in coffee cups for pudding, that sumptuous hazelnut meringue cake with apricot conserve and last year's raspberries from the deep freeze and a big tarte aux pommes with windfall apples still lying about in the garden.

We had a big soft Brie and Italian Flatbread with raisins and grapes. I cheat with that, making the dough in the bread maker then dividing it in half and pulling each half into a thin flat circle. I put the first circle onto a baking tray and smother it with fat raisins and grapes. Then the second circle goes on top and I press more grapes into the dough, sprinkle with sugar and put it somewhere warm to rise for at least half an hour to an hour. It takes about 25 minutes to bake in a hot oven at 200°C. Served slightly warm and gooey it's delicious with any soft cheese.

To make the Galantine of Chicken I need a large free-range fresh chicken and a sharp filleting knife with a flexible blade. Also, a couple of big shallots or a large onion, 500g of minced pork, 200g of chicken livers, a few juniper berries, a couple of fat cloves of garlic, mixed dried herbs and the zest and juice of a lemon. Add to that a good splash of red wine, a couple of handfuls of blanched spinach leaves and, of course, salt and pepper.

I chop the onion, crush the juniper berries in a pestle and mortar and crush the garlic to a paste with a little salt. I strip the zest from the lemon and squeeze the juice and stir all this together into the pork with the mixed herbs, red wine, salt and pepper.

While that is infusing, I bone the chicken with a sharp knife, being careful not to puncture the skin. I leave the wing bones in to give a little structure.

When the carcass and the thigh bones are removed, I open the meat out flat and season it well. I press half the pork mixture into the chicken followed by half the blanched spinach then arrange the chicken livers on the spinach, then repeat the layers with the remaining spinach and pork.

Carefully, I close the chicken and sew up using fine string and a larding needle. I gently try to press the chicken roughly back into a chicken shape so it doesn't look as if it's been run over! I wrap it in foil and place in a close-fitting dish. I stand the dish in a bain-marie (a roasting tin half-filled with hot water) and cook at 180°C for about 1½ hours.

I do keep testing with a skewer; if the juices run clear it is cooked through. If the juices are pink, I continue cooking for a further few minutes and test again.

Once I'm satisfied it's cooked, I take it out of the oven, drain the bain-marie and put a heavy weight on top of the chicken until it is cool, then, into the fridge.

I serve it sliced on a large plate decorated with fresh lemons and salad leaves.

A Hazelnut Meringue Cake must be one of the best!

For the meringue I need two 20cm cake tins, four egg whites, 250g of sugar and about 150g of hazelnuts.

First, I grease the tins and line them with non-stick baking paper and oil again.

I preheat the oven to 190°C. Next I brown the hazelnuts and, when cool, grind them until fine in my coffee grinder; it works well!

To make the meringue I whisk the egg whites with half the sugar until stiff, then gently fold in the remaining sugar. In go the groundnuts, then into the oven for 30–40 minutes. I check regularly; all ovens differ! The meringue should be lightly browned, dry and slightly chewy.

While it cools on a rack, I whip some cream to soft peaks and mix it with a compote of apricots. I sandwich this between the two halves and decorate with raspberries and icing sugar. It really is one of the best!

A FRESH START

Despite the love and laughter of family and friends over Christmas, I find myself entering the New Year with a certain gloom and trepidation that I have rarely, if ever, experienced at this time of year. Usually, with the dark days of November and December behind me, I find, with delight, the first snowdrop, watch with anticipation the fat expectant ewes, and, walking over crisp sunny hills, my thoughts turn optimistically to an early spring.

This year I am confused. On the one hand, I am dogged by despair. War rages in the Gaza Strip, famine and disease is left unaddressed in Zimbabwe and all over Africa. In the US and Britain businesses and banks are going bust, people are losing jobs and homes. We are being urged to spend our way out of debt, and, by increasing our debts save the economy. How mad is that, or have I missed something somewhere?

And yet and yet at the same time I feel a strange niggle of hope for, well, maybe, perhaps a tiny hint of something changing, values shifting, ideas being challenged? Just recently I begin to detect a subtle change in the use of words in the media. Words I haven't seen for years are creeping back, words like love, kindness, friendship, caring, compassion and altruism or am I just caught in a trap of wishful thinking?

A strange thing happened yesterday. I was searching for some photographs for a friend when I came upon an old tatty photo album of my mother's, stuffed unceremoniously into the back of a bookshelf. There were indeed a few of the sought-after old pictures but as I turned the pages out fell a copy of *Picture Post*, 3 May 1941: Morning After the Blitz, 3d.

My morning disappeared as I read my way from front to back. Fascinating wartime adverts for every sort of remedy, letters from readers, some touching, some furious. And then there were the photographs of devastation that was London. The account by one, Louis MacNeice, is so moving – his walk through the wreckage the next morning fired by the sense of defiance, sharp humour and survival of men and women caught in the midst of it. But it was the photographs that really moved me. I grew up in London in the aftermath of World War II. The bombs had stopped just before I was born, as had the guns and the air raids, but London was ravaged, full of ruins, smog and desolation. Here were the pictures of how it happened when it happened and, to my horror, they were no different to the pictures of the Gaza Strip in my paper today. Hospitals destroyed, homes wrecked, people wounded, people standing in the street in despair, people coping, helping, clearing. What have we learned? Why is it still happening?

Riveted, I turned the pages, mesmerised by each article, until I reached the back – the farming page, 'Does Backyard Farming Pay?'

Mr Jones, a London businessman apparently, started his smallholding after the outbreak of war. He soon discovered that to be totally self-supporting with milk and eggs he needed 20 acres of land. Remember, he tells us, that he needed not only grazing land, but land for growing the feed, as food stuff was not available with rationing and it was no good buying animals he was unable to feed. On 20 acres he found it just possible to keep two cows, a calf or two, fifty poultry and a horse for ploughing. Five of the twenty acres was for grazing, ten reserved for hay, four under a cereal crop, and one under root crops.

He goes on to explain in detail the yield from each crop, feeding instructions for livestock, indeed every detail of a smallholding. If you have a mere 2 acres, he says, then your approach will be different. Geese are good, as are hens and goats. But Mr Jones is strongly anti-pig, as they eat so voraciously! Everything you need to know to get you started in farming is here on one back page of *Picture Post* 1941 together with wonderful photographs of Mr Jones in action!

I had to smile. As waiting lists for allotments grow and credit-crunched homeowners are urged to grow their own, here is advice of all those years ago that stands up, oh, *so* well right now! Indeed, it has a lot in common with how we have been farming here in this valley, unfashionably, for all these years! Add this to Thomas Tusser's advice of 1557 with his *Five Hundred Points of Good Husbandry* and you're in business! Well almost; we do have a 1964 Dexta tractor and an old 1970s Lamborghini one instead of a horse. Donkeys don't plough so well, or maybe I simply haven't tried hard enough to teach them!

How is it that as the postwar years of prosperity have gone rolling by, we have not only, by and large, lost many of these skills but also the respect for those who still have them? Could it be that my funny little optimistic niggle is about a return of respect and a revaluing of these disappearing skills and the people who do still have them?

And that brings me naturally, as you may guess, to the question of food. Will old-fashioned straightforward food creep back on to menus too? Will we be spared a 'jus' underneath everything, raspberry vinegar, and even perhaps that strange modern interpretation of food cooked 'sous vide'. Please may we have a properly cooked straightforward plate of locally and ethically produced, seasonal food? It must be the dreary dark days of January but no sooner had I finished reading *Picture Post* than I was shuffling through my box file of recipes from my student days of cooking!

Oh my, what's this: boiled cod and egg sauce, oh no, memories of childhood! This one sounds a little better: cod dimitri. Bake the fish and serve with a white sauce, anchovies and parsleyed potatoes. Not quite so bad!

Cauliflower Mornay, blanched cauliflower finished in the oven or under the grill with white sauce and grated cheese, merits two cards. It is an incredibly complicated affair apparently. The milk for the sauce is first infused with peppercorns, a blade of mace and sliced onion. The cauliflower is broken into sprigs, well washed in those pre-hydroponic days; vegetables still touched real soil then and needed washing! Next, it is boiled, so I read, for an incredible 12–15 minutes. Don't do it!

What did I say about straightforward food? On go the instructions. 'Butter a pudding basin. Arrange sprigs in basin, stalks inwards so as to completely fill basin, seasoning between the layers. Dot with butter and press down lightly. Now turn it out onto a fireproof dish, cover with the prepared sauce made with the infused milk. Cover with breadcrumbs and grated cheese and brown in a hot oven for 12–15 minutes.' Wasn't it Shirley Conran who said life's too short to stuff a mushroom?

This next one sounds good: Veal and Ham Pie, a rare and delicious thing these days. Despite giving quantities there are no instructions for making the required 8oz of flaky pastry, so best just buy it ready-made! It improves if it's rolled out twice adding more butter between the layers to make it a bit flakier.

Now here are my student instructions for the pie!

Cut 1½lb of shoulder or pie veal into pieces 1½ inches square…sorry, nothing metric then… Cut 4oz ham or gammon rashers into thin strips. If gammon is used remove the rind and the rust? I'm not too sure what that means! Cut it into strips and blanch. Arrange the meat, ham and three quartered hard-boiled eggs, a dessert spoon of finely chopped onion and the same of parsley, in layers until a pie dish is filled and doming slightly. Pour in enough stock to fill dish three parts full. Cover with pastry. Knock up the edges. Make a small hole in the centre of the pie. Decorate with pastry leaves and brush with a little beaten egg containing a pinch of salt.

Put pie to cook at Reg 7/425°F for approx. 30 minutes.

Then wrap the pie in the double sheet of wet greaseproof paper; replace in the oven and lower the temperature to Reg 4/350°F. Continue cooking for 1 hour, or until meat is tender when tested with a thin skewer. Serve hot or cold. If cold, add more stock to the filling through the hole in the crust. I can't help wondering how the pastry stands up to this!

It probably does make a delicious pie *but* I fear that maybe these instructions demonstrate why so many of us have lost the will to cook! Now, without doubt, I would gently cook the veal and gammon filing first. Then assemble the pie with the eggs, etc. and simply put it into the oven long enough to cook the pastry; none of this wet greaseproof paper palaver.

Happy New Year!

RAIN, SNOW AND LAMBS

No time for writing, no time for cooking or gardening, no time to plan next summer's planting, no time to keep in touch with friends, no time to read, sit still, just be, no time to sleep, no time for anything except lambing and fighting the elements. Lambs were born in record time this year; never have we had so many so quickly, all entering such an unusually cold, dismal world. For several weeks before the first babies were due, we started bringing the ewes down from the fields every evening as usual. We were so glad to have our big old sheds in the farmyard where they could find food and shelter each night, protected from the wild weather.

Every year, after they have lambed, we move the ewes into individual pens and leave them for a day or two to get them started and make sure all is well. Then they join the others in the 'nursery' where lambs play together and mothers eat hay and rest before going back into the fields: the annual routine.

This year was so different. Snow followed by sleet followed by rain and gales forced us to keep everyone in for weeks instead of days. Despite heavy snow falls, little settled, and snowflakes quickly turned to sleet, whipped up by an icy north wind. Then the old familiar 'stair rod' rain returned; nothing 'sideways' about it, just a relentless pouring torrent transforming fields into muddy swamps – grey days, cold and dark, following one upon another. We are not used to this weather in Devon and Cornwall.

Now suddenly the sky turns blue, we see the sun again for a brief spell, there seems to be a hint of spring in the air. Even the white snowy sugar sprinkle on Haytor, far away in distant Dartmoor, has gone. It hung around long after the snow on the rest of the Moor had melted, a crisp and lingering reminder of paralysing cold, so rare in this Gulf Stream-warmed peninsula.

It is half-term and the children are here for a week. There is great competition to feed Dinky, our one bottle-fed lamb. A beautiful little ewe, one of twins, her mother rejected her. Usually this means something is wrong, but Dinky seems to be going from strength to strength, thriving on all the human attention.

At last Paul and Harry, now seven, were able to move the ewes and lambs up onto fresh grass this morning. They walked up the hill to the beautiful top field we call 'Dainty' after an erstwhile pony of that name. A sheltered spot despite its height, it looks towards Dartmoor to the north and the river to the east. A little old barn in the corner offers sheep extra shelter if the bad weather does return.

Birds are singing. All sorts of tits, blue, long-tailed, coal, are pushing and shoving one another on the bird feeder. I watched anxiously this morning, ready to warn a magnificent green woodpecker, as he marched daringly about the back lawn, of advancing kittens. Huge swathes of snowdrops, unchecked by the terrible weather, tumble down the orchard in celebration once more, liberated by all the cutting and clearing last autumn. Now that it's dry, a stone wall will be finished to hold back the bank where rhododendrons and camellias grow. Hellebores are creeping into flower and the first daffodil is showing a yellow glow on its dropped head. A few early celandines and primroses poke their tiny heads through the tangled grass.

A certain anxiety is beginning to grip me as weeks fly past and the bad weather prevents me from working outside. There is just so much to do in preparation for our first open day in

June for the National Garden Scheme: a new adventure and not an easy one in a frozen then soggy landscape.

I have almost cleared the polytunnel and replanted the strawberries. Sweet peas, sown before Christmas, are looking promising. Broad beans are starting off inside in boxes this year, an attempt to beat slugs and rabbits. The vegetable garden needs digging and the tomato greenhouse is a shambles, in need of a complete makeover, after the eviction of a bantam squatter and her large and raucous family.

Rosa rugosa, pruned hard for their health, on the advice of my gardening neighbour, resemble dead twigs and make me nervous. I examine them daily for signs of life. The fig tree is in line for a severe pruning too, in a couple of weeks, in an attempt to tame its rampant growth. Herbaceous borders need digging and restocking; plants need splitting and dividing. I even dream, rather optimistically, of new, safe steps leading onto the grass from the back door, if time permits.

In the grape house the tender plants are hanging on to life despite the cold. A tiny heater holds the temperature just above freezing and seems to be winning. The olive tree looks all right, the avocados and the oleander too. But some pelargoniums are suffering and the plumbago looks very sad and cold. The banana has taken a turn for the worse and I'm not convinced that Ali's mum's *Datura* is going to make it either. I rather dread telling her I've failed so soon after it was gifted to me!

Oh, how I long for some warm spring sunshine.

A dear friend gave me some goose fat before she fled this freezing winter and flew away to the warmth of California. I keep imagining her sitting on her hill in the sun looking out across the treetops at Mount Tam, under a bright blue sky in a balmy breeze…

In haste I used the goose fat to 'confit' some duck while the children were here, forgetting I must climb the hill with them to feed Dinky. Time passed and, on my return, I found what I fear will be a rather crispy frazzled version of confit of duck to crunch with chips or disguise in cassoulet in weeks to come!

So time to cook something else to warm and comfort us all this half-term: a traditional free-range roast chicken maybe, with bacon and stuffing, bread sauce, gravy, roast potatoes and a huge dish of mixed vegetables in white sauce. We'll have plums fried in sugar and butter, topped with ice cream and chocolate sauce for pudding and a big piece of ripe Brie to finish.

Then tomorrow I'll make chicken, sweet potato and tomato soup using stock made from the chicken bones. We'll have a giant chicken and mushroom vol-au-vent made from the leftovers for supper. And the very final bits of chicken will go into sandwiches for lunch.

I love half-term!

A LATE SPRING

'Weed, weed, weed', the words of the National Garden Scheme chairman still ring in my ears. Daily, as I struggle to prepare the valley for public gaze once more, I am grateful for last year's dress rehearsal. But I do wonder why I allowed myself to be persuaded to open the garden in June again, this time to raise money for the nursing charities supported by the National Garden Scheme. Then as I dig, weed, weed and dig, a quiet inward smile spreads through me until, laughing out loud, a picture rises up before my inner eye of the barren landscape I took on all those years ago.

I kick off my boots and go to the book shelf to seek out an old photograph album. Surely my memory must be playing tricks but, no; there it all is, just as I remember, my recall accurate: no garden, no garden at all. I find pictures of the huge tumbledown derelict greenhouses that had housed our predecessor's chickens and threatened me with serious injury from falling glass. There are pictures of 'garden fences' made from those old gas cooker parts and corrugated tin. Towering brassicas, higher than me, march up the hill behind the house. A dark, dank tractor shed, full of junk and buried treasure, crowded out the sun where the pond now twinkles. There's our teenage son, Tom, knocking down the breeze block walls; our Aussie friend, Alan, building the pond, laying paths, building steps; a young Paul driving a digger to move earth from the back of the house to fight the damp; me chopping my way through the undergrowth, laying cobbles, digging flowerbeds. There we all are taming the wilderness.

Then there are pictures of the felling of the great Wellingtonia in the front garden after the huge storm in 1989 and the eucalyptus swaying hazardously near the back of the house, threatening the roof in another later gale. We think we make progress but nature always has her way and will take back the valley in no time when I step back and no one follows me.

And I can hardly believe the photographs of that flood water crashing through the valley devastating all in its path – and pictures of the ravaged landscape when the water had subsided. I can still smell the rank mud as I look at the pages. I remember my old goose floating in his water-filled house, banging his poor old head on the roof, chickens quickly learning to swim, our huge old tractor sliding and aquaplaning in the yard. Sheep fleeing safely up the hill and donkeys paddling in their stables, puzzled eeyores filling the air.

It would be years before I could grow anything in the vegetable garden again without plants turning sad and yellow. We never knew what chemical horrors had been washed down the valley in the flood water.

So to have a garden is wonder enough; to have one deemed good enough to open for the National Garden Scheme is truly extraordinary and a huge incentive to make it look as good as I can in order to raise as much as possible for such a wonderful charity, hence my smile!

The unusually cold winter has held me in limbo for weeks until suddenly snow and sleet gave way to blue skies and sun. A swingeing north wind still whistled round us as we moved ewes and lambs to fresh grass up on the top fields but, sheltered by hedges on south-facing slopes, they shook off winter blues and blossomed in the improving weather.

Held back by the cold, all flowers exploded into bloom at once. The early double daffs of February hid underground, only emerging weeks late with their tender cousins – everything happening at once. I keep promising myself that one day I will try to count the different varieties of narcissi cascading through orchard and garden but I have never managed it. Just as I think I'm there another beauty opens. I have no idea where they come from, who planted them or what they are called but as fast as we clear the undergrowth, more and more appear – a nodding blaze of yellow and cream, orange and white singing through the whole garden standing above a glistening carpet of aconite and soft yellow primroses, Leucojum, grape hyacinths and the last hellebores, clashing wonderfully and wildly with blousy pink camellias.

Buds are swelling on all the trees. The first cherry blossom sparkles against blue sky and scudding clouds. Damson trees, covered in fine white snow, scatter their petals in the strong wind and *Caltha* glistens golden by the pond. Big old chickens have returned to their refurbished summer quarters, bantams are rehoused too and cockerel numbers are thankfully reduced. Donkeys climb happily to the top of the hill, glad to stretch their legs and feel the wind on their backs. The kittens, sleek now, fat and fully grown, sneak out at night on hunting expeditions. Fred, old and grouchy, growls as they pass, reminding him of the feline haunts of his youth. Elderly sheepdogs gamble like puppies in the sun. And I do so miss little Cairn, Min.

Warmer weather at last means work in the garden is beginning in earnest. Stephan has nearly finished the new wall that will hold back the hill, should it rain like last year. Ali and I are digging borders, splitting plants, reshaping and redesigning. I go through a bed only to turn and find her working over the same place; I must improve my weeding technique! Paul is fixing pond pumps again, painting chicken houses, mending, making, moving, mentoring!

Sweet peas sown last October are planted out. Broad beans are ready to follow. Courgettes, gourds and melons wait their turn to be liberated from their pots and tomatoes and tomatillos are germinating rather slowly. Peas are starting in the polytunnel too, together with mixed salad leaves, lettuce and early carrots. The herb garden has suffered very badly from the cold and some plants will have to be replaced. My treasured new tiny box hedge, which I planted with such trepidation last year does seem to have survived the cold. Oh my, there is so much to do I can hardly sit still to write.

But it's time to stop anyway and cook meatballs in tomato sauce with garlic and shallots and red wine for supper. We'll have it with spaghetti before we rush out to a meeting this evening. Cooking is a pleasure once more with my terrific new cooker. After all the years spent cooking on my erratic old range it is a joy to know that the temperature is not only what it says it is, but stays there too! Last week I cooked pheasant with celeriac, cider and cream slowly in the bottom oven for 2 hours while I went out. The result was delicious and so easy; meat was cooked and tender but not dry and the sauce slightly thickened. We had boiled potatoes, garlicky flageolet beans with mixed herbs and some of last summer's frozen runner beans followed by local cheese then blackcurrants, strawberries and ice cream.

I even managed a quickly cooked rare roast beef in the very hot new oven recently, the first time for years. My old fellow never reached a high enough temperature to seal the meat and leave the inside pink. I sliced it thick and served it with a dressing of fresh herbs crushed in the pestle and mortar with garlic and olive oil, stir-fried vegetables and, I'm ashamed to say, out of season new potatoes. It was nice though! I poached pears in white wine, reducing the syrup until it coated both pears and ice cream with a sticky golden shine.

Tomorrow I think we'll have sausages with Puy lentils. I'll cook the lentils with shallots, garlic and finely sliced carrots and I'll stir in fresh wild garlic leaves from the garden at the last moment... when I'm gardening, I daydream a lot about cooking...

SUMMERTIME

Days, weeks, months have flown by. Spring has slipped silently into the lush green of summer. As apple blossom fades, roses prepare for their annual show. Will they perform in time? I gaze at them pleadingly. Our first National Garden Scheme open days loom very close now. Will the *Embothrium* still blaze scarlet against the sky? Will the sky be blue or filled with rain and thunder? Will anyone visit. Will there be enough cream teas? Will we get the photography exhibition hung in time? Are my photos good enough? Is my garden good enough? Oh, oh, doubts, doubts haunt me in the early hours.

Serried rows of vegetables are standing to attention in the vegetable garden. Those little box hedge plants are growing, big enough now to hold hands and encircle the herbs. Potatoes, blight-free so far, are sitting snugly in their earthed-up bed. Broad beans begin to flower and French and runners are striking out boldly up their poles. Peas peep somewhat coyly at their twiggy supports, prompting me to cheer them on daily. Gladioli spears stand in rows like little scimitars, sweet peas rush ahead crazily missing their supports in their exuberance and strawberries glisten enticingly in the fruit cage. Summer is surely here.

Lambs, so fat and sturdy now, rush round, trying to find their newly shorn mothers who wearily baa a gentle acknowledgement as they relax, cool at last. Dinky, this year's hand-reared lamb, still unsure of her identity, lives apart from the flock limbo-ing under the gate whenever she gets the chance, in search of human company. Donkeys climb to the top of a well-grazed 'Steep Field' in search of the best grass, basking in sunshine and shedding their winter coats.

But it is not all good news. Last Friday the fox was here again in mid-afternoon and took all but three of my chickens as they pecked happily in the sunshine. A terrible silence met us in the evening when we went to close their house, the orchard full of feathers. Even dear Oddie, my funny long-legged cockerel I hatched last year, lay dead in the grass, too heavy for Reynard to carry away for tea. Sadly, we gathered up the bodies if only to deprive him of a second helping. Now a net covers the chicken run and the survivors must stay imprisoned for their safety for a long while until cubs are grown and the fox family forget about this convenient teashop.

UNTIDY JULY

June has given way to the chaos that is July. Our Open Garden weekend was almost a huge success. Well, that is to say it was a huge success on day one when the torrential rain of the previous day gave way to beautiful blustery summer sunshine. Hordes of people flowed back and forth through the garden all afternoon. Scones smothered in clotted cream and strawberry jam flew off the shelves. My stalwart garden tea team and I dished out teas and washed up until our arms and feet ached – a triumph. And our photography exhibition drew an enthusiastic crowd.

Complacently we launched forth into Monday opening, day two. Serves us right. Grey skies, drizzle followed by chilly, blustery showers should have been an omen. 'It'll clear up,' I said in a half-cheerful voice. Then we heard that the local council had decided to dig a big hole in the road in the nearby village of Tuckenhay, the main route here. 'Oh well,' I said in a slightly less enthusiastic voice. It was just then that the vast lorry arrived outside the gate. Despite numerous phone calls with directions to his destination, the driver decided he or his satnav knew best; a quicker route could be achieved, he thought, by squeezing through the tiny Devon lanes.

Reaching us, he finally realised his error, panicked and tried to turn. Alas he was wedged, unable to manoeuvre either left or right, completely stuck and blocking access to the garden, farmyard parking, and, of course, cream teas! We were open from two o'clock until five-thirty. He arrived at two-thirty and was finally bounced out – rescued by a neighbouring farmer with a mighty JCB. He finally turned to retrace his ill-advised steps at four-thirty!

Nevertheless a few stalwart garden visitors braved a detour and walked round a damp windy garden. We did raise a little more money for the National Garden Scheme but hardly the sum of the previous day. They say things come along in threes and they certainly did that day. It was so bad we could only throw up our hands and laugh.

So now July bounds through the valley unchecked. So different from last year's soaking, the fields are brown, grass dry and sheep and donkeys scratching what they can. Yesterday's welcome rain is already being sucked back into the sky aided by a drying wind brushing through the long grass. We moved lambs and ewes onto a field with something slightly better this morning and Paul topped Quarry Field, knocking down great spiky thistles and wispy hay. More rain, please, to renew and restore the vital nutrients needed by the grazing incumbents.

Down at the bottom of the valley the garden does its usual trick of running away in July. It's a race to cut back the wild garden, the banks and long grass in the orchard before it engulfs us completely. Strimmers whizz and mowers roar, racing together against nature's relentless march.

The great splash of rampant roses, 'Seagull' and 'Kiftsgate', are fading beside the pond, replaced by a yellow border of loosestrife (*Lysimachia punctata*), yellow daylilies (*Hemerocallis lilioasphodelos*) and the last efforts of golden and orange candelabra primulas. Wild crocosmia and, I hope in time, its scarlet cousin 'Lucifer' push through spikes of vibrant yellow *Ligularia stenocephala*. Their flowers, daintily hanging from black stems, are framed by their jagged leaves. They shimmer in the breeze next to their purple-leaved relation, 'Desdemona'. Delphiniums soldier on and cosmos sneaks up shaggily, buds about to burst and clash marvellously in time with this year's planting of *Echinacea*.

Sweet peas are something of a triumph too. I'm having trouble keeping up with them as they riot up and over and beyond their supports. Each day I pick armfuls of long-stemmed, sweetly scented blooms and fill the house with the smell of summer. I do thank my daughter's neighbours, the spinster Miss Vaizey sisters, for their invaluable advice to plant the seeds in October. I have never had such robust and rampant plants.

And, of course, the vegetable crop has begun. The broad beans are just wonderful this year: such a contrast to last year's dreadful vegetable crop. We've already eaten them quickly blanched and tossed in butter, accompanied by a light béchamel sauce and, the other day, turned in a hot pan with finely diced pancetta – delicious. They will go into salads, tortillas and risottos and as they toughen through the summer, I'll take off their jackets to prolong their season! Finally, those that have not been eaten or made it into the deep freeze for winter, will be transformed into a light fresh-tasting soup with chicken stock and crème fraîche; so nice!

This year I have grown two sorts of courgette, the round 'Tonda Chiara di Nizza', which is good if picked really small but, left to expand, it has that old childhood memory of watery marrow. Courgette 'Cavili' F1, on the other hand, is a real success. Pale green and firm, it stays dry and crisp when quickly cooked in butter and olive oil and served with chopped parsley, really good and versatile – it's definitely one I'll grow again.

'Painted Lady' is daintily and decoratively climbing her bean poles promising beautiful runner beans in a couple of weeks. French beans are looking good too. Not so my brassicas! An error here, I thought I was planting purple-sprouting broccoli but seem to have muddled the packets with a summer variety that goes to seed before my eyes, very disappointing. Then my good friend, Julia, she of allotment fame, sent me seeds germinated, she assured me, from a packet of cavolo nero I had previously sent to her. Alas they are certainly not the strappy Italian cabbages I anticipated. We wait to see what they will produce, surprise sprouts for Christmas perhaps.

I have a strange resistance, I don't know why, to taking off the sideshoots of tomatoes. So, of course, my tomato greenhouse is a wonderful rampant jungle of wildly hanging vines covered in an abundance of yellow flowers. I look on nervously, daring to hope for a crop this year instead of a wipeout by the dreaded potato blight that took all last year's plants together with all their *Solanum* relations onto the bonfire without a single edible specimen.

My ridiculous pride and glory is a small but expanding melon in the polytunnel. It has grown thus far from a seed from my sister-in-law in California. So excited am I that I have made it a little supporting snood from a supermarket satsuma net, should it eventually grow too heavy for its stalk; such an optimist, me!

Strawberries were good this year after being dug up, divided and moved to pastures new – a tedious exercise which did pay off. They are all finished now, not enough to turn into jam and so disappointing when frozen we simply kept on eating them. Raspberries are ripening, gooseberries, red- and blackcurrants too. Some will be eaten and the rest will climb into the deep freeze or turn into jam to cheer long winter months.

So much to do in the garden as the year marches on but now, as the sun continues to shine, I am sitting with a cup of tea enjoying a blackbird's song break the silence of a perfect summer afternoon.

THE ARRIVAL OF MR PORTER

Year after year the seasons roll reliably along just as they always have since time began, moving in such timeless momentum we hardly notice their passing. Spring blends into summer, summer slides into autumn and suddenly we wake up and realise that winter is breaking over us again. It all feels so predictable and yet each day, week, month that passes, unfolds, unwraps in its own unique and inimitable way – the same but not at all the same, the same but absolutely different.

August raced past in a mizzelly, damp wave of family birthday parties, regattas, Red Arrows, judging sheep at the Totnes Show, judging cakes at the fête, picnics in the rain, dinghy sailing, rowing races. Children made bread and pasta at Manna from Devon Cooking School. They camped in the garden, climbed the wall in the old barn, ran through the fields, rode bicycles and barbecued swiftly between showers. There were damp forays to the beach, icy dips in the paddling pool, noisy, joyous family meals around the kitchen table, talking, laughing, cooking, oh and so, so much more. Days and weeks rolled along in a very English summer sort of way. Then family returned home, children returned to school, holidays ended and we were left, tired and happy, basking, briefly in the illusive sunshine we had longed for in the previous weeks. Autumn had crept up on us again.

Suddenly it's September. Warm sunny autumn days are encircled by that zing in the air. Sharp mornings and raw evenings foretell what is ahead. Leaves begin to change colour and a certain tiredness seems to sweep over the landscape, bringing with it just a hint of decay, of early signs of an ensuing hibernation. Geese are back, buzzards conduct loud flying lessons teaching their young how to rise and fall on the warm thermals and as usual house martins swirl overhead preparing to leave.

Combines rumble in the fields along the valley bringing in the last of the harvest and a very new ram eyes up the girls over the gate. Funny little newly shorn lambs stride like skinny, awkward teenagers up the steep field we call Sunday Orchard trying to look cool and grown up. They are alone now without their mothers who, relaxing for a while up the hill, prepare for the cycle of lambing and motherhood to begin all over again.

But there is something different or rather, someone different in our midst this autumn. Mr Porter has arrived. In fact, he's been with us now nearly ten weeks, a sort of mad spontaneous birthday present for me. In July, gripped by another of those recurring waves of sadness, missing the terrible, wonderful, Min, I google Cairn Rescue only to be reminded almost at once of the countless hours, days, spent searching for the dear departed delinquent Cairn Terrier. On the spur of the moment, I type in 'Labrador Rescue' instead and the rest is history. Mr Porter is here.

We were visited, viewed and vetted, carefully, closely questioned about our doggy credentials. We both recounted the many dogs we'd loved, both together and separately, since birth. We produced photographs of dogs past and brought forth the present incumbents for interview. We all passed.

All four of us, that is to say Paul, me, Border Collie Meg and, her dear, daft daughter, Wellie, climbed into the Land Rover and drove some fifty miles across the county to meet possible contenders. A beautiful yellow lab curled his lip and backed away, growling and terrified; perhaps not that poor fellow. A gorgeous puppy bounded up to us. Alas, he was blind and, with tractors and farmyards, our lifestyle would be far too dangerous for him. Another chap limped up with a very bad hip, again a no no on the farm. We sadly prepared to leave when out came a small, wobbly, painfully skinny black, half-grown pup with beautiful soft, kind brown eyes.

Papers signed and we were in the car travelling home again. No room in the back, so the little chap sat at my feet gazing at me nervously, licking me and making appalling smells. He was so thin I could count his ribs between my fingers. He didn't seem to have any tummy muscles nor any in his back legs. He was so weak he was unable to jump and simply fell out of the car when we arrived home. We fed him a small supper with the other dogs then took him through the garden and farmyard into a field. I feel certain grass was new to him, so was the lashing rain, but he sniffed and wobbled his way across the field running in a zigzag between us, never for one moment letting us out of his sight.

With regular meals, morning and evening, he is turning into a beautiful strong Labrador with a handsome broad head. He is about eighteen months old we are told, and is determinedly catching up on the puppy hood he hasn't had. On the vet's advice we have been very careful not to overwalk him in order to give him a chance to build up muscle strength. Now he bounces around the garden, has no brakes and hurls himself through the air as he races across the fields. He tries so hard to make the older ladies play and ignores them rudely if they tick him off.

He adored playing with the children in the summer and was ecstatic to find their spaniel puppy would play too. He fell in the pond not once, not twice but three times and found, to his surprise that he was a great swimmer in true Labrador fashion. He races round the garden, tail tucked under tum, in mad celebration of his new-found skill! He was amazed at the chickens and had a go at chasing them, which was terrific fun, for him. He did, however, stop abruptly when he discovered we did not consider this a very popular sport!

He licked the donkeys' noses and made good friends with all three cats, licking them too and entreating them constantly and without success, to play. As for sheep, well they will keep running away in such a satisfactory manner that he must wear a long lead in their company until he may, one day, realise they just hate the idea of playing with him and have much better and more serious things to do and see to.

A neglected, starved, caged, pathetic little dog has turned into the most delightful, happy, sweet-natured chap I could possibly imagine. He's even quite intelligent, well, for a Labrador who, as we know, are more famous for their love of food and love of love than intellect!

This morning as we walked to the farmyard, a chill wind swept wistfully through the valley. A dark grey sky began to split and curdle with the growing heat of a silvery sun eventually fading into blue. Older dogs walked quietly up the hill, poor Wellie still limping on her bandaged and stitched foot after her mysterious accident last week. We will never know what happened, only that we let dogs out as usual last thing in the evening. Two frightened dogs ran back almost immediately. Then seconds later, a terrible screech of pain and Wellie limped in with such a badly damaged foot the vet had to remove her toe. No traps or sharp tin in our garden, so was it a badger perhaps feasting on apples, who perceiving himself cornered, lashed out, catching his claw in her foot? Usually badgers run at the very first sound of a dog and Wellie is no fierce little terrier like the erstwhile Min; she's a bit of a wimp, in fact. So, who knows, poor girl – a mystery and a very sore foot.

Porter, abandoning any hope of a game, gambles up the hill inventing his own entertainment by tossing a feather in the air and catching it. Sheep go peacefully about their business: some graze, some doze in the long grass, all still eyed longingly by the boy next door. Pausing for a while, we lean on the gate to enjoy the sunshine and look across the fields to a misty blue-tinged Dartmoor in the far distance. Slowly we turn and walk down the hill, let out chickens, feed donkeys, checking first for warm feet, before letting them out into a small fenced area. The grass is still growing fast and full of sugar, which bodes ill for those prone to laminitis, so restricted grazing and straw not hay are the order of the day, much to their annoyance. Donkeys and Labrador have a similar attitude to food; neither have a built-in stop button!

Food has been on my mind too lately. An abundance of fruit and vegetables have been making their progress from garden to deep freeze for the winter. Raspberries followed gooseberries, followed red- and blackcurrants. Figs in vanilla syrup will make rich comforting flans and damsons topped with breadcrumbs, oats, butter and sugar will turn into unctuous, rich crumbles to cheer cold November days. November is the low spot of my year! October is golden, December brings Christmas, January delights with the first snowdrops, ditto February with daffodils, March is lambing and so the years unfolds; but, oh, tell me, what is good about November? Maybe its virtue lies in helping me to enjoy and appreciate the rest of the year.

This year's courgettes were, by chance, wonderful, pale and crisp; they held both texture and flavour when cooked. I'll grow them again, good little 'Cavili' F1. Ridge cucumbers, 'Restini', were sweet and prolific, even the ones I missed and allowed to swell beyond their rightful size. Big orange pumpkins promise more chutney and maybe will sneak into a lasagne without Paul noticing. He is not a fan of that gorgeous gourd.

Beans, broad, runner and even French, were wonderful this year, particularly the latter 'Cosse Violette' who, in the chaos of summer, were left until big and purple on the plants. Nevertheless, snapped into pieces, blanched and served in a thick tomato and garlic sauce, they are deliciously tender without a hint of stringiness. Sadly, the tomato sauce was not of my making as tomato blight struck again despite my best efforts. Next year I will grow tomatoes in the polytunnel and give my little greenhouse a rest.

It is a year now since a large supermarket appeared on our horizon, just 15 seductive minutes from our once isolated front door. I try, I really do, not to be drawn in, but, of course, I do succumb. It says it does its best to be as eco as it can, windmills whirring to produce electricity for the tills. Local produce does appear on the shelves and, yes, it does give us greater variety all year round, bargains too sometimes, I suppose.

Last week I spotted a half-price duck; what a treat, on a high shelf. Being very small I often struggle to reach anything on the top shelves but I persevered to reach this bargain bird. And what a bargain it turned out to be. Roasted with sage and a ham hock and served with braised celery, the aforesaid beans, my blight-free crushed potatoes, and redcurrant-enriched gravy, it fed five of us, deliciously, for dinner.

The next day, alone, we had a cold duck leg each with chutney, salad and baked potatoes. On the third day, this sounds faintly ecclesiastic, I stripped the remaining meat from the carcass, added it to a velouté sauce containing mushrooms and shallots and filled up some crisp vol-au-vent cases for supper. We ate them with Puy lentils cooked in a duck stock.

NOVEMBER BLUES

Dark skies belie the time of day, three in the afternoon in mid-November and the light is fading fast. Rain lashes sideways outside my window. Trees, almost leafless now, outlined black against a slate grey ceiling, bend double in the gale. Once again, the huge *Araucaria araucana* dances its terrifying corkscrew dance, swivelling its vast great trunk this way and that. The radio blares warnings of eighty mile an hour winds, floods, devastation. Dogs and I huddle by the fire in the study wondering if we can pull down the blind and shut out the world. But, no, first we must struggle up to the yard in the howling wind, heads down against the thrust. Soaked once more, we shut up wet little chickens. We feed gloomy, bored donkeys, saying goodnight and shutting their door tight against the storm. We must check the ewes and Big Chris, the new ram in Sunday Orchard, before struggling up to the top fields to feed the yearlings and make sure they too are safe. What a storm. Even Mr Porter views this expedition with a lack of enthusiasm.

The garden, which had opened its heart to the public in the summer, basking in glowing June sunshine, has gone to sleep. *Liriodendron tulipifera* sheds leaves as big as plates in the path as we walk. Katsura, almost bare now, still tries to warm us with the mouthwatering smell of boiling caramel. All around us the air is alive with leaves, golden, yellow, brown flying past as trees close down all systems until spring. We tiptoe through a perpetual fruit salad on the ground. As fast as I collect apples, quince, medlars, walnuts, more cascade through the air landing at my feet.

A few leeks still stand forlornly by the shrivelled bean poles. A clump of scarlet chard stands alone majestic, glowing like a tiny fire. Nasturtium flowers cling on defiantly until the first frost. A few roses bloom their swan song.

Apples are pressed, juice strained and stored. Quinces are transformed into deep crimson twinkling jelly, thick golden jam and sticky squares of sweet chewy membrillo – Christmas presents waiting in the storecupboard. Medlars, once bletted, will also become a translucent jelly to cheer up winter meals.

Wet walnuts are a treat with a glass of wine on a dark cold evening by the fire. Now we must fall back on all the harvested and stored produce of summer and autumn.

It was an autumn that whirled past in the glow of golden sunshine, long shadows across the windswept fields. After a quiet, peaceful week away on the Isles of Scilly we returned to a feast of friends and family.

Sheep were brought into the yard for judging, sheep escaped; judges ran amuck snatching and catching at ram lamb horns, all flying horizontal across the yard pursuing Big Chris before he ran off with the now plump ewe lambs. Older ladies scattered; chaos reigned. Guests looked on amazed and we won the Whiteface Dartmoor Sheep Breeders' Association prize for the best flock of under fifty breeding pedigree ewes!

Half-term found us looking after grandchildren once more while parents absconded to Paris. It took two days to build a huge climbing frame gifted to us by a very generous friend. We heaved ladders, ropes, slides and swings into place. I was sent aloft to align higher beams and tighten nuts. Harry trimmed back bolts with a hack saw, Bee wielded a huge spanner and Flo gave us directions while retrieving the instructions from the mud.

We had unsuitable chocolate-rich picnics in the top barn. Walls were scaled and courage screwed up to jump from the top barn door on to the soggy soft grass below. Trees were climbed, races run across Sunday Orchard, chickens cleaned out, donkeys stroked and brushed, the yard circumnavigated many times on bicycles; we all slept soundly helped by big bowls of pasta.

A simplified version of the classic Italian Tagliatelle Bolognese did the trick. I left out the minced prosciutto fat but added a little chopped streaky bacon instead. To feed the five of us I heated 60g of butter in a heavy-based pan and added the bacon with finely chopped carrot, celery and onion. I cooked it all gently without browning for about 10 minutes. Next, I stirred in 300g of lean minced beef and continued cooking for a few more minutes. Then in went a tin of tomatoes or a little beef stock and tomato purée to loosen the mixture. I left out the glass of red wine as my fellow diners were rather small! I left it all in the bottom of the range to cook very gently for a couple of hours. We ate it with freshly boiled tagliatelle and lots of grated Parmesan followed by plenty of ice cream and chocolate sauce!

NEW YEAR FOR OLD

Snow has melted, now sleet drives sideways across the valley. As early afternoon darkness falls, icy shards bounce off frozen ground. This is our twenty-eighth January in this beautiful valley and it is the very first one without the reassurance of a New Year snowdrop.

Rain fell relentlessly all through November. We slid muddily around the farmyard, squelching through soggy fields, crushing any precious remaining grass despite our best efforts. Then it froze. Muddy farmyard turned to an ice rink. Tractors slid around and so did we. All pipes ceased to yield water to thirsty animals. Thick ice sealed off all water troughs. At first a good kick shattered the surface. It got colder: a hammer became necessary to render a trickle. The temperature continued to plummet, ice welded to plastic and the whole became a solid shining mass. We rigged up a bucket on a rope over the still flowing stream and laboriously heaved out gallons morning and evening. Sheep eating oats, beet shreds and haylage instead of watery grass, sucked it up thirstily as fast as we could scoop.

Then the snow arrived. We don't get snow in South Devon, at least not often. The last really bad winter here was in 1986! I had forgotten just how upside down it turns our unaccustomed lives. Dogs, cats, donkeys, sheep have never seen anything like it. Chickens, crowded at their pop hole, tentatively placed an outstretched claw on the strange shining white stuff – loud squawks and they flew clumsily into the air. I laughed as I watched them dare to land, peck gingerly then retreat hastily into their shed in disgust, only to try again minutes later in disbelief.

The donkeys have spent most of their time in their big barn for weeks now with just the occasional foray into the field. Rain, ice and snow are no friends to them. Dear old Dandy finally gave up the fight on a cold Friday evening just before Christmas. He died quietly in true stoical donkey fashion, no fuss, no struggle. On the Wednesday evening he eeyored to me across a wet field, warm inside his big blue coat, reluctant to walk down the slope into the yard for tea. I coaxed him and talked to him and, oh so slowly, he tottered stiffly into the big barn. On Thursday I kept them all inside. He seemed a little better but on Friday morning we found him lying in the straw exhausted. We propped his head on a thick hay bale, covered him with his coat and took it in turns to sit with him, his head in our lap, stroking his big soft ears, tears gently rolling down our cheeks as we came to terms with his inevitable departure. He simply faded gently away and by evening he had left us.

Dear boy had a wonderful fifteen years here. Although very, very old indeed, about thirty-eight we think, he left us as a well-fed happy donkey. A far cry from the skinny, mangy fellow we loaded into a trailer with his balding friend, dear old Sweep, all those years ago. We buried him beside her and once the ground allows, we will plant a walnut tree nearby to give him summer shade. He was the sweetest, most gentle fellow, friend to so many children, frequent star of nativities and Easter processions. We miss him badly.

Christmas came and went happily, despite Dandy's demise, with all the fun that children bring to the yearly ritual: decorating the tree, hanging up stockings, Father Christmas, unwrapping presents, struggling to church on Christmas morning on the ice, roast turkey, mistletoe, Christmas pud, friends, laughter, love, happiness, five dogs, crackers, chaos, treasure hunt, champagne, regular sorties to the farmyard to feed animals, kiss donkeys, play on the climbing frame, try out new roller blades, trudge through muddy icy fields, sing carols, eat too much. And then New Year found us with our dear old friends once again for a quiet delicious dinner, a good omen for the year ahead.

This is the time of the year to gather friends around for long warming delicious lunches; to eat comforting food and drink wine by a log fire; to exchange stories, love and laughter until the snowdrops finally arrive and the first daffodils peer nervously above crumpled grass assuring me that spring really will roll around again.

CHICKEN WITH GARLIC, CHORIZO AND FENNEL

Just before Christmas our local theatre group came to lunch. Some twenty-two of us all squashed up together into our dining room. I cooked a huge dish of chicken with shallots, fennel, celeriac, pancetta, chorizo, potatoes, olives and whole cloves of garlic – a kind of Italian Orvieto Chicken with Spanish overtones! It worked surprisingly well! We ate it with baked vegetables in cheese sauce, boiled potatoes and green salad followed by apricot and apple tarts, ice cream and cheese and biscuits.

I browned the chicken pieces in olive oil before stirring in plenty of sliced chorizo sausage, crushed garlic and chopped shallots. I left it to sizzle for a few minutes to soften then added stock and white wine stirring well and scraping gently with a wooden spoon to deglaze the pan. Then it all went into a moderate oven for half an hour or so until the chicken was cooked.

Meanwhile, I blanched sliced fennel and celeriac with whole garlic cloves for 2 minutes, plunging all into fast boiling water.

Once thoroughly drained, I added it to the chicken and chorizo to cook for a few more minutes. I made a velouté sauce with butter, flour, stock and the juices drained from the chicken. To serve, I piled the chicken up in a big serving dish, poured the sauce over it all and finally scattered it with chopped black olives.

FEBRUARY RAIN AND
WARMING FARE

Snowdrops cascade down the hillside in an avalanche of petals
once more. As they push their tiny tips up through a ravaged
landscape, we feel our spirits climb from the despair of winter.
A tiny blue iris has exploded through crystallised soil by the
back door, a camellia winks at me through the kitchen window
and yellow crocuses struggle to make themselves seen. The
smallest vestige of hope tingles within; it will be spring again.

In gentle South Devon, warmed by the Gulf Stream, we
rarely feel the biting cold of morning frost. This year has been,
oh, so different. November's relentless rain drenched our souls.
December ice and snow found us skating on frozen farmyard,
collecting water for thirsty animals, bucket by bucket, from the
stream, once more the only source of unfrozen water. January
brought swingeing north winds, hail and sparkling, spectacular
heavy frosts and now February rains again.

The ground has been frozen for weeks but now we slip
and slide on mud. Tractors travel back and forth collecting
big bales of haylage to keep hunger at bay. Ewes come down
to the yard at night for tea and night-time shelter; lambs are
born thick and fast. Each new mother is penned up with her
offspring in the dry until babies are seen to be thriving and
feeding well. The ladies-in-waiting huddle into another shed

sheltering from the elements, awaiting admittance to the maternity wing.

Wethers and last year's ewe lambs nibble at what they can find on top fields. As they hear the tractor, each afternoon they race to their respective gates waiting anxiously for tea, pushing and shoving to get to the hay and the trough first. Unlike commercial breeds Whiteface Dartmoors mature slowly so may stay with us for up to a year before being sold either for breeding or meat.

Just three donkeys now glean what they can by stretching necks over fences for a little sweet delicacy here and there, bramble or ivy, supplementing a manger of haylage and the breakfast and tea served daily in their stable. Thick coats keep them warm but, unlike horses, they have no oil in their coats to keep them dry so must always come in when the rain lashes sideways across the valley.

Time now between visits to the farmyard to catch up on all the inside jobs so tedious when the sun shines: mend the leaking ceiling in a shed, make plans for the garden, plant seeds, redecorate a bedroom, clear desks and file all those papers, tidy cupboards, take a trip to the recycling depot! And try, oh try to sit now and then by the fire and read.

It's time, too, to use up all the food harvested from farm and garden in the summer: Now is the weather for real comfort eating while we wait for spring! Old English boiled beef and carrots, Italian minestrone, Welsh cawl, Suffolk stew.

And then there's Garbure. Somehow this last wonderful pot from Southwest France brings so many regional dishes together. And as an English woman, all be it with a tiny amount of French ancestry, who am I to say how it should be cooked! Well bravely, here's my Anglicised version!

To begin I make a good rich stock with a chicken or duck carcass in the usual way. I soak 500g of dried white beans overnight. The next day, I begin by draining and rinsing the soaked beans then bringing them to the boil in a heavy-based pan. I boil briskly for 10 minutes, rinse and drain again while I blanch a 500g piece of belly of pork.

The pork belly, a ham hock, an onion stuck with cloves and the blanched beans go into the strained stock and are simmered for about 1 hour. I add a couple of diced potatoes, a large leek, a turnip, a few carrots, green or red pepper, salt, pepper, crushed garlic, a little paprika and a big spoonful of dried herbs. When the vegetables are nearly cooked, I add shredded white cabbage, 500g of garlic sausage and most importantly, a tin or jar of confit of duck. Opinion varies as to whether or not the duck fat is added too. It's a matter of taste: a little will enrich the whole, I think. Just before serving I take the meat from the pot and keep it warm. We have the broth with thick slices of bread as a first course and followed by the meat and vegetables – a really warming supper on a cold winter's evening.

One of the most versatile and handsome vegetables standing majestically in the vegetable garden this winter is the Italian cabbage, cavolo nero. Its thin, long dark green leaves are the essential part of Ribollita, the famous Tuscan bean and cabbage soup, made a day in advance and 'reboiled'. Yesterday's minestrone!

Walking back from the farmyard to the house today, I picked a handful of leaves and pulled up a leek. With the addition of a couple of carrots and potatoes, a parsnip, a shallot, a tin of haricot beans and a tin of tomatoes, and a handful of scraps of ham we will have a thick and delicious soup for supper tomorrow: Ribollita.

I grew my cavolo nero plants from seed for the first time last year. I planted them out in blocks where they now stand like little green palms in the bare earth. The narrow green leaves can be snapped off the plant encouraging new growth. Tiny new leaves are wonderful in winter salad with the variegated chicory, radicchio Sottomarina, mizuna and land cress all over wintering in the polytunnel.

Cavolo nero can be braised with garlic and ham and become a meal in itself. My favourite way to use it, though, is with rich garlicky flageolet beans. Rinse the dried beans and then soak for 30 minutes. Bring to a fast boil for 15 minutes. It's important to preboil all dried beans because some contain toxins and the best rule of thumb is preboil them all! Now drain them, rinse again and simmer gently for about 1 hour. Do not salt the water; this toughens the skins of the beans.

You can of course simply open a tin of flageolet beans! Put the cooked beans into a pan with a dash of olive oil, a crushed clove of garlic and a teaspoon of dried herbs and leave to infuse. Then strip the tough stalks from the cabbage leaves and blanch for a couple of minutes in boiling water. Drain thoroughly and stir into the beans. Warm through gently. It is delicious with any grilled meat, roast shoulder of lamb or braised sausages with gravy and mashed potato for a comforting meal on another cold evening.

Spring is surely on its way!

WAITING FOR GRASS AND
MEETING THE QUEEN

Gentle rain is falling on brown fields at last. Although we long for the warmth of the sun, we need rain badly. We have no grass for sheep or new lambs, for donkeys or chickens. The temperature has risen but the hills are bare after the terrible winter. Everyone is struggling to feed livestock even though spring hints its arrival at last. Snowdrops fade as February daffodils burst into flower, joining their March cousins a month late. Crocuses glowed briefly in the sun last week, flattened now by rain. Camellias appear all at once. I pray they will be spared by the frost. Just one more icy sparkling morning and all bushes will be garlanded in brown limp blooms.

But the dry cold has been good for lambing – not one bottle-fed lamb this year. Usually, I am dashing up to the yard every four hours to juggle more bottles than I have hands to feed hungry pushy babies. Or I'm in a pen soothing a ewe with no milk while trying to help her little scrap survive, or bringing orphans back to the kitchen for warmth. But not this year; healthy lambs bounce around the field playing together as mothers feed. Every afternoon they rush to meet us as we climb the hill with high-protein feed, mixed with oats and malt shreds to try to supplement the lack of grass. Great bales of haylage sit in the fields and farmyard making up for the lack of pasture.

We live in a part of England that is often so mild that the grass grows all year round. This has indeed been a strange year for us.

More strange things have happened recently away from the farmyard too, not least an unexpected invitation from the Trustees of Dartington Hall to a lunch in the Great Hall. Mystified we accepted only then to be told we would be lunching with the Queen and the Duke of Edinburgh. We were amazed and still have no idea why we were invited; maybe names from a hat, some charity work perhaps, we will never know!

Security was tight but relaxed, protocol detailed. We were escorted to the reception area where we were offered a glass of Prosecco and asked to wait in small groups with our table host, for the Queen to arrive. We did as we were told in that delightful, relaxed slightly anarchic style of Dartington, a feeling of childhood excitement and giggles floating through the room. Then, all at once a hush fell as a very small elderly lady in mauve and orange quietly arrived. She went from group to group shaking hands and speaking to everyone. Suddenly it was our turn. 'Mr and Mrs Vincent have a small rare breed sheep farm on the River Dart.' We each shook her gloved hand and I did the tiny bob required these days, in place of the low curtsy of years gone by. Her face, so familiar yet often so stern in photographs, on stamps and five pound notes, broke into a twinkling smile. 'What sort of sheep?' she asked.

'Whiteface Dartmoors; we're lambing', we said, bathing in the smile. She chatted with us for a little while but it was so surreal to be standing talking to her that I can't remember what else she said before she moved with grace and interest to the next person!

Lunch was served in the magnificent hall. Local Sharpham wine, grapes grown on the estate, accompanied a local cheese salad, followed by chicken breast then crème brûlée. All held up the standard of Dartington's restaurant, The White Hart.

The Dartington Hall estate dates back a thousand years and more. There is said to be evidence of occupation of the sight by the Romans. The first written record is a mention in a Royal Charter of 833 AD. But it was not until 1384 that it really came into its own when Richard II granted the estate to his half-brother, John Holand, later Earl of Huntingdon and Duke of Exeter. It was he who built the Great Hall and Courtyard sometime between 1388 and 1400.

Richard's reign was troubled at a time when the country was immersed in the struggles of the Wars of the Roses. He came to the throne at the age of ten, son of the Black Prince and grandson of the Plantagenet Edward III. Although a colourful king and patron of the arts, including famously Chaucer, who visited Dartmouth to try to reclaim taxes and goods stolen from looted ships, he was not a popular monarch. In 1399 he was ousted by his cousin, Henry Bolingbroke, and murdered in Pontefract Castle.

Despite all this Dartington remained in the hands of the Earls of Huntingdon until 1476 when the estate passed briefly to the St Leger family before passing to the Crown. It had a succession of owners and tenants including Henry VIII's wives Catherine Howard and Catherine Parr before passing to Sir Arthur Champernowne, Admiral to Elizabeth I in 1559. It remained in the same family until the Elmhirsts bought it in 1925.

Their vision and commitment, so in tune with Richard II's patronage of the arts all those years before, made it the place of excellence it is today, working 'for advancement of art, sustainability and social justice' – a suitable venue for a visit from the Queen and the Duke of Edinburgh if ever there was one.

We drove home to the sharp reality of lambing and feeding stock, but with that slightly bemused feeling of a fading dream, pinching ourselves for a reality check and still completely unaware of why we had been invited!

HEATWAVE AND SUMMER FOOD

Day after day the sun beats down unblinking from a cloudless, rainless, azure sky. Grass has long since stopped growing and crunches brownly underfoot. The garden quietly fries and the fields are barren. We continue to move sheep from field to field as we imagine we see a tiny haze of green appear. Each day ewes and lambs follow me to the gate baaing to come through in case the grass really is greener on the other side but, alas, it is not. Day after day we look at the local weather forecast praying for rain; tomorrow and tomorrow it teases, only to drift away day after day like a mirage on the screen. Spring water still fills troughs in the fields and the pond pumps water from a trickling stream but for how much longer, I wonder.

It's weeks since it last rained and we should be so happy to have a beautiful summer at last. Instead we're pondering the future price of hay and wondering if there will be any available for next winter. The whole valley has a brownish yellow haze. We are all in the same predicament.

The garden opening was a huge success. No lorries jammed the lane this year, no rain either. Visitors poured in, basking in the blistering sunshine. Weeds almost eliminated, temporarily at least, lawns mowed; everything bursting into flower, all the effort really did seem worthwhile.

A garden stroll completed; an afternoon-long queue formed for cream teas! We set tables and chairs in the now tidy farmyard among tubs of lavender and daisies. Plate after plate of scones, clotted cream and strawberry jam flew out of our makeshift kitchen. Will, from the wonderful The Anchorstone Café in the village, had generously baked piles and piles of gloriously light golden scones. Of course, the cream debate re-emerged; in Devon, jam then cream, in Cornwall, cream then jam or is that the other way round? My roots are in Devon, my husband, a Cornishman; the debate continues! But the teas were a triumph!

Good friends pitched in to help; big thank you to them all. My neighbour, a professional horticulturist, acted as my plant memory for the afternoon: such a help as we walked around talking to our visitors doing our best to answer their questions about the house and garden. We explained how the garden had gradually evolved from nothing over the last twenty-eight years, about the origins of the house built in 1767. We recounted the rumour that the Reverend Francis Lyte wrote 'Abide with Me' during his brief tenure here. I wonder if he did?

We had two glorious afternoons after weeks of hard work and, best of all, thanks to the generosity of all our visitors, we were able to make a big donation to the nursing charities supported by the National Garden Scheme. A big team effort, thanks to everyone.

As vegetables burst forth in the vegetable garden in the relentless heat and the house fills with summer guests, I seem to have been swept up once more in a cooking whirlwind. Summer days lead me back to my much-loved Elizabeth David, Jane Grigson and the River Café books.

As a result of the dry weather the strawberry crop is somewhat overwhelming. I'm pondering how to use them, having found in the past that freezing is not a success. So, jam will be made and I will try a strawberry and rhubarb crumble. A good friend tells me it's delicious.

Broad beans abound, courgettes too. The pea plants looked so small and feeble but have somehow still produced a bumper crop. I'm not sure where all the slugs have gone this year; maybe they hate the drought too. The result is the brassicas are doing really well, cavolo nero majestic already. And the sweet peas are so long stemmed and sweet smelling this year.

I baked a huge Polenta Cake for the first time for a friend's League of Friends. It looked so inviting it was hard to give it away! I whizzed up 450g of unsalted butter with 450g of caster sugar, then stirred in 450g of ground almonds, a dash of vanilla essence, six eggs and the grated zest and juice of a lemon. A small teaspoon of baking powder, a good pinch of salt and, of course, 225g of polenta completed the mix. It went into a 30cm oiled and floured cake tin, then into the oven at 160°C for about 45 minutes until firm and golden; very nice!

The following weekend some friends from childhood arrived for a long weekend. We were fourteen for dinner so I 'butterflied' a large leg of our own Whiteface Dartmoor lamb by removing the bone and pressing it flat. It cooks so quickly and nicely like this without drying out and is so easy to serve. We ate it pink and warm with steamed samphire, lemon, mint and olive oil – a really good combination.

I made a big terrine of pork and chicken with crushed juniper berries, green peppercorns and fresh herbs from the garden. We had a salad of broad beans, roasted peppers and a small private triumph, my own baby carrots! A green salad from the garden, new potatoes with grilled artichoke and a big bowl of homemade aioli completed the feast. For pudding, I made a big fig flan and a kissel of blackcurrants and strawberries both served, of course, with Devon clotted cream.

TERRINE OF PORK AND CHICKEN

I always prepare the terrine at least a day in advance. First, I mince 500g of belly of pork with 250g boneless chicken meat. I mix the pork with the chicken, before adding three cloves of crushed garlic, two finely chopped shallots, a teaspoon of green peppercorns and five or six crushed juniper berries. I pour on a glass of red wine and allow it all to marinate.

I line a 450g loaf tin or similar shaped ovenproof pie dish with streaky bacon taking each rasher and stretching it out with the back of a knife on the chopping board. As the terrine cooks the stretched bacon tightens round the meat mixture. I line the dish with the bacon so that each rasher covers the bottom and one side with the end hanging over the edge.

I fill the dish with half of the minced meat and sprinkle it with chopped herbs. I cut another 250g of chicken into strips and place this down the centre of the meat with 100g of chicken livers. Another couple of teaspoons of chopped herbs, and in goes the rest of the minced meat. I press down gently and wrap the bacon over the top. I decorate with lemon slices and a couple of bay leaves, cover with foil and place in a bain-marie – a roasting tin, in other words, half-filled with hot water.

It goes into a moderate oven for 1½ hours. I check it regularly, topping up the water in the bain-marie when necessary.

To be sure it is cooked I pierce with a long skewer. If the juice is clear the terrine is cooked; if it is still pink, I cook a little more.

When I'm confident it is cooked, I take it out of the oven, lifting it carefully from the bain-marie. I tip the water out and return the cooked terrine to the dish. I put a heavy weight on the top: a well-washed brick and the weights from Granny's old-fashioned kitchen scales! The juices will overflow a little. When it is quite cool, I put it into the fridge to be eaten the following day.

HARVEST TIME

Buzzards circle overhead once more calling to their young; autumn flying lessons have begun again. As geese arrive, so house martins and swallows prepare to leave for their long journey south. The trees are looking tired and the whole valley resembles a great fruit salad.

It's been a funny year. A winter of relentless rain, ice and snow was followed by a devastating spring draught; blazing sunshine but no grass for tired ewes and growing lambs. We fretted, we worried, we moved sheep from field to field following every tiny flush of green. Then rain arrived in August just as the holiday season dawned, lush grass appeared once more, sheep grew fat again. Now autumn days bring mixed fortune. Gentle mizzle soaks fleece and fur. A golden sun warms us briefly as it casts long strange shadows across the hills before slipping from the sky.

It is time for us to take stock, to go through the sheep to select ewes for next year's breeding and send off hogs for meat or market. This year's lambs are sturdy now, plenty of ewe lamb followers to ensure the future of the breed. Chris has done a fine job. His new companion, Cliff or Gake, so named by our Japanese grandchildren based on some complicated pun, is developing into a strong young ram ready to join Chris for duty at the end of the month.

We plan a whole new chicken complex in the spring – a major undertaking requiring the manhandling of old sheds into the orchard and the creation of yet another anti-fox/badger fortification. Meanwhile, all birds have been moved from what had threatened to become a slum dwelling in the autumn rain. They are now in luxury dry winter quarters in the farmyard. Chicks are growing fast too; their beautiful varied colours tell me they are descendants of my dear old Araucana chap who vanished several weeks ago; more tea for a fox, I fear.

Despite the drought the wild harvest is once more prolific.

Apples trees are bowed low with the promise of a huge harvest in October. With the closure of our local cider press I will have to find another destination for our crop. I cannot bear to see them simply rot on the ground.

Huge horse mushrooms appear beside the little old barn on the top field, so large that just one makes a substantial meal with a sausage and a fried potato or two. I found parasol mushrooms too. But I wasn't sure, so I gave some to my dear Czech friends, fungi experts, who fell on them with glee. Confident now, I cooked ours and regretted giving so many away! Fry in egg and breadcrumbs says Carluccio – very, very nice indeed.

The fig trees have also surpassed themselves again. I picked thirty fruits on just one day alone last week. Some I poached in vanilla syrup as last year, some I baked and lots simply disappeared immediately with slices of prosciutto. But my best find, by far, is a recipe in *The Cooking of South West France* by Paula Wolfert. The combination of fig, lemon and walnuts is magical. Served with soft cheese it will be an ongoing winter treat.

Friends arrive from Brittany next week, an excuse for another feast or two. I'm planning that butterflied leg of lamb with samphire, lemon and mint again; it was such a success in the summer. I'll make paella and cook a duck. We'll eat more figs with clotted cream and bake the first quince. I'll make chicken liver pâté to have with bread from our wonderful French patisserie, coals to Newcastle for them, I know, but still a treat for us and on our doorstep.

And then it will be time to tackle that pumpkin and make chutney.

FIG FLAN

Each time we visit Brittany I buy lots of wonderful ready-made pastry from a French supermarket nearby and put it into my freezer. It fits a 26cm metal flan ring exactly, no rolling out or trimming necessary!

I cover the pastry with baking paper and bake blind in a hot oven until golden and crisp. There's nothing worse than a soggy bottomed flan.

As it cools, I poach ten or so figs in sugar syrup made up of a cup of water to an equal cup of sugar and a dash of vanilla essence or a vanilla pod.

I make a custard of 50g each of unsalted butter, icing sugar and ground almonds mixed together with a large egg and a generous tablespoon of double cream. I spread the mixture onto the cool pastry base and arrange the figs in a neat circle much as I would when making Tarte aux Pommes. I sprinkle with caster sugar and cook for 20–30 minutes in a moderate oven until the custard is set. When all is cool, I melt a tablespoon of redcurrant jelly and 'paint' the cool flan and pastry with the shiny glaze. We must eat it the same day with cream or ice cream.

FIG CONSERVE WITH LEMON AND WALNUTS

I take about sixteen figs or 1kg, two lemons, 750g of sugar and 125g of shelled walnuts, fresh if possible.

I zest the lemons either with a potato peeler or slice the peel into tiny julienne strips. Removing the pith, I cut the flesh into slices retaining all the juice and save the pips, which I put into a little piece of muslin.

I halve the figs and remove the tough stem tips.

I make a syrup with the sugar and 300ml of water. When the sugar has dissolved, I add figs, lemon rind and slices and a muslin bag of pips (this aids setting).

I cook it all gently until setting point is reached. To test for setting point, I put a teaspoonful of liquid on a saucer and put the saucer into the freezer or fridge until cool. If it wrinkles the jam is ready. In go the walnuts followed by a good stir and it's done.

I pot the conserve into small sterilised jars while still hot and cover and seal. I prefer to use small Kilner jars and store the jam in the fridge after opening.

ARCTIC DECEMBER

Snow, ice, sleet, fog, gale force winds, rain, more heavy snow; only once do I remember anything like this in South Devon. Thick snow, huge drifts and frozen pipes, and here we are again, a second year running – early frost followed by ice and snow and it's only December.

For so many years we have lived in this valley unthreatened by harsh weather. Winters are mild; grass usually continues to grow, slowly of course and sugar free, throughout the coldest months. Our hardy Dartmoor sheep graze happily on the hills all year round.

I leave dahlias in the ground, risk the odd geranium by the back door, the pond never freezes, chicks hatch in January, donkeys rarely have to stay in their stables during the day. Rain and mud are our usual winter companions.

Yes, we West Country people are very spoiled and that's why we stay here. My neighbouring farmer flagged me down on icy roads last week to pass the time of day. Chatting in the lanes is a local tradition.

'All right?' A local salutation. 'All right, cold though,' I say.

'Them's got snow in Scotland,' he continues cheerfully. 'Them like it and them can keep it.' Oh, how I agree!

Alas, the next day more heavy snow fell here.

What has happened to that Gulf Stream that's supposed to whirl so warmly round us and keep the west coast of the British Isles safe from those Canadian winters whose latitude we share? The Gulf Stream has been responsible for rendering us our mild weather in this, our southernmost British peninsular since time began. Where has it gone?

Pondering, I google Gulf Stream. I am told this warm Atlantic Ocean current, one of the strongest in the world, starts in the Gulf of Mexico, bringing warmth northwards towards us, as it flows past Florida driven by the prevailing southwest winds. As it flows north the warm water evaporates and becomes increasingly salty. In the north Atlantic this warm water meets the Arctic cold, the heavy saltwater sinks forming a deep current that sets up a pulling mechanism splitting the Gulf Stream and drawing it to the northwest coast of Africa and towards the western part of the UK and Europe, warming us and thus stopping us experiencing our rightful lot of those icy Canadian winters. Are you with me so far? I think I'm somewhat out of my depth.

Now, scientists say global warming is causing the melting of the Arctic and disrupting this pattern and, ironically, causing colder winters. The science, I have to admit, is hard for me to grasp but as I tramp unaccustomed across fields of ice and snow, lower buckets into an icy stream, stamp on frozen water troughs hoping to release just a tiny trickle for the sheep and donkeys, I know something is afoot. It just isn't usually like this!

The valley is transformed into a sparkling white alien wonderland backed by an azure sky. It is bathed in the golden glow of a low winter sun that, in turn, casts wild distorted shadows on the ground. A flock of redwings are feeding on frozen windfall apples and blue tits jostle for the bird feeders.

The farmyard is an ice rink, the lanes resemble the Cresta Run, most of the villagers are snowed in at the bottom of steep

South Hams hills. I watch children hurling themselves down a neighbour's field on a wobbly toboggan.

Suddenly the sun vanishes, the sky turns black, a northeasterly wind swings in across the hills bringing yet more snow. Even the dogs look dejected as we slide down 'Steep Field' into the valley.

After such a dry summer, hay and straw prices are at a premium as we feared. Careful feeding is essential – no margin for waste this year. Today we brought the ewes down from the top of the hill to Sunday Orchard, the big steep field nearest the farmyard. So enthusiastic were they, they nearly had us off our feet. From here we will feed them every day and keep them in tiptop condition until lambing starts on Valentine's Day.

Well done Chris, our handsome Whiteface ram. Having given us wonderful lambs for the past two years, he will go to pastures new this year so that we may introduce new blood and avoid inbreeding. We will miss such a gentle chap so expertly bred and raised by farmer Claire Butcher, our Whiteface Dartmoor chairperson.

Meanwhile, up the road, the brown cross-bred ewes are with our homegrown ram, the grumpy Cliff. His fate rests with the configuration of his progeny; I fear his temperament might influence his future.

Seven hoggets came back from the abattoir last week, beautifully butchered this time. It hasn't always been the case and is somewhat depressing to have to hand my faithful customers meat that is not presented as well as I would like. But until I find another butcher or master the art myself, I must put up and shut up!

I am always amazed at how quickly our lamb sells. Once they have tried it, people love it and keep coming back. Whiteface Dartmoor sheep are an old-fashioned breed and the lambs mature slowly. They reach maturity much later than commercial breeds. This has its drawbacks; we must keep them and feed them for longer. But the result is meat with the depth of flavour of mutton, but without the fat – rich dark tender meat. They call it Angel Meat on the Moor!

LAMB TAGINE WITH CHICKPEAS AND APRICOTS

Last week a friend gave a big birthday party and asked several of us to help her cook. Our Whiteface lamb was just right for her recipe. For eight people I cut up 1kg of lamb from a shoulder into large cubes removing any fat or sinew. I put the meat into a bowl and added a teaspoon each of ground cumin, cinnamon, ginger, black pepper and paprika, gently turning the meat over until it was thoroughly coated in the spices.

I left it in the fridge for a couple of hours to allow the flavours to penetrate. Meanwhile, I chopped two large shallots, crushed two cloves of garlic and peeled and diced a small butternut squash.

I heated four tablespoons of oil in a heavy-based pan and browned the meat in batches. Each batch then went into the tagine. I softened the shallots, garlic and squash in the remaining oil. I stirred all this into the meat in the tagine, together with a tin of chickpeas and about 500g of dried apricots. I added just enough good stock to cover the meat. It all cooked gently for about 1½ hours in a moderate oven until the meat was tender and the sauce thick and reduced. I tasted it and added salt and pepper; it's always best to leave the salt until the end of cooking as it has a tendency to toughen even the most tender cuts of meat. Finally, I sprinkled it with flaked almonds. We ate it with couscous and a green salad.

MARMALADE AND ORANGES

January and, as shops fill with Seville oranges, it's time I made marmalade. This year the airwaves have been full of advice. We are told that sales of marmalade have fallen away dramatically, that the nation's breakfast diet has changed or vanished completely. But not for me: I love the winter comfort of both making marmalade and eating it! I love the warm, sweet, spicy orangey smell that fills the kitchen as it boils to setting point. I love the satisfaction of a row of glistening jars – the promise of a slice of toast, a croissant, a cup of coffee.

All this media attention set me thinking, of course, searching for the origins of this unusually British conserve. Where else in the world can you buy a jar of citrus fruit boiled up in sugar? The first marmalades or marmelado were thick pastes or fruit cheeses made from the Portuguese *marmelo*, a kind of quince. Gervase Markham, in his 1615 book *The English Huswife*, instructs us to 'boyl it till stiff enough to mould, and when it is cold, then role it: print it', which sounds more like membrillo, that Spanish sweetmeat so delicious eaten with cheese, than our present-day marmalade.

In her delightful transcription of the seventeenth-century manuscript of recipes *Booke of Cookery and book of Sweetmeats*, edited by Martha Washington, Karen Hess quotes this quince marmalade of 1608: 'To make a marmalet that was presented to

Ye Queene for a New Year gift: Take a pond & halfe of sugar, boyle it with a pinte of water till it comes to manus Christi. Then take 3 or 4 quinces; A good orring pill preserved and finely beaten; 3 ounces almonds blanch'd & finely beaten by themselves; oringo roots preserved, 2 ounces & a half. Stir these with ye sugar in a basin over a chafing dish of coles till it will come from the sides of ye bason, & thene put in a little musk and ambergreece dissolved in rosewater, of each 4 greyns; of cinnamon, ginger, cloves, and mace, of each 3 drams: & put in 2 drops of oyle of cinnamon. This being done, box it up & present it to whom you please.'

These pastes and fruit leathers, valued for soothing the stomach after a large meal, still sound appetising to me although I would omit the ambergris in modern deference to the sperm whale. The oringo roots or candied sea holly roots (*Eryngium maritimum*) are not essential either, although highly praised by Gerard for their efficacious properties. The therapeutic and medicinal qualities of these preserves were highly prized by the Tudors and Stuarts. Richard Surflet's 1666 translation of *A Countrey Farme* tells us that 'some make a confection of Quinces, called Marmalade, which is verie soveraigne against flux of the bellie'. It was apparently also often prescribed for various 'diseases of the head' including headaches, madness, epilepsies and something somewhat alarmingly described as 'fits of the mother'.

By the end of the fifteenth century and beginning of the sixteenth, citrus fruit was moving west, quietly usurping the now very English quince. Although oranges had been known in China since about 2000 BC their progress to Europe was slow. The Romans are believed to have enjoyed oranges at their banquets. The fruit was imported from the Palestinians who constructed an irrigation system of earthenware pipes, still working today, to water their citrus trees.

And there is, of course, the Malaysian legend of oranges and the elephant in the days before the empire of Srivijaya, when animals could speak. The greedy elephant, finding a tree laden with fruit, ate all the oranges and burst. Many years later when humankind had been invented, a traveller came to the place of the unfortunate animals' demise and found on the spot an orange tree laden with 1000 golden fruit. Which is why the words 'naga ranga' mean both 'orange' and 'fatal indigestion for elephants' in Sanskrit. So says Maguelonne Toussaint-Samat in her wonderfully entertaining *History of Food*.

Columbus is said to have planted the first oranges in Haiti on his voyage of 1493. The fruit trees spread through the islands eventually reaching mainland America where the first orange plantation began to flourish in Florida in 1579. Meanwhile, our own Gervais Markham was extolling the virtues of a 'cutting paste of oranges' in 1615 and Martha Washington was turning her attention to 'preserue orringes and leamons'.

Gradually the delights of citrus fruit took hold and the medicinal advantages became apparent. During the Gold Rush oranges were taken with difficulty by wagon from Florida to California where it was noticed that they had an extraordinarily efficacious effect on the badly nourished early settlers and gold prospectors, preventing scurvy. Sometime earlier in 1747 a ship's doctor, one Dr Lend, experimented with his sickly crew by feeding half with the juice of two oranges a day and the rest none. He noted that those drinking orange juice recovered from the scurvy while the others perished!

From the eighteenth century more and more varieties of oranges were being developed across the warm regions of the world; marmalade recipes became prolific. Eliza Acton gives a recipe in her classic *Modern Cookery for Private Families* of 1845 for Genuine Scottish Marmalade: oranges, 3lb; water, 3 quarts; sugar, 6lb.

Mrs Beeton follows suite with a plethora of examples. In my own old broken 1880 edition there are no less than five orange marmalade recipes. Mary A. Everard is very concise in her little book of 1888 *The Handy Dictionary of Cookery* 'simply cut up twelve Seville oranges into strips; put them in six quarts of water. Allow them to stand for twenty-four hours. Boil till reduced by half; then add eight pounds of sugar. Boil one and a half hours till set.'

Even today we eat oranges to top up our vitamin C intake and drink orange juice as part of our government recommended five a day. But I rest my case for oranges in every form, be they fresh or as marmalade. Maguelonne Toussaint-Samat tells us that to eat an orange is to travel in imagination to countries where the climate is heavenly, the sun kind, water abundant and pure, the breeze caressing, the soil light, the nights cool, and man skilful, patient, careful and well organised.

SEVILLE ORANGE MARMALADE

My favourite marmalade recipe, the one I use year after year, comes from Jane Grigson's beautiful *Fruit Book* first published by Michael Joseph in 1982 – the simplest, easiest and best-flavoured marmalade, she says. I agree.

So this is what I do. First, I scrub 1.5kg of Seville oranges and put them into a pan with 3.5 litres of water and simmer until the skin is tender, about 1½ hours. I take soft oranges out of the water, cool, halve and remove the pips. The pips go into a piece of muslin. I cut up the orange flesh or pulse it into a liquidiser, being careful not to reduce it to a mush. Then back it goes into the water with 3kg of preserving sugar and the little bag of pips, which I hang over the side of the pan on a piece of string. The pips will bubble along with the fruit and release their pectin. I stir gently over the heat while the sugar dissolves before bringing it to a vigorous boil until setting point is reached. I test for setting by placing a tiny spoonful of syrup on a cold saucer and putting it into the fridge or freezer for a few minutes. If setting point is reached a wrinkled skin will form.

I usually leave the marmalade to stand for 15 minutes to allow the peel to settle. Then I remove the bag of pips and pot the warm marmalade into warm sterilised jars and cover: so nice!

APRIL

Lambs and ewes bask in the sunshine on top of the hill sheltered from the strong southwesterly: a wind so strong this Sunday morning that it pushes me back as I scramble up to the top of Steep Field as fast as I can. I stumble through the gate following the distressed cry of a lamb and the frantic baaing of a ewe. As I run, its cries move away from me. Eventually I track it down in the next field occupied by my neighbours' visiting alpacas. As I struggle to undo the gate before they spot the tiny chap, the ewe races towards me ignoring all dogs; a quick shoo from me and a loud call from her and the lamb dashes safely back through the gate. Chaos is averted.

Panting, I turn back and walk slowly down to the house. Across the valley neighbouring farmer, Richard, is ploughing a chocolate furrow against the backdrop of Dartmoor. The sky is white with seagulls following his tractor. The River Dart below us sings azure blue in the sun.

Lambing was a strange business this year, dragging on for weeks. The Whiteface sheep breeders on the Moor put it down to the wet cold autumn and the heavy snow of early winter that seemed to upset the natural rhythm of tupping and gestation. We have several barren ewes too, which is a first. Larry, the only orphan lamb, has gone to live with our friend Alison and her pygmy goats, so he's in clover. She's taken two older ewes too so now she's a sheep farmer, I tell her!

Late spring is bursting prematurely into summer. A gaggle of sweltering bank holidays encompassing Easter and the Royal Wedding together with a severe drought has plunged the garden into confusion; everything is at least two weeks early. And now with gentle rain and this warm wind, everything is racing ahead of itself. In classic gardener's anxiety, I'm wondering what will be at its peak when we open the garden in mid-June. I feel that old 'If only you could have seen it last week' cliché coming on!

It's not yet mid-May and the *Embothrium* is already scarlet against a blue sky while bluebells still carpet the banks. Peonies are breaking open from fat buds, roses even creep furtively into flower, *euphorbia* fires up the border as iris spike blue with gentle *Mecanopsis* and yet we are still not safely into frost-free territory. *Pelargoniums* clutter the greenhouse and I dare not let the great avocado into the garden yet. He towers over me magnificently inside the back door, some ten feet tall now, far too big for the little glass house.

The polytunnel is gone, bought by an enthusiastic new couple in the village. I feel wonderfully liberated! Beans and peas will grow on its site until autumn when the small glass greenhouse will take its place once the tomatoes have cropped, provided of course that we are blight free at last. I have lost tomatoes despite my best efforts for the last two years.

The old chicken houses, having been carefully moved, mended and painted green, now stand in the orchard behind a smart new post and rail fence; chickens, liberated at last from their winter quarters in the farmyard, scratch and squabble happily in the long grass, laying prolifically. I await a visit by fox or badger!

A wonderful clutch of eggs enabled me to make a traditional Simnel Cake for Easter.

This cake used to be baked for Mothering Sunday but has now become more popular at Easter. It is so light and fresh and lemony, just right for spring!

I begin by greasing and lining a 18cm cake tin. I set the oven at 165°C. Then I cream together 230g of unsalted butter with the grated rind of two lemons and 230g of caster sugar until light and fluffy. In go four eggs. I add them slowly, beating as I go.

Next, I stir in 200g of mixed candied peel, 200g of sultanas and 500g of currants. I sift together 400g of plain flour with a pinch of salt and a small teaspoon of baking powder and mixed spice and gently fold it in. If the mixture seems very stiff, I loosen it with a dash of milk. I spoon the mixture into the prepared tin and cook for about 3 hours, testing with a skewer to see if it's cooked. If it comes out of the cake tin still sticky, I cook it a little longer. Once I'm happy it is cooked, I turn it onto a rack to cool and make the almond topping.

For this, I mix together 120g of ground almonds with 120g of icing sugar, half a lightly beaten egg and a few drops of lemon juice. I knead the paste until it's smooth. Then I roll out two-thirds of the paste into a 18cm circle to fit the top of the cake. I form little balls with the remaining paste, which traditionally represented the eleven Apostles, Judas being excluded, of course. Next, on go crystallised flowers and some very pre-Christian Easter eggs to celebrate spring!

BREAD

Last week brought a special treat. A friend invited me to bake bread in her huge outdoor bread oven. Although I have been cooking for years enthusiastically both professionally and for friends and family, my knowledge of bread making would fit tidily on the back of a large postage stamp. The reasons are twofold, or maybe three: first, I was given a bread machine years ago; second, we have a fantastic French pâtisserie in our local town, as good as any you will find anywhere in France and lastly, I've just been too idle to try! Just one day, and all is changed. Fresh yeast is already sitting in the fridge and a new enthusiasm has been ignited.

Felicity's oven is a very large affair standing in a corner of her beautiful garden in mid-Devon. It was built by her son, Fred, a couple of years ago. Fred has been the driving force behind Slow Food Devon for a number of years now and his enthusiasm and knowledge of bread making has culminated into this wonderful project.

The day before my visit I dive into Tom Jaine's *Making Bread at Home* and David Jones's excellent bread-making notes, which I gleaned from a wonderful day's cookery at Manna From Devon Cooking School.

A biga, that's what I must make. I mix 8g of fresh yeast with 150ml of warm water and 150g strong bread flour and I leave it overnight.

The next morning, I use Tom Jaine's Italian Country Bread recipe: 200g of my biga, 300ml tepid water, 15g fresh yeast, 2 teaspoons of salt, 2 tablespoons olive oil and 250g each of white and wholemeal flour. I mix the dough, knead it for 10 minutes and let it rise. I put it into a covered bowl in my car and drive across Devon.

When I arrive, Felicity is in her kitchen surrounded by huge quantities of risen dough. My little bowl looks somewhat inadequate but I'm on a steep learning curve today, so watch and listen. Together we knock down, shape and set bread to prove for a second time in cotton-lined baskets. Fred and Felicity's husband, Simon, lit the oven early in the morning, so the temperature is already rising promisingly. Fred bakes focaccia.

We have lunch in the garden: tomato soup. 'Last year's tomatoes and the contents of the bread bin,' Felicity says. Eaten with the warm, rosemary-tinged focaccia – delicious.

Fred checks the oven; our dough is risen and ready. He rakes out the ashes, in go the loaves. The 'door' is sealed. We sit near the oven in the sun listening to the sheep over the hedge and wait as the air is filled with the sweet smell of baking bread.

Out they come one at a time on the great metal peel. We stand around congratulating one another and admiring the day's work. I leave with my loaf and Felicity fills the still-hot oven with a great dish of beans and deliciousness for their supper. I've had a wonderful day.

SUMMER AGAIN

As Devon fills up once more with holiday makers, we somehow remain untouched in our silent valley, the world passing us by. A few more cars hoot on the bend by the gate, voices and laughter occasionally waft across the hillside but mostly our silence is punctuated by the call of the buzzards overhead, a baaing sheep on the top of the hill, the donkeys in the distance reminding me it's teatime again and, just sometimes, on a very still day, the whistle of the steam train away down river in Kingswear.

It's been a dry hot spring followed by a still and humid summer with just enough rain to give us grazing. That is except for 12 June, the second of our National Garden Scheme open days. Saturday was warm and sunny and we had an excellent turnout and sold more than a hundred cream teas, courtesy, once again, of The Anchorestone Café who donated their huge delicious scones. The garden seemed to glow under scrutiny as smiling visitors flocked through. Wild spikes of foxgloves jostled for a place among *Rosa mundi* and *R. rugosa*, astrantia and huge white daisies dominated the sunken border. *Rosa* 'Seagull', recovered from last year's disastrous storm damage, hung on the pergola by the pond, itself like a great snowstorm. Even the *Embothrium* clung on to its scarletness for just a few more days, fiery once more, against the blue sky.

Then Sunday dawned and the world changed. Trees bent double in the gale, rain lashing through the valley. Just twelve stalwart people passed through the dancing entrance marquee, sheltering inside to bravely eat a scone and drink a warming cup of tea. We were not alone; some 300 National Garden Scheme openings were rained off right across the country that day. A day that will go down in the history of this charity!

Now that slightly tired August look is descending on the valley. Trees seem to be preparing for an early autumn, lack of water taking its toll. The stream is down to a trickle and I'm fighting blanket weed in the pond. But despite the lack of rain the harvest is beginning. Broad beans were wonderful, peas are prolific, runners look promising. Turnips picked small are delicious quickly cooked in butter, beetroots are swelling and this year's small round courgettes are really delicious. Spinach and chard are nearly ready and I have fingers crossed for blight-free potatoes and tomatoes in a week or so. Sweetcorn love this weather but I do wonder if I'll enjoy them before the badgers this time round.

The lambs, big and fat now, will be shorn next Monday, having been separated from their mothers. The ewes graze quietly on their own at last, their job done for this year. The last of the hogs have gone to the butcher and big boys Chris and Cliff will go to pastures new. A new ram will soon be joining the flock ready for the cycle to start all over again in the autumn.

So for now we enjoy gentle sunny summer days – a Crab Day celebration in Dartmouth, feasts of our own rare cooked lamb, garden vegetables, salads full of herbs and flowers, flans of local seafood with ginger and lemon, delicious cakes made from the German Friendship cake, passed on as a sourdough, from friend to friend – Felicity again, of course!

And soon it will be time to fly away to visit family in Japan – exciting new food, Tokyo, Shikoku, the Inland Sea, Korea, Seoul!

SEAFOOD FLAN

Supper in the garden on a warm summer's evening and a seafood flan with a glass of white wine, seem the perfect choice. I choose the fish according to the bounty the Brixham fishing boats have brought in and, of course, whatever I find on Mark Lobb's fish stall. It may be some fresh crabmeat, scallops, a handful of large prawns or a crayfish tail or two. I may mix and match and add some firm white fish as well, like monkfish tail. It all depends on the boats and the weather.

Once home, I line a metal flan ring with ready-made pastry, cover with greaseproof paper and dried beans or rice and bake the tart blind in a hot oven until dry and crisp but still pale.

Then to the fish. Raw fish gets a quick turn in some olive oil in a hot pan just to seal it. I combine it all in a bowl, mixing it gently to avoid it breaking up. I add the grated zest and juice of a lemon, chopped parsley and coriander and a small piece of fresh ginger chopped very small. I soften a shallot or two depending on their size, in some oil together with a couple of cloves of crushed garlic and add it to the fish mixture. I season it with salt and pepper then pile it gently into the cooked flan case.

I beat together two eggs plus two egg yolks with equal quantities of double cream and milk and pour the custard over the fish. It goes back into the oven for 30–40 minutes until the custard is just set. I let it rest for a few minutes before serving with a green salad and maybe a few new potatoes.

PLUMS, PLUMS, PLUMS

As torrential rain washes away the last remnants of summer, so the remains of this year's bumper crop of plums moulder and fall to the ground. But not before we have managed to gather bucket loads. It has been a wonderful year for all fruit in the garden despite the weather and the plums have been no exception. The orchard overflowed with the unique Dit'sum plum – boughs weighed down to the ground by the prolific harvest. Soaked grandchildren staggered into the kitchen with load after load as I looked on bewildered, wondering what I could find to do with such a bounteous crop.

Years go by with no plums – a cold spring destroys the blossom, early rain rots the unripe fruit, silver leaf disease rampages through the orchard attacking tree after tree. Then once in a while we are overwhelmed by pounds and pounds of beautiful reddish, purple fruit.

The plum as we know it today, *Prunus domestica (rosaceae)*, has been growing across Europe and Asia, Syria and Iraq, since before Roman times. Plum stones have been found in the ancient tombs of Damascus and in the tomb of Kha, Egyptian architect of Thebes. Pliny talks of 'ingens turba prunorum', great crowds of plums in Roman orchards. The mischievous Roman satirist and poet Marcus Valerius Martialis (*c*.38–*c*.104 AD) wrote of plums as 'frigida sunt, laxant, multum prosunt tibi pruna' – 'Plums are cold, relaxing to the stomach and very good for you!'We all remember those school prunes and custard!

In the Middle Ages we hear of the dark damask plums of Tours and Brignoles in France, forerunners of the famous Agen prune, and the bittersweet *Prunus salicina* from Japan introduced to the United States in the late nineteenth century. A small fruit, delicious raw, used in sweet-sour pickles as well as Sumomo Shu, a plum liqueur. In the nineteenth century there were some twenty-six varieties of plums that, a London nurseryman, formerly of the Royal gardens, says were some of the best varieties grown in the garden. Among those listed are the greengage, common damson and the red and white Magnum Bonham. The varieties of plum are legion.

Then there is, of course, our famous Victoria plum similar in appearance to the Dit'sum Ploughman, although not as delicious and definitely not regarded with delight by Jane Grigson. She didn't like it and called it the apotheosis of a long reign in a flood of bland boring plums. Poor Victoria, she began life in 1840, a stray seedling found in Sussex and introduced by a nurseryman in Brixton...

Victorias are for plums and custard, that crowning moment of the school, hospital, prison and boarding house midday meal.

And, of course, Mr Bird invented his custard powder in about the same time: a Pooteresque ménage à trois of plum, nurseryman and custard! I cannot agree that Victorias are quite that bad but there is no doubt our own Dit'sum plum has a superior flavour!

But what is the origin of this very local Dit'sum Ploughman plum, growing only in Dittisham on the banks of the River Dart in South Devon? As I dug deeper into numerous books and the Internet the answer became more and more obscure. Village myth or rumour has it that a German ship was wrecked off the coast near the mouth of the river carrying a cargo of trees or, maybe, prunes. Washed up on the village quay, barrels of prunes or maybe trees were collected by the villagers. This may be why the plums are also said to be related to the German 'fluegal' plum. Interestingly the trees are raised from suckers and not grafted or budded, which may be why they became unique to the valley.

There was a time when the village crop was so prolific that the plums were sold in Brixham, Paignton and Torquay, taken from the village by donkey cart and ferry across the river.

The plum was registered at Brogdale, home of the National Fruit Collection in 1949. They were kind enough to send me the limited information they have on record:

'Thank you for your enquiry on the Dit'sum plum (listed as Dittisham Ploughman in the National Fruit Collection). There are currently 325 varieties of plum in our Collection, of which we maintain two trees of each. The majority of the information we keep on file for the different varieties relates to tree and fruit characteristics which helps for comparing and identifying varieties. For example, the notes on the Dittisham Ploughman fruit include 'Season: early to mid-August Size: medium to large Shape: oval-oblong, slightly unequal sides, slightly flattened on suture; slightly tapering to base, slightly flattened at base, standing; slightly tapering to apex, slightly flattened at apex, not standing. Stalk: medium to medium long, 11–16mm Av.15mm; medium to slender, hairy, fairly conspicuous; inserted in a medium to deep cavity Flavour: sub acid; moderately sweet; little rich.'

There is no doubt that, whatever their mysterious origin, they are beautiful plums. They have an excellent flavour straight from the tree and great setting quality for jams, jellies and puddings.

Delicious recipes abound. I will be trying Josceline Dimbleby's Plums in Red Wine Syrup – sounds so simple and delicious. Simply stone the plums then make syrup of sugar, red wine and the juice of an orange and a lemon. Pour the thick syrup over the plums and leave to stand for a few hours. Serve with cream. And I love the sound of Nigel Slater's Plum Crisp, a sort of cinnamon plum crumble but with a 'rubble' of breadcrumbs and butter to make the crispy topping. Some of my frozen plums will certainly be transformed into this on cold winter days to come.

I have already made some of this year's glut into an East European soft plum jam similar to fruit cheese called Povidle. The recipe is remarkably similar to the plum jam recipe made with Orlean or Magnum Bonham plums in my 1880 edition of Mrs Beeton.

Stone and chop 2kg of purple plums. Layer the plums in a preserving pan with 1kg of sugar. Cover with a cloth and leave for a few hours until the juices start to run. Then bring the mixture gently to the boil, stirring until the sugar is melted. Simmer for 1–2 hours, stirring occasionally until thick and dark. Ladle into hot sterilised jars and seal in the usual way. The jam can be eaten immediately but improves with keeping.

PLUM JELLY

Stone and chop the plums. Put into a preserving pan and add a little water not quite covering the fruit. Bring to the boil, then simmer until the fruit is cooked and breaking up. Tip the fruit purée into a jelly bag and allow it to strain overnight. I use a piece of muslin on an upturned stool! Do not be tempted to speed up the process by pressing the fruit; this will result in cloudy jelly!

Tip the red juice into a measuring jug and allow 500ml of fruit to 500g of sugar (i.e., equal amounts). Now return both to the pan and boil to setting point. A good way to test for setting is to spoon a tiny bit of the jelly onto a saucer as we did with the marmalade, and put it into the ice box of the fridge for a few minutes until chilled. If when you touch it, it wrinkles across the top, your jelly is ready to put into hot sterilised pots.

PLUM CHUTNEY

I love this old recipe and use it all the time, adapting it to the quantity of plums and apples according to the harvest.

Stone and chop 2lb of plums and 1lb of raisins. Cook plums and raisins with ½lb of apples, two chopped onions, two cloves of crushed garlic, a dried chilli, ½oz of allspice, ½oz of ginger and ½ teaspoon of salt in 1 pint of the vinegar until soft.

Pour another ½ pint of vinegar over 1½lb of sugar and put into a warm place to dissolve. When the fruit is cooked, add the sugar and vinegar and continue cooking in an uncovered pan until thick and dark. Put into hot sterilised jars and cover. Although the chutney can be eaten right away it does improve with keeping.

BOTTLED PLUMS

Prick the plums all over with a cocktail stick and pack into Kilner jars. Half cover with a spirit of your choice.

Last year I added a dash of cherry brandy and a vanilla pod for an extraordinarily lovely haunting scent, but this year I decided to go East European again and try vodka.

Top up and cover the plums with strong sugar syrup made with equal quantities of sugar and water. Seal the jars and put away in a dark cupboard for a couple of months.

PIGS AT LAST!

Autumn glowed gentle and golden right into November. Sunny days outnumbered rain. Roses flowered into December and the nights were frost free until last week. I threw myself into the garden joyfully replanning and replanting for next summer.

But my main job for the last three months has been Number One Farmer! I have made the transition from Farmer's Wife and Farming Assistant to being 'The One', not, of course, the boss, you understand, but the One Who Does The Farming! Paul, at last, has had the long-awaited complete knee replacement operation. It all went wonderfully well but as he makes a steady excellent recovery, animals must be cared for and farming jobs done. So, it is I who must step into the breach and up to the plate, etc.!

It has been such a wonderful autumn for everything including apples and yet, with so much extra to do, cider and apple juice was simply beyond me. What else to do with all these lovely apples I pondered every morning as I walked up to the yard.

Piggies, of course!

In all the years of Mondays that Stephen has been working with us, we've said to each other, he and I, year on year, one of these days we'll get some pigs. Then suddenly this autumn we made a plan. Paul, with time on his hands, studied the Internet, made phone calls, found weaners and did research. Stephen and I drove across the county to fetch the little chaps, three

Berkshires and three Middle Whites. We bought them from Ian Todd; a champion breeder near Honiton who not only sold them to us but also gave us a thorough piggy tutorial.

This was a steep learning curve for us. I can speak pretty fluent 'sheep'; in fact we've just won second prize for our Whiteface Dartmoor breeding ewes at the Flock Competition this autumn against the really professional big boys up on the Moor – no mean feat! But my pig knowledge is minimal. Thankfully Stephen has a little more experience.

Last week I visited champion pig breeder Sue Fildes on her farm nearby. She also shows winners and bought her first Berkshires from Ian Todd too. Little did he know all those years ago that she would be bitten by the piggy bug and become one of his biggest competitors at shows! Her pigs, like his, are superb specimens, living out on the hill in a piggy paradise. It was so good to talk to her and she, like Ian, was so generous with her huge knowledge and expertise. I came away feeling that we were definitely on the right track with our boys.

I have been amused at the reaction of friends and neighbours at my new venture. I can hear them thinking 'at your age' although too polite to say. And then the question, 'And what will you do with them?' inevitably follows that first unspoken thought!

'Well, eat them of course,' I reply. A horrified 'Eat them!' follows if they are not of the farming or foodie fraternity or, worse still, and a real faux pas on my part, vegetarians! 'My, they'll taste good!' say the others.

I smile to myself and think of all the possibilities in Fergus Henderson's wonderful book *Nose to Tail Eating*. I was even lucky enough to meet him briefly when he was demonstrating in the Cookery Theatre where I was helping at the Dartmouth Food Festival in October this year.

I'm dreaming of curing and salting, of hams and brawn, terrines and big roasts. How heartless am I, I hear you ask? But no, I have a much more serious ulterior motive. Yes, I do want to cook and eat good-quality pork and yes, I am fed up with the nasty stuff imported into this country masquerading as the real thing. Here we have legislation for the humane treatment of pigs. In Britain it is illegal to use sow stalls, sometimes known as gestation crates that prevent the pregnant sow from any movement. The majority of sows live outside in this country and have access to straw bedding and freedom of movement. It is also illegal to castrate young males, a practice widely used abroad, without aesthetic.

These are but two examples of better animal husbandry in the UK that, in turn, inevitably makes our pork more expensive. So many supermarkets are importing vast quantities of cheap pork raised in countries without humane animal welfare legislation where pigs are bred and raised in appalling conditions. This has of course led to a reduction in UK pig farming. I want to support British farmers and do my minute bit to champion our high animal welfare standards in the UK.

So, my first weaners will have a short but happy life. They will be well cared for and well fed. Stephen and I enjoy them hugely and with the help of other pig farmers, our excellent local abattoir and our butcher we and our friends will enjoy some really good old-fashioned pork in the New Year.

In the meantime, I am reading up on all that curing and salting, sausages, hams! Watch this space…

SLOW-ROAST PORK

Ideally, if I have time, I stuff a boned shoulder of pork with apples and celery, onion and breadcrumbs, sage and lemon all bound together with soft butter and a beaten egg and salt and pepper of course.

But if I'm in a hurry, I leave out the stuffing or cook it later separately. I score the pork skin with a sharp knife and rub in plenty of oil and salt. It can be done the evening before and left in the fridge overnight. In the morning I shove it into a hot oven as I grab a coffee, read emails and dash up to the yard. But I must remember to turn the oven down after 30 minutes to a low temperature, 140°C, and pour over a glass of cider and a little water. Once this is done it can be left alone for 4–5 hours. The bottom oven of my range is ideal here.

About an hour before supper, I move it up to the hot top oven to crisp the crackling on the pork. And, if the stuffing is separate, now is the time to cook it in a dish beside the pork. I keep an eye on the meat while I peel, cook and mash potatoes and sauté cabbage or leeks to go with the meat. Once out of the oven, I allow the pork to rest. This is essential to allow the juices to soak back into the meat. Meanwhile, I finish the vegetables and make gravy in the roasting dish deglazing the residue with the vegetable water or a little stock and thickening with a little slaked cornflour (i.e., cornflour mixed with a little water) and salt and pepper.

To serve, I cut the crackling from the meat and break into crisp pieces. I tear the meat into shreds and serve it with the stuffing, gravy, the mashed potatoes and vegetables – just the thing for a cold December evening with good friends.

As I write sitting warm and snug by the fire in the study, so the weather changes – a tremendous gale is lashing South Devon. This morning dogs and I set off once more for the farmyard in drizzle and semi-darkness, the sky slate grey and the air damp and misty. It never did get light today. Now as evening falls, a huge storm rages on the hills above us. The wind is so strong dogs and I could barely struggle against it as we climbed the vertiginous slopes of Steep Field to check the flock. Rain swept sideways in a great curtain across the hills driven by the southwesterly gale. Dartmoor was swallowed in cloud and the river below me barely visible. Old ewes, driven by the ancient instinct of their moorland forebears, sheltered in the hedge safe from the onslaught. Down the hill to the farmyard again the wind threatened to make our descent airborne. Dogs raced ahead, the wind in their tales. We fed donkeys and pigs, collected eggs and shut the chickens up for the night. Soggily we squelched home through the driving rain as the light faded. What a contrast to this time last year when all was still, silent, white and frozen.

HAPPY NEW YEAR!

This morning's hard frost came as quite a surprise. The mild, damp weather of the last two months has lulled us into a sense of false security. No snow, no frozen water troughs or icy farmyard. No heaving of water buckets from the stream to quench the thirst of chilly livestock. No throbbing, freezy fingers, no numb toes paralysed with cold inside unrelenting wellies, no scarlet, stinging nose poking out of a balaclava, whipped numb by the east wind; well, not yet anyway.

The grass continues to grow, spring bulbs push up through mud, snowdrops promise another avalanche of white, while camellias take enormous risks bursting into a profusion of pinks, forgetting completely the perils of early morning sun on icy petals. Even roses continue to produce funny ragged little flowers. It can't last. A cold snap is bound to arrive but for now the garden seems to think spring is already on its way; I wish!

Fat ewes munch happily in the rain. The wethers, growing fast, race up to me each morning. Bucket tame, they jostle for their breakfast. Last year's ewe lambs, round and fat now, graze quietly on the top field we call 'Dainty' after that naughty erstwhile pony.

As for the pigs they are getting so big. To quote Hugh Fearnley-Whittingstall's description of his porkers in his *The River Cottage Meat Book*: 'they arrived as fat puppies and now resemble small hippos'. Little hippos they are, indeed, I'm learning why it is that so many people love pigs; they are so intelligent, so entertaining. They just make me smile! But sadly, it is also becoming clear to me why they are the most abused of farm animals. They require such different husbandry to sheep and cattle.

Pigs need regular feeding and attention twice a day. Since the foot-and-mouth outbreak some years ago strict laws are in place in this country controlling their diet; no more kitchen scraps or 'pig swill'. We must feed only certified pig nuts. Pigs eat neither grass nor straw but love to rootle round in search of tasty morsels in the ground, truffles if possible! Such enthusiasm leads to large holes and much mud. But despite this fun they are extraordinarily clean, keeping their sleeping quarters immaculate and pooing only in one designated place. The defamatory 'Living like Pigs' is, without doubt, a reflection not of the creatures themselves but of their human captors. My weaners demand and deserve respect and care during their short lives and they will reward that care and attention with wonderful pork.

No pigs to be seen at this year's Dartmouth Fat Stock Show. There were sheep, all breeds and sizes, cattle, massive, large and small and yards and yards of trestle tables groaning under the weight of ready-dressed turkeys. The beautifully restored and refurbished market place was filled once more with livestock and deadstock, as it has been for so many years. All the local farming community, young and old, were there for this historic annual meet. Rain, sleet and sunshine took turns with an icy wind that curled around the market walls.

With its smart new plate glass and stainless steel, the market place houses even more businesses than ever, while still remaining true to its roots. Weekly markets and the farmers' market flourish and of course the wonderful Fat Stock Show takes over for a day each December.

So home now to my kitchen. My freezer is filled with my own lamb and vegetables, local beef from Farmer Phil Bond, Mark Lobb's wonderful fish, another delicious Oakcroft chicken from Mr Rogers of Beaworthy, and soon my own pork too – winter suppers are looking promising.

But first I need a warming Vegetable Soup for a quick lunch. There's nothing as comforting as a big bowl of homemade soup when dogs and I have been blown home from the farmyard by a sharp south easterly.

I choose the ingredients for soup according to the homemade stock I have in the freezer. This time it's ham. Onions or shallots are a must and peas go so well with ham. The other ingredients just happen to be in the fridge or larder: the last piece of a large pumpkin, a potato, two big garlic cloves, some parsley stalks, pepper and maybe a little salt, but I taste first as ham stock can be salty.

The principle is the same for most soup: sweat the chopped shallots or onions, garlic too, if you like. Add a peeled diced potato; this will act as the thickening agent. Add diced pumpkin, carrot or other root vegetable but keep the balance of flavour in mind. Remember, for example, that parsnips, although delicious, are much more dominant than a carrot, pumpkin is mild but will enhance texture and so on. Once your chosen vegetables are sweated, that is, softened in their own steam and a little oil in a pan with a heavy lid, you can stir in the stock; simmer gently for about 20 minutes, taste and season. To liquidise or not to liquidise is a matter of taste: soup smooth or soup with bits!

It's so warm and restorative on a cold winter's day with hot crusty bread and good slightly salted butter!

FARMING BEGINS

I've just found the old copy of *Country Living Magazine* February 1994: 'HOW TO SURVIVE REDUNDANCY, A SECOND CAREER'. My, that took me back a bit! There we are photographed climbing the hill, pitchforks in hand and dogs in tow, starting our new life.

We had already lived in our funny old house for a number of years when Thames Television lost its franchise to broadcast and Paul found himself in charge of closing down technical operations at Thames' Euston Studios. The process was agonisingly slow; months passed as transmission wound down until finally, he was able to write himself out of the script. He walked out of the studios after twenty-seven years in television: 'Can I have your car keys, please, sir?' and suddenly it was all over. It seems a lifetime away now.

That same year our farming neighbour born in our house, decided to sell up and move away. Most of the land went to his relation, up the valley, in farming tradition – brother's wife's sister's husband, just a few minutes' walk from us across the fields. But his relation didn't want it all; he didn't want the steep thirty something acres that had once belonged to our house or the large ugly 1970s ramshackle farmyard.

We pondered our options; not a very promising farming potential. We bought four sheep, a couple of Dexter cows, a few chickens and some turkey poults and quite a few books. But, most important of all, our neighbouring farmers overwhelmed us with unbelievable kindness and generosity, sharing their knowledge, help and support.

In time we built up a thriving little business breeding Whiteface Dartmoor sheep, producing free-range eggs, raising table birds for delivery every week and turkeys for Christmas. We began making up salad bags long before the supermarkets caught on to the idea. All this we delivered in our minute, elderly refrigerated van to a quickly growing list of regular customers. And soon we supplied local businesses with our eggs and local hotels and pubs with lamb and chicken.

A summer visitor in a big queue in our village shop was heard to ask the sell-by date of our eggs. 'About half an hour,' replied a local wag. We knew we had arrived!

One day we were surprised to turn up on BBC *Spotlight*, the Devon TV news programme; it helped our sales no end. A little later the *Times Weekend* did a half-page feature of us called 'Farming for Fun'! Despite the terrific input of the regional director of the National Farmers' Union, South West, the journalist clearly knew little about farming and described us, rather disparagingly, as 'hobby farmers'! Some things don't change.

Our weeks followed a regular pattern. From Monday to Wednesday I ran courses for the University of Plymouth and my own psychotherapy practice in Totnes as well as providing clinical supervision for NHS GP counsellors. Paul farmed.

On Thursdays I joined him and began preparing the chickens he had plucked. I drew and trussed them then packed, weighed and labelled them. I took the orders, worked out the delivery route, wrote recipes to accompany them, picked salad and herbs from my polytunnel and made up the salad bags. I collected, graded, packed and labelled the eggs.

We were approved and regularly visited by Health and Safety, Trading Standards, Environmental Health and the Ministry of Agriculture, Fisheries and Food (MAFF), which preceded the Department for Environment, Food and Rural Affairs (DEFRA) and the 'egg inspector' who always made me giggle, poor man. Fancy being called an egg inspector, but someone has to do it...and Paul had, of course, done the appropriate training to be awarded a professional poultry slaughter man's licence; not so glamourous either!

On Friday and Saturday Paul did deliveries while I cleared up, cleaned and caught up with paperwork. On Sunday we crawled to church, planned the new week ahead, fed the animals (no one told them it was Sunday!), cooked supper and collapsed – some 'hobby'!

THE DILEMMAS OF SPRING

Winter is behind us once more. Clocks have sprung forward and British summer time has arrived; light evenings back at last. A fierce March sun blazes down across the valley. Unusually strong for the time of year, it warms our backs and coaxes tired old grass into growth. Newly ploughed fields glow like dark melting chocolate under a cloudless blue sky. Ecstatic birds fill the air with their rejoicing. A heron dives optimistically into the stream and the swans are back on the creek. The millpond is a cacophony of quacking. Daffodils, yellow, orange, white, spread across the orchard. They seem to sing in harmony above the primrose carpet. Camellias, planted just a few years ago, are suddenly overburdened with huge blooms; flowering for weeks, they defy wind and frost. And yet, I am told from all sides, I must not celebrate any of this gloriousness because, despite recent downpours and heavy morning dew, down here in the Southwest at least, this wonderful weather threatens future drought.

We're lambing again too, of course. This gentle weather is perfect for new life; nine strong babies so far in rapid succession. Yet all the while we are reminded not to rejoice at this either; our next infants may be born severely deformed, infected with the Schmallenberg virus, a deadly threat lurking in the wings. Just one case so far in the Southwest but news bulletins keep us constantly in fear. Apparently, the infection is carried across Europe by midges. There is absolutely nothing we can do to control the situation but cross fingers and pray. I must not enjoy the sun because it may not rain, my lambs may all be born deformed or dead, so says the media.

As I drive through narrow Devon lanes, having just filled my very ordinary car with an eye-wateringly expensive tank of diesel, I am reminded that fuel cost has become so huge few of us can move about freely any more. And if the threatened tanker driver's strike comes to fruition none of us will be going anywhere at all.

I am told I must not share a bottle of wine with my partner because we will surely become ill and die of cancer or heart disease. Old people with dementia, of which I will doubtless soon become, according to statistics, if, of course, I live, are being starved by overworked hospital staff or locked up in wards 'for their own safety'. As the government are damned if they do and damned if they don't, whichever way they try to tackle this national malaise, I begin to feel overwhelmed by an epidemic of despair and fear. A 'what if' culture seems to have us by the throat.

But, hey, it may rain very soon, as it always does just in time for the Easter holiday! Our lambs may all be born strong and healthy after all. The fuel strike may not happen. I may live to 103 like my father who still loves to discuss current affairs over a glass of sherry. This evening on the phone: 'Will this Granny Tax affect you? Who's suffering from all this dementia? Should Cameron have had these people to supper…? And how is the economy?' I may even escape hospital and any medication and maybe even die without ever suffering the downward spiral of Alzheimer's just like him.

So I tend the ewes with new lambs, feed the wethers and the yearlings, talk to the donkeys, dig the garden, celebrate my newly reconstructed old greenhouse, clear mud from the pond, collect eggs and clean out the chickens, walk over the hills with my dogs and my camera, ponder when to get more pigs, do the accounts, cook kitchen suppers for my friends and risk that second glass of wine. I feel inclined to rejoice, regardless, at what we have, rather than negate the beauty of the present by fretting about what may never happen in the future.

Oh, and the pork was wonderful too – the pigs a great success. Richard Pollard, our butcher, did an excellent job: delicious sausages, bacon and gammon, shoulders and legs neatly boned and rolled ready for stuffing, belly boned for slow roasting until crisp and cracklingly, loin chops cut thick to cook slowly under the grill until dark and golden.

Pork as it used to taste. 'Have you any left?', 'When can we have some more?' I must get more pigs!

Postscript: Today we lost our beloved old sheepdog, Meg, loyal friend and wonderful working dog of fifteen years. We miss her terribly but she had a long and happy doggy life, sweet girl.

FILLET OF PORK WITH SAUSAGEMEAT AND PRUNES

Friends for supper last week, so I thought I would do something with the pork fillet, but it looked a little small for four of us. Trawling idly through my mass of cookery books, Hugh Fearnley-Whittingstall's *Meat Book* came up trumps again, but of course I didn't have exactly the required ingredients. So, instead of the mincemeat and dried chestnuts that he suggests I used my own prunes; last summer's Dit'sum plums dried slowly overnight in the bottom oven of the Everhot then stored in an airtight jar.

I split my little fillet nearly in half and filled the cavity with our sausagemeat, salt, fresh ground black pepper and the pitted prunes. I tied the whole with string to make a big oblong, then wrapped it loosely in foil leaving the top exposed, poured lemon juice over it and chilled it in the fridge while I went into the garden to dig the very last Pink Fir Apple potatoes and pick winter spinach.

The pork went into a hot oven, 200°C, for an hour until well done and golden. As the potatoes cooked, I took the meat out of the oven, covered it and let it rest in a warm place on top of the cooker. I made a sauce with chicken stock, a tablespoon of redcurrant jelly and a pinch of cinnamon.

I slaked a dessertspoon of cornflour into a little extra stock, stirred that into the sauce and brought it just to the boil, stirring all the time until it thickened. Finally, I stirred in a couple of tablespoons of cream, tasted the sauce and added seasoning.

I washed the spinach I had picked from the garden that morning and wilted it quickly in its own water in a pan. The secret with spinach is no extra water and the quickest possible cooking. I still needed to drain it thoroughly and press it down in the colander to really get it dry. A quick stir over the heat with a knob of butter and it was ready too.

As I sliced the pork and served my friends it suddenly occurred to me that I had produced everything on the plate! Not pudding though; I found Nigel Slater's wonderful quick lemon curd ice cream recipe in his lovely book, *Kitchen Diaries*. Speedy to make, it is sharp and delicious after the rich unctuous pork.

SEASON OF MISTS AND NOT SO MELLOW FRUITFULNESS

The wettest summer on record has come to an end. Dartmouth Regatta marked the close of the holiday season once more. Boats were moored up, caravans towed away, tents packed, holiday cottages emptied, children returned to school and, of course, the rain stopped. Here we are once more in a soft September, bathed by the gently sinking sun. My long-legged shadow precedes me as I climb the hill to the top fields. Morning mist hangs over the river and steam seems to rise from the grass as it warms in the sunlight. Autumn is here again.

The land has suffered from so much summer rain. The wettest June for years was followed by a soaking July and August. And now mildew creeps stealthily through the garden. Vegetables rot in the ground never having matured; beans brown on their supports. All my potatoes, infested with wireworm, must be burned. Sweetcorn refuses to ripen; courgettes wither. The vegetable garden is a disaster. The quince tree has some strange disease making me fear for its future. No wild plums glisten in the hedgerows; apples are sparse, blackberries too. Only the tomato seeds out shine expectation. Although late, they are producing abundant weird and wonderful fruit.

And the cosmos is magnificent this year. Just one little packet of seeds has overwhelmed the garden in an uplifting blousy pink and white froth. I had so many seedlings I just shoved them in everywhere and anywhere and the result is unexpectedly wonderful. They sway gently in the breeze among giant anemones, hollyhocks and *Verbena bonariensis*. They crowd in between the roses and fall over the *Hydrangea paniculata*. What a bargain.

This is my second year of pigs. Paul is facing another new knee operation in a few weeks; I'm so glad he only has two legs not four. My partner in pigs is once again Stephen. Last year we had three Middle Whites and three Berkshire between us. Having decided Middle Whites were favourite, six little fellows arrived last Monday. This time we have put them out in our big field, Sunday Orchard, where they are already busy wrecking the joint as only piglets can. Our neighbour and ex-pig farmer kindly supplied us with a big ark, which is fine now but may prove very cosy as they grow. They look so happy and inquisitive, digging and snuffling through the grass; so much nicer to see them in the fresh air rather than in a barn, however spacious.

The donkeys came to take a look when they arrived, first the beautiful Nutmeg, then fat Luke and finally old Bunty: 'What on earth do you call those?' They stood peering at the newcomers over their fence for a very long time! This year's ewe lambs ran down the hill too, took a look, but quickly lost interest and returned to serious grazing. The wethers and rams were more curious and peered at them for some time drawn by the sight and sound of a bucket of food. They came closer and closer to the electric fence led by the, now recovered, senior pedigree ram, Big Dez. Poor old chap, having had his ingrowing horns removed, a somewhat traumatic event for all concerned, his face has healed and he's able to chew properly again. He is putting on weight and back to his old self; sad though to have to lose those magnificent horns.

Soon Dez will begin work again. In a few weeks he will be in with ewes once more, busy making next year's lambs. The pigs will grow fat and roast pork, sausages and bacon sandwiches will be back on the menu. And so the cycle continues; summer ends, autumn gentles us into winter and Christmas snowdrops point us towards the welcome of spring. Round and round we go watching the valley change colour with each season's individual beauty.

MEATBALLS WITH SPAGHETTI

Today another quick supper that will use up the last of the pork mince – so good with a big bowl of spaghetti on an autumnal evening.

I start by soaking a large slice of bread in some milk and mix it with the minced pork meat, gently kneading it with my hands to break up the bread. I add chopped parsley, a finely chopped shallot, a crushed clove of garlic and salt and pepper. I bind the mixture with just enough egg to enable me to roll and shape it into balls. I fry them in a little oil until brown all over. Then into the pan goes more crushed garlic, a tin of tomatoes or, better still, some of this year's prolific tomato crop! I add a dash of red wine or water and simmer it all gently for about half an hour until the sauce is creamy and the meatballs cooked through. We eat it with the boiled spaghetti and lots of grated Parmesan cheese.

TOMATOES

Amazingly I have a tomato glut this year despite the sodden winter and return of the blight! Every year a dear friend sources wonderful heritage seed for me. I grow enough for both of us and when she returns from a warm winter on the other side of the world, we share the seedlings – a very satisfactory arrangement for us both!

This year I grew 'Yellow Brandywine', 'Black Cherry' and the amazing giants, 'Cherokee', as well as modern 'Pomodoro Red Cherry' and a funny pointed fellow called 'Follia' F1. Last year saw success with 'Striped Cavern', 'Ivory Egg', 'Copia' and 'Japanese Black Trifele'. Of course, I've grown good old 'Gardeners Delight' and 'Moneymaker' too, many times, but the heritage ones are fun and a bit of a challenge. The flavour is often better too.

For years *Solanum lycopersicum* were considered poisonous in this country. Gerard dismisses them out of hand in his *The Herbal or General History of Plants* of 1597: '*Poma Amoris,* Apples of Love. ...In Spaine and those hot Regions they vse to eat the Apples prepared and boiled with pepper, salt, and oile: but they yeeld very little nourishment to the bodie, and the same nought and corrupt. Likewise, they doe eat the Apples with oile, vineger and pepper mixed together for sauce to their meate, euen as we in these cold Countries doe Mustard.'

Tomatoes were already being eaten in Italy and Spain by then, brought back from the Andes by the Spanish Conquistadors. The word tomato comes from 'tomatl' in Nahuatl, the language of the Aztecs. The Italians called it *pomo dei Mori*, apple of the Moors. The first reference to the cooking of tomatoes in Italy can be found in Vincenzo Corrado's 1773 *Il Cuoco Galante* (The Gallant Cook). In his wonderful book, *Complete Italian Food*, Antonio Carluccio states that Italians now consume an astonishing 50kg per head per year, mostly in the form of sauce and purées on their pasta!

In France it was named *pomme d'amour* and in time was embraced as warmly as in Spain and Italy. In contrast we cautious Brits only began to let the 'Love Apple' creep into our diet in about 1820 still clinging to the dire warnings of Gerard two hundred years earlier and despite the best efforts of the Quaker merchant, Peter Collinson. He reported in 1742 that the apples of love 'are very much in Italy to putt when ripe into their Brooths & Soops giving it a pretty Tart Taste. A Lady Just come from Leghorn says she thinks it gives an Agreeable tartness and Relish to them & she likes it Much.' But tomatoes were still considered as 'chill to the stomach', the cause of maladies such as gout and a dangerous aphrodisiac. How times have changed!

So, what to do with all this deliciousness? I will be halving the small red tomatoes and putting them into a cool oven overnight to half-dry them. Then I will bottle them in olive oil with a sprig of basil and store them in the fridge for winter treats, such as a tiny salad with grated Parmesan, a quick pasta topping or a filling for a baked potato.

One of my own favourite ways to cook tomatoes takes me back to a tiny village in the hills in Provence many years ago, when Madam cooked just one set meal in her tiny restaurant in the village square – no choice and the food was served in big dishes straight to the table. I can't remember the rest of the meal only the exquisite beans and tomatoes!

Blanch French beans, drain carefully and return to the pan with olive oil. Add a clove of crushed garlic and freshly chopped tomatoes. Simmer gently for a few minutes. Add salt and pepper and serve with more really good olive oil. That's it – truly wonderful if the beans are tender, the tomatoes full of flavour and the olive oil thick and green.

The big boys such as 'Cherokee' will be a meal in themselves. I will scoop out their middles, make a stuffing, top them with breadcrumbs and cheese and bake them in the oven. Others will be made into sauce with shallots, herbs and garlic, then frozen ready to go into winter ragouts and pasta sauces. Some I will simply whizz in the blender and freeze. And, of course, the green tomatoes will join apples, sugar, shallots, chilli and vinegar to become thick dark chutney. I love tomatoes!

FARMING, FLOODS AND FESTIVITIES

It's stopped raining! Hurrah, but for how long I wonder.

So much water has gone under and over the bridge, literally and metaphorically since September. The sodden ground can take no more. The rain started in the spring, continued throughout the summer, drenched us in the autumn and continues unabated. Floods spread across Britain; we're sinking into the sea or so it feels. Devon has been particularly hard hit; towns and villages under water, farmland devastated, railway lines washed away. Now and then the sun tried to break through to remind us of times past, but not for long, just as we gazed in wonder at the golden autumn light casting long shadows on the grass, storm clouds gathered again, trees danced manically in the returning wind and the heavens opened once more.

Again and again I catch myself looking at the local weather forecast praying aloud, 'Please, no more flood alerts, no more amber warnings, grey clouds, rain symbols'. Dry till Monday it says today; a brief lull and, maybe, time for some water to drain down the hill into the raging torrent that was once a gentle stream.

But we've been lucky this time. The flood protection put in some years ago after the terrible night of 24 December 1999 has mostly held up at least for us. The house is dry, so is the cottage and all the animals are safe. Just one big shed, thankfully empty of livestock at the moment, is still under water. Only our drive is washed away again, pipework not large enough to carry the cascading torrent underground from the stream, out of our gate beneath the road into the river beyond.

As the rain fell relentlessly once more, I went out last evening to check the place at the end of our drive where the stream is supposed to disappear underground. It was very dark, and suddenly I found myself struggling to stay standing in the raging water. The gates were jammed open the wrong way, the great refuse wheelie bins trapped against them forming a perfect dam. I pushed through the water, managing to release the bins and watched helpless as they disappeared at speed down the flooded road towards the river.

Water rushed round the old Land Rover parked at the gate. I watched in horror as water rose higher and higher over the wheels and up the bonnet. I forced my way through the water, scrambled into the driver's seat and drove up the drive just in time. As I looked behind me the drive collapsed and a huge crater appeared filling with water in seconds, just where the car had stood two minutes earlier. Shaking a bit, I went into the house, took off my soaking clothes before making light of it to Paul, who was still unable to walk after his second knee replacement operation at the beginning of November.

Knee surgery has stopped him doing anything for the last two months so I've been promoted again to (acting!) head farmer and general factotum once more – a demanding role! My days have been divided up into small chunks reminiscent of a time when the children were tiny and everything had to be shoe horned in between everything else and done at speed – a time and motion masterclass.

Seven o'clock the alarm clock shouts. It's still dark outside. I make a cup of coffee for Paul, scramble into boots and waterproofs, serve breakfast to surprised cats and dogs and venture up to the yard in the grey light of yet another wet murky dawn.

By the end of September all dreams of piggies living happy autumn days foraging in the field had disappeared. Rain and mud forced us to move them back into the big barn. So, first job is always to assuage their voracious appetites, refill water trough and re-straw their sleeping quarters. It never fails to surprise me how clean and tidy they are if given enough space. I scatter chopped carrots and apples among the clean straw so they can at least pretend to be foraging outside.

One morning, a few weeks ago, as I filled their food troughs, I glanced towards the water trough and gaped in disbelief; it had gone, vanished, disappeared. I looked down at my boots squelching in the straw, covered in water, then at the trickle coming from the disconnected pipe. The water had frozen the day before and, even though I had filled the trough with buckets to the brim, my fat, pink boys had furiously removed the trough and footballed it away across the barn in protest. Oh, mud inside as well as outside now! Fortunately, Stephen arrived and quickly replaced it with a solid concrete trough unsuitable for rugby tackles or scoring goals! I live and learn.

Next, donkeys have breakfast. Bunty must have hers separately being almost the oldest donk in Devon and therefore the slowest eater in the world. Given half a chance the other two, big fat Luke and prima donna Nutmeg, will elbow her out of the way and scoff hers as well as their own. The waterlogged barn adds to the complicated logistics of keeping them separate but fortunately their stable stands on higher ground and has remained completely dry throughout the deluge.

As donkeys eat, dogs and I take a bucket of oats out to the wethers and rams in Sunday Orchard. Then I clean the stable as donkeys, food finished, climb the hill to drier ground. For once, such steep land has its merits. When all that is done dogs and I set off up to the top fields to feed the ewes. They're alone now without the boys, big Dez and young Ernie. They will lamb at the end of March, the next big event in the farming calendar. Down the hill again we go to the yard then up the lane to a neighbour's field to check out yearling ewe lambs before finally going home to make breakfast.

Each day Paul becomes a little more mobile. Gradually the magic of modern medicine is working, the pain diminishing and mobility returning – each day a little better than the last. 'You've grown, you're taller. Hey, you look ten years younger,' our friends shouted when he finally emerged from the house without crutches or a stick.

Meanwhile, my days pass in a whirl of farming, shopping, washing, cleaning, lunch, back to the yard for the evening feeds before dark at 4.30 p.m., then cooking again and finally sleep… full-on days and always raining of course! No time to sit and ponder or to write.

And so the weeks have passed, punctuated by appointments at the hospital in Torquay and play rehearsals in the evenings for our village Christmas production of Alan Shaffer's hilarious *Black Comedy*, a hugely demanding and exhausting success.

Then suddenly Christmas. I baked the cake, made the pudding, stuffed the turkey and cooked one of our hams. I made a brawn terrine from my pork and a giant, not so traditional, shepherd's pie with our lamb, tomatoes, red peppers, parsley and sliced potatoes. I made up beds, went shopping, wrapped presents, decorated the tree, hung up the Christmas cards and laid the Christmas table. And then all at once they were here: first son and family from Japan, then daughter and family from Bath – the first Christmas we have had all together for twelve years.

On Christmas Eve we ate a huge pot of bourride for supper, based on Claudia Roden's wonderful recipe in her *Mediterranean*

Cookery published in 1987, an old favourite of mine. Then it was a Midnight Service in St Georges Church, Dittisham – readings and carols led by Paul. On Christmas morning I was up to the yard as usual to feed the animals before cooking the turkey. We had a huge traditional Christmas lunch – turkey, ham, chestnut stuffing, Brussels sprouts, more chestnuts, bread sauce, cranberry jelly, roast potatoes and gravy all followed by ice cream, clotted cream, Christmas pud and brandy butter made, as in the old days, by our son Tom, home briefly from Tokyo, who still remembered how delicious he always used to know it was! We pulled crackers, opened presents, hugged one another, laughed, played games and climbed the hills to feed sheep and donkeys and take photos of fat pigs munching their supper.

On Boxing Day, I had lots of help in the farmyard! The next day, we set off for the village along the riverbank sliding on the seaweed, watching the birds, paddling in the water, then lunch in the Ferry Boat Inn. We visited Totnes market and had supper in Harberton's Church House Inn. Friends dropped by to say hello. Suddenly the six days had disappeared, it was all over and time to say goodbye.

Happy, sad and exhausted, Paul and I quietly dismantled the traditions of Christmas as the week gradually floated away behind us changing by stealth into a precious dream to be held in a memory bubble forever.

And now it's time to go and feed the animals again and it's still raining sideways…

BOURRIDE

This is, of course, just my version of this delicious fish stew, depending, as usual, on whatever fish I can get! Firm white fish is best – monkfish, bream or bass, for example. I have used cod and haddock. They taste fine but are inclined to fall to bits.

Squid, mussels and large prawns are good additions too. I make sure I clean the mussels carefully, rinsing out the grit, pulling off the beards and discarding any open or broken ones.

I start by making the aioli with four eggs yolks, six cloves of garlic and about 500ml of olive oil. I make it in the usual way for mayonnaise but put the garlic in at the beginning with the egg yolks. Slow is the word here! Once it's thick and creamy I set it to one side.

I peel and blanch about 1.5kg of potatoes and cut up a few sticks of celery, four or five tomatoes, a fennel bulb, some thyme and summer savory and a good handful of chopped parsley. If I have any garden peas or broad beans left, I add these too.

Once everything is prepared, I heat some oil in a big pan. The vegetables go in first then the mussels and a layer of fish. I cover it with about 2 litres of fish stock or water. I sometimes use a tin of chopped tomatoes or some from the garden, instead of some of the water.

I let it all come gently to the boil, add 300ml of white wine and let it simmer for 10 minutes. Then I carefully take out all the fish leaving a little potato behind. Having carefully discarded any mussels that have not opened, I keep the fish warm while I crush the potato into the sauce before stirring in half the aioli and warming it through.

I spoon fish and broth into individual bowls and serve with the remaining aioli and crusty bread. A good crisp white wine completes the feast.

DEVON RAIN

And still it rains, relentlessly, torrentially, day in, day out, week after week. Once again, we've become obsessed with the weather forecast, tuning into radio and television at every opportunity, checking our phones, computers, tablets every hour. Low after low swirl across the Atlantic, bringing more and more severe flooding, leaving more and more devastation in their wake. Flooding, waterlogged fields, storm force winds, it feels as if the whole of the British Isles is sinking below the sea again.

As we travelled right across England from west to east last week to the memorial service of a dear friend, the roads seemed to snail their way like great grey slime trails across mile after mile of submerged farmland. News flashes told us of the desperate plight of the Somerset Levels and we saw for ourselves the same in Avon, Wiltshire, North Oxfordshire, everywhere. And now it has reached us here in the West Country; the rail connection gone from Exeter to Penzance, the track at Dawlish washed away. Catastrophe after catastrophe spreading right across Devon and Cornwall.

Day in day out the forecast is the same: rain and wind, wind and rain. A brief respite and we rush to the yard to try to do a few long overdue jobs. Then in comes the next storm. Gale force winds rock the very fabric of the buildings, trees sway precariously on the steep hills above us. Day in day out, slipping and sliding on waterlogged ground, we trudge up to the top fields to feed the sheep. Today I could barely stay upright in the wind as I called the girls to tea. For once we are grateful to have such steep land where ewes can graze safely on high ground with a little barn for shelter.

No serious flooding here yet – no flooded barns or collapsing driveways so far this year. The flood defences we put in place after last year's deluge are so far holding up. The stream is still just about contained, as it roars through the valley. Frothing brown, it crashes its way to the mud-streaked creek taking all in its path. Each high tide finds us cut off from the village as gale force winds hold back the huge volume of water coming off the hills, interrupting the natural tidal flow of the river. The geese arrived last week but didn't stay long this year. Resting and feeding briefly, even they found the river too wild and soon moved on.

I heard on the radio the other day that someone somewhere has unearthed old records that show we are experiencing the highest rainfall since 1767, the year our house was built. As I watch our twenty-first century builders equipped with all the latest gear struggle to climb the scaffolding in howling winds and rain to mend our leaking roof and replace our rotten windows, I try to image the scene in the eighteenth century as men dug into the muddy Devon hillside in torrential rain, toiling to build this strange, narrow four-storey folly – a local rector's dream house for his daughter.

Some folly indeed, down a muddy track almost a mile from a steep riverside village, it stood at the head of a creek looking east towards the River Dart. There was a ford running at the gate, no heating, no plumbing. There was certainly no little shop in a village that could only be reached on foot or by horse and cart. Dartmouth, the local town, was only accessible by water. One token to modernity, if you can call it that, in this quirky house, were the coal grates. Very unusual for the time, they replaced the usual woodburning hearth. Coal barges unloaded their cargo at the head of the creek onto horse and carts just outside our gate, so coal was available to warm the two main rooms – so very modern for 1767. But I keep imagining just how hard and bleak life must have been.

Dartmouth is still our nearest little town. A town with an extraordinary history, it has managed to reinvent itself in a quite remarkable way, time and again, across the centuries. It sits at the mouth of the Dart, a river that rises 550 metres above sea level on the acidic peat bogs high up on Dartmoor. Dartmouth perches at its mouth, a town with a history of ships and shipping and a story dominated by the sea. In the twelfth century Dartmouth was the fourth most important town in Devon after Exeter, Plymouth and Barnstaple.

The First Crusade left in 1147 and the third in 1190. Dartmouth was already meeting the needs of commercial shipping. Smith Street, Higher Street and Lower Street formed the town centre on the water's edge; merchant houses and warehouses backed onto the river making it easy to load and unload cargoes straight from the ships. Boats lay alongside for repairs and the quayside was a thriving marketplace, the earliest recorded in 1231. Plenty of fresh water flowed from the hills above the town filling conduits that were still in use in the twentieth century. The water supply made Dartmouth a popular place with brewers and vintners and in 1364 it received the Charter of Merchant Vintners, increasing the trade in cloth and herring as well as wine.

There were brewers, bakers, butchers and craftsmen. There was the pillory, stocks and a cucking stool in the waterside churchyard of St Saviours. Laws were plenty to dissuade the unscrupulous tradesman; a millar must only have three hens and a cock in case he should feed a client's grain to his poultry. If he gave short weight, he was fined for the first two offences then, if he offended again, he was into the pillory. A similar fate awaited the brewer who sold short measure. On his third offence it was into the cucking stool then into the pillory soaking wet – a nasty deterrent. And so on for the fishmonger and cook. Taverners were forbidden to make their own wine and one innkeeper who used his premises as a brothel was simply expelled from the town.

The strength behind the success of the town for many years was the great merchant and shipmaster John Hawley, *c.*1340–1408. It was he who fortified the town with a great chain that could be cast across the mouth of the river thus giving the town the power to stop enemy ships entering or leaving. So impressed was Chaucer when he met Hawley while visiting Dartmouth in his role as customs officer on behalf of the king in 1373, that he is believed to have based the famous Shipman upon him in *The Canterbury Tales*. Hawley's achievements are legendry, mayor many times, a privateer of huge reputation and some say, possibly something of a pirate too. On his death the town mourned the loss of one of its greatest and began to decline.

But not for long, as the fishing trade increased, so Dartmouth was to become famous for the Newfoundland fisheries. Sir Walter Raleigh, 'a local', described the fishery as 'the mainstay of the West'. So important was Newfoundland fishing that crews were exempt press-ganging into the navy at times of war. The ships were away for half the year salting and drying the cod on board and trading it with goods from Spain, France and Portugal on their return en route to Dartmouth. As time passed fishing became more local and by the eighteenth century Devon boats were sending fish to Bristol, Bath, Portsmouth, London and the Channel Islands. The fish was kept alive in huge tanks onboard ship.

Gradually the town began to change. It is hard to imagine now Victoria Road under water until the beginning of the nineteenth century, crossing places at North Ford and South Ford uniting the two small towns of Hardness and Clifton, which together formed Dartmouth. Drainage and land reclamation began in earnest. By the 1820s Foss Street was dry land leading to the new market place. But it was not until 1823 that the town became accessible by land for wheeled vehicles, almost sixty years after our house was built. Up until that time only pack horses or ponies could manage the steep descent; the river was the motorway to the town.

Wheeled vehicles began to come down the hill into the town at last. Local trade increased as farmers were able to bring more produce to market and supply local shops. Burgoyne's the Butcher and Oldreive Brothers in Fairfax Place victualled the ships and fed the town. The display of poultry and game hanging from the first floor of Oldreives was such that they employed staff all night to prevent 'pilfering'.

And so the town swung into the twentieth century and then the twenty-first. Small traders like Mr Shillibeare and Mr Cutmore the butchers, Crisp and Green the greengrocers, 'Dave Killer the chemist' and 'Cundells the grocer' have all given way to the supermarkets. There is just one butcher now run by the Pollards who cut up our lamb and pork so beautifully for our customers. Jilly's Farm Shop sells local produce every week day. High-quality restaurants, cafés and pubs abound. The old bakery is gone but the fabulous pâtisserie, Saveurs, has arrived from France. The old market has recently been magnificently refurbished: the fat stock show and the farmers' market keep the old traditions, not just alive, but thriving there. Local food producers bring their produce to the town as they have done for centuries, then by boat, by cart or pack horse, now by car or van.

The fishing fleet mostly trade from nearby Brixham now but the crabbers still come into the river and wonderful fresh fish is still available in abundance; local food producers are once more thriving and multiplying and local food is slowly being valued once again. Times change, and as in the past, Dartmouth adjusts to the needs of the moment – the multiplicity of a present built upon hundreds of years of the past.

CHICKEN SUPPERS

A delicious smell of chicken stock floats into the study as I write from the very last vestiges of a delicious local free-range bird bought from the Pollards last week. We're hard to please when it comes to chickens having spent so many years raising table birds ourselves. But this was as good as anything we used to sell! And it provided so many meals.

Our first meal was traditional roast chicken. The following day a wonderful cold chicken salad, then a chicken and mushroom pie with added Hogs Pudding. The latter made in Devon by the aforesaid Richard Pollard even won the approval of my Cornish husband! This evening a risotto and still to go, stock for soup and even scraps as a treat for the dogs! Not bad for one small chicken.

LEFTOVER CHICKEN PIE

I strip the last pieces of meat from the carcass, saving the bones to make stock for soup later. I finely chop a small onion or shallot and soften it in a little butter and oil (the oil stops the butter burning). When it's soft but not coloured, I add sliced mushrooms, a little chopped bacon, a sausage maybe or hog's pudding if I have any in the fridge. The latter tends to be available only in the West Country.

I cook it gently for a few minutes then stir in stock or leftover gravy. I use a little cornflour, if necessary, to thicken it to a creamy consistency. Then in goes the chicken and some chopped parsley. I add seasoning to taste, tip it all into a pie dish and cover it with ready-made puff pastry, brush with beaten egg and bake until crisp and golden in a hot oven at 200°C.

THE CHAIN OF EVENTS:
ONE SMALL FARMER'S PERSPECTIVE

Gradually the land is draining, floodwater subsides, our barns dry out, the stream slows to its usual sombre pace. Rain, gentle now, wraps us in a fine mist, the air is warmer, the wind has dropped. Maybe spring will arrive after all. Snowdrops fade as primroses and daffodils push their way through the sodden ground. Crocuses wait for a rare flash of sunlight to transform their petals into silk. Camellias are late this year and early blossom hardly shows against a steel grey sky.

We fled to sunshine in the hills of southern Portugal last week for six days of silence. We gazed out across another world to a distant ocean under a blue sky. Bougainvillea flowered above the door, lemons, ripe for picking, glistened in the little garden, goats meandered in the neighbour's field and the air was rich with the heady scent of oranges carpeting the ground.

Home again refreshed after such a dismal January and February; our hopes turn now to March to cheer us up. Ewes are getting rounder as lambing approaches but grass is sparse. Excitement is tinged with anxiety this year with stories in the local press of ewes in lamb being slaughtered in the field just miles from here. And once again we will not be sure we have escaped the dreadful Schmallenberg virus until our lambs are born. So bittersweet weeks lie ahead as we face the inevitable exhaustion of lambing – that strange tiredness outweighed by the joy of new life. Let us hope that, after all, this year will be no different.

Rain, flooding, lack of grass, anxieties about the safety of our livestock, the horrors of the Schmallenberg virus and now the food contamination scandal, all in just a few short weeks – farming is tougher than usual right now. It's a lifestyle we either inherit or become addicted too, a way of being not easily abandoned. And yet farmers, who, contrary to an urban myth, are not the complainers the press would have you believe, are becoming ground down – the wettest winter for some hundred years, flooding, poor crops, rising price of fuel and fodder, and now the horsemeat scandal.

Personally, I believe this exposure of the dreadful deception of food production and food labelling is a good thing. For too long the finger has pointed in the wrong direction or in no direction at all. Few people know exactly what they are eating or are aware of just how many hoops farmers have to jump through, how much legislation and control surround the breeding and movement of farm animals. Before any animal leaves the farm, all must have ear tags in place, one of which must be electronic. The tags must give the flock number on one side and the animal's individual number on the other.

Four copies of movement forms must be completed before any animal is taken anywhere. The white copy must go to the local authority of the destination premises within three days of movement. The pink copy is given to the receiving location and must record the keeper's holding number and slaughterhouse number, if relevant, as well as arrival time and time animals are unloaded. This must be signed by the Keeper.

The blue copy is for the haulier who must hold a City & Guilds NPTC Animal Transport Licence. The yellow copy, retained by the keeper, records the keepers holding number of his or her land, name and address, flock identification number, individual animal number, declaration that animals are fit for the food chain, departure date, loading time and duration of journey. Are you with me so far...? I could go on.

This is just what we do with sheep and pigs but I have been scouring the net for all the other regulations recently, that is, cows and equines, that is to say my donkeys, all have 'passports'. A ministry vet must be present when all animals arrive at the abattoir; the Little Red Tractor insists on the highest welfare standards. There are movement restrictions on animals arriving and leaving any new premises, etc.

We are lucky. Our local abattoir is small and excellently run and, most importantly, nearby. Having pressure washed our Land Rover and our trailer inside and out before loading, as per the regulations, we take our animals early in the morning. They are unloaded and quickly and humanely despatched. The minimum delay not only spares the animals unnecessary distress but enhances the quality of the meat. Distressed, frightened animals produce adrenaline, which in turn makes the meat tough.

Once dead, the animals are skinned and their heads removed – no more ear tag identification. 'So how do you know your butcher can identify your lambs when he collects them for butchery?' a customer asked me recently. Confident in the integrity, efficiency and honesty of the abattoir I use, I assured them they were indeed eating my lamb and pork. But it started me thinking and as I read more and more alarming stories in the press, I realised how fortunate we are to have a small, honest, efficient, hygienic, humane abattoir just a few miles from our farm.

But what of the huge commercial outfits where lorries come and go all day long unloading animals that have been transported to the very brink of their legal allowance? Abattoirs where animals, held for hours in pens before slaughter, smell death.

Once killed they travel along the conveyor belt, heads gone, tags gone, identity gone – where then traceability, the form filling, ear tagging, haulage regulations? In the light of all the recent horrifying press coverage are all these exercises in form filling worth any more than the papers they are written on?

A supermarket executive said at a recent National Farmers' Union Conference, 'Customers don't like what they've been hearing about how some of the meat they put on their plates is produced.' How right he is. It is hard to believe that the huge supermarkets have not played some indirect part in all this. Not in any way by intending to mislead customers but by pressuring suppliers perhaps, to come up with the cheapest option regardless of content. Labelling has become meaningless. And it is the people on the lowest incomes who have the least choice and, I fear, are being taken advantage of the most. They have little choice but to buy the cheapest food in good faith, only to learn now that the content is not what they expected. It may even contain something unidentifiable called MSM used to keep price down and bind and bulk up processed meat products.

MSM, mechanically separated meat, replaces the now disallowed MRM, mechanically recovered meat, the residue left on the carcass after butchering, which was pressure washed off the bones by machinery. The reddish slurry resembling runny mince has been replaced by MSM, low pressure desinewed meat that looks more like mince. So now MSM replaces MRM, which was banned by the EU after fears it might contain traces of BSE contaminated spinal cord.

Suddenly it becomes clear to me how traces of pork might turn up in burgers served to Muslim prisoners or to the Orthodox Jewish community, when MSM is used as a filler. It doesn't sound too promising either for the quality of food served in schools and hospitals on tight catering budgets.

And then there is the whole question of horse meat. It is an emotive issue. I personally don't want to eat horse meat. Horses are not bred on the farm for meat. They have, as far as I'm concerned, a completely other purpose. But many people do not share my reservations and eat horse meat happily. There are perfectly clean wholesome horse butchers all over Europe.

But what of the race horses that are no longer winning, the barren mares, all those now unwanted children's ponies bought on a whim, Romanian cart horses made redundant under new highway legislation? They all cost money to feed, take time and money to care for. So much simpler to offload them to some unscrupulous dealer, maybe, who will ease them into the food chain, regardless of performance-enhancing drugs, antibiotics and anything else unsuitable for human consumption, no questions asked.

Once again with all meat production and consumption, the real issue is human responsibility towards animal welfare and traceability.

And what of the abattoirs who ask no questions? Go to the press for some truly shocking footage of horses and ponies being hit with iron bars to force them into the slaughter pens and thence into the food chain regardless of any regulations. And some of these places I am ashamed and disgusted to say are here in Britain.

So as that Exec said, 'Where it is reasonable to do so, we will source from British producers... I am in no doubt that we will find things we don't like. But when we find them, we will change them.'

I hope he means it and I hope others will follow.

The NFU president used his opening address to the conference to call on supermarkets to source more from British farmers and growers

It is true that the longer a supply chain and the more borders it crosses, the less traceable our food becomes and the more the chain is open to negligence at best, fraud and criminal activity at worst. We need the supermarkets to stop scouring the world for the cheapest products they can find and start sourcing high-quality, traceable products from farmers here at home.

Farmers so often get a bad press at worst or misunderstood press at best: 'farmers complaining again' goes the strap line. Most of us work hard and do our best; certainly, all the farmers I know put their heart and soul into their farms and the care and welfare of their livestock. We are inundated by inspectors: Trading Standards, Health and Safety, Environmental Health, Food Standards Agency, DEFRA, EU regulations to name but a few and, although sometimes irksome, a very good thing it is too. But this surveillance is meaningless unless it follows the product right through to the customer who puts the food on their plate.

The old mantra holds firm: buy local, check the provenance of your food, ask hard questions, talk to farmers if you can and talk to the butchers, be they on the high street or in the supermarket. Demand the best. Learn to cook!

ORANGES IN COINTREAU!

Speaking of learning to cook, I bought an absurdly large net of ripe aromatic oranges in Portugal last week. They were irresistible, for sale by the side of the road direct from the farmer, for just 2 Euros. Ripe and soft they bore no resemblance to the hard, artificially ripened, waxed orange tennis balls I find at home.

But, what to do with them: I realised greed had driven me to weigh down my bag! I scoured my not so small collection of cookery books. No more marmalade this year; I've made too much already and spiced orange in vinegar just doesn't appeal.

So, I sliced the whole fruit very thinly, poached the slices quickly in a strong sugar syrup, an equal quantity of water to sugar, until slightly sticky and shiny. I potted up the glistening fruit into large Kilner jars and topped up the syrup with orange liqueur. The smell was wonderful. I sealed the jars and put them at the back of the fridge to mature. We'll see!

THE COLDEST SPRING

Mid-April and still we wait for the gentle warmth of spring. For weeks now, just as we looked forward to the end of a long hard winter, a searing east wind has held us in its grip. It howls through the valley, over the hilltops to the sea, across the Moor carrying lashing rain in a freezing sideways curtain in its wake. Plants stand in limbo, camellias brown on the bushes, daffodils bow their heads in submission, no blossom yet, no greening on the branches. Our drive was washed away again, fields waterlogged, grass nowhere to be seen. We pumped for two hours to get rid of a foot of water inside the sheep shed. A digger arrived and stayed a week redirecting the underground stream, a one-time ford we are told, by our gate. Land drains were dug, the stream dredged and still we squelch across the fields and welcome brown muddy sheep into the yard for tea.

But we're not in Wales, Cumbria or Scotland. Hard and wild as the winter has been for South Devon, we have not had to face the unbearable tragedy of the hill farmers whose flocks have been lost under snowdrifts so huge, in winds so strong they had to abandon their search or be lost themselves. The heartbreak, the hardship, the sadness and the cost are almost unbearable to even think about but those farmers have had to face it all. And many now face ruin as well, as a result of this extraordinary winter. A winter only matched by the national farming tragedy all those years ago in 1946–47.

Down south we're all in it together too, as we ask each one another who has grass, who has some straw, who has hay. Our hay was baled damp last soaking summer so it emits clouds of mould when each bale is broken open. Sheep and donkeys are not impressed. 'Water it with liquid molasses,' said Keith, our farming neighbour. 'It washes off the mould, makes it palatable and does them good.'

It's these tips from long-term farming friends that help so much. 'Don't go buying hay,' says Farmer Phil. 'Have a bale of mine. No, I don't want anything for it.' So I'll be at the farmers' market tomorrow with some of my own sausages and bacon for him; he's a sheep farmer so I hope pork will make a change!

It's years now since we bought our first sheep but we're still nowhere near these boys and girls whose families have been farming for generations. It takes a long time to be accepted into the farming community but once in, the support is wonderful. Paul has just been voted from chairman to president of the Whiteface Dartmoor Sheep Breeders' Association. And, as if that's not enough of an honour in itself, he's a Cornishman in Devon; some achievement!

The association was formed in 1950 when farmers on Dartmoor realised the breed was on its way to extinction. They realised too, the value of these ancient sheep that can withstand the freezing conditions of the Moor surviving on pastures from 500 to 2000 feet above sea level. In better times, way back in the eighteenth century when they were also known as Widecombe Whitefaces, the breed spread right across the West Country but as their numbers diminished, they retreated to the Moor. Today they are listed as 'Breed at Risk' on the Natural England register.

Happily, numbers are now gradually beginning to grow as farmers across the country realise their value when crossed with other breeds. The great mothering instincts of the Whiteface crossed with a Teeswater or Blue-faced Leicester produce a very hardy mule capable of raising multiple lambs. Cross a Whiteface with a Suffolk, or, as we do sometimes, a Jacob and you will have truly delicious roast lamb!

And here we are lambing again in this coldest of springs. I like to think the ewes are holding on to their babies to keep them warm inside but I know the real reason is that Big Dez, our ram, didn't show much interest in his task for the first couple of weeks of his 'tup'. Two weeks into lambing and we have just three lambs. No doubt they will soon start arriving in a rush all at once. As the east wind drops and the temperature creeps up this may not be such a bad thing after all. Maybe spring will burst upon us at last and the grass will even begin to grow and there will be something for them to eat on the hills when they finally decide to be born.

MAKING THE MOST OF ANOTHER SMALL CHICKEN!

Time is limited as we paddle up to the yard in the pouring rain, feed sheep, wait for reluctant lambs to be born and return to the house soaking wet, hungry and tired.

On Monday I spatchcocked a chicken; that is to say, I turned it upside down, cut out the backbone and squashed it flat!

The expression spatchcock is said to have come from eighteenth-century Ireland; a farmyard chicken was quickly *dis*patched, split and fried or grilled to provide a quick meal for an unexpected guest.

Mine went into a hot oven for about half an hour having been spread generously with olive oil, crushed garlic, dried herbs, coarse sea salt and black pepper – delicious, warming and quick.

On Tuesday we had a chicken and avocado salad with a baked potato and on Wednesday evening I put the bones in the pressure cooker with a shallot and made a quick stock. With this I made a simple mushroom and chicken risotto topped with Parmesan cheese. Three quick meals from one small bird!

SUMMER GARDENS

As I stare out of the study window at relentless rain, I realise that no sooner had I celebrated the gloriousness of May sunshine lighting up the scarlet *Embothrium* against an azure blue sky, than the heavens opened yet again. It has rained almost continuously ever since.

Rain, rain, rain, not the sideways rain of summer that drifts gently in a delicate curtain across the valley, refreshing crops and clearing the humid summer air. No, just a straightforward, straight down deluge, which has brought still more devastating flooding all across Britain; no sun, no break in the cloud, no comforting summer warmth, no uplifting glow of sunlight, just grey skies, low temperatures and rain.

Donkeys get fractious in their big barn day after day eating straw instead of wet grass. Desert animals by origin, they don't do well outside in wet weather unlike the sturdy ponies on the Moor. Shorn sheep shelter with their fat lambs in the hedgerows and the chickens vote with their feet and stay inside. Cats race round the house playing rough games instead of hunting in the fields. Even the dogs give me a funny look when I suggest a walk over the hills.

This year the National Garden Scheme (NGS) declared 15–16 June would be their first Festival Weekend. It put us all in a flurry; some 800 gardens would open on the same weekend nationwide. How on earth could we do it, a festival of any sort by June? Gardens up and down the country had been devastated by the rain, snow, flooding – how would we all pull our gardens round to something worthy of a visit?

Digging was almost impossible; plants stood in limbo in the ground for months. My heart sank and I was not alone; every gardener I spoke to, talked of years of work gone by the board. Very slowly, tiny signs of spring appeared at last, our spirits rose, well, just a tad. Then suddenly everything burst out all at once. Daffodils so late, lingered with the primroses while snowdrops, still fading, hung about defiantly around them. Rhododendrons mixed with forget-me-nots and the first blue geraniums. The *Embothrium* continued to sing scarlet against the heavens for weeks right into the middle of June; azaleas loitered but cold roses kept us guessing, reluctant to open their buds until they felt the sun on their petals. How strange it was!

Would the rain stop briefly for our open days? After frantic preparations dashing out between showers or simply getting soaked again and again, we managed to be ready to open despite the weather.

Grass was cut, edges trimmed, beds weeded, planting out completed but, best of all, my tiny new parterre was ready in the nick of time. Well, a grandiose name for my small space, but nevertheless a little terrace of box hedge, narrow paths and gravel, all beautifully laid out by Stephen who somehow managed to replicate the picture in my head. A huge old stone roller, a relic of the days of horse-drawn farming, was moved, in the manner of Stonehenge, across the garden to form a centrepiece upon which to display a little bronze bird by sculptor, Bridget McCrum.

Despite depressing weather forecasts, we finally downed tools and opened our gates in mid-June. I was still far from optimistic that anyone would turn up and risk a soaking just to look at our horticultural efforts. I was wrong. We had two dry afternoons and the visitors flocked in. Cream teas disappeared at an amazing rate and everybody seemed to enjoy themselves, delighted, they told me, to be out in the sunshine at last. We had no rain; instead we broke our own record in this, our fifth year of opening. We welcomed more than 160 visitors to our garden over the two afternoons.

Contrary to those dire weather warnings, the storm never happened and the sun burst upon us, burning down at last. Those reluctant roses sprang into life more dramatically than I can ever remember. *Rosa* 'Seagull' cascaded over the pond, 'Margaret Merril' bent low under great clusters of flowers, the new rugosas flourished and *Rosa mundi* stole the show. Even the feeble little Icebergs, planted in such terrible soggy soil, rallied stoically. Warmed by the sun, buds unfurled their damp little petals. Waterlilies, so unceremoniously divided and replanted by me last winter, suddenly exploded into a mass of waxy white flowers. Foxgloves and delphiniums stood to attention beside spiky *Verbena bonariensis*. A bank of blue geraniums nodded in the gentle warmth. Hostas and Solomon's seal stood up against the slugs. Poppies of all varieties sprang up uninvited everywhere; even hostas were extraordinarily slug free.

Even the vegetable garden put on a brave face with neatly strimmed grass and crisply trimmed box hedge. The vegetables suddenly began to catch up – planting having been so late into cold waterlogged ground. Beans reached the top of their canes at last and sweet peas decided to put on a brilliant show after all. Majestic old cavolo nero thrives between the giant leaves of *Inula* and horseradish. Red cabbage is statuesque, a glut in store that will at least thrill the chickens! Only the tomatoes continue to look a little less robust, while aubergines flourish, the largest I have ever grown.

RATATOUILLE

So thrilled am I to have grown my own aubergines successfully for the first time, I determine to make ratatouille! It hasn't been the best year for tomatoes or courgettes but I have just enough to make an attempt worthwhile.

I slice the unpeeled aubergine and courgette, put them into a colander and sprinkle with salt, leaving them for an hour or so to drain. I dry them thoroughly with kitchen paper and set about chopping tomatoes. I chop an onion, crush a few garlic cloves and deseed and cut some peppers into strips.

I soften the onion in olive oil, add the aubergine and peppers and cook covered for 20 minutes. Next, in go the tomatoes and courgette to cook, covered this time, for a further 40–50 minutes. I stir occasionally, being careful not to break up the vegetables. The sauce should be fairly thick with no sign of wateriness. Finally, I stir in chopped parsley, coriander and maybe a little basil.

VILLAGE GARDENS

And now, as summer progresses, after months, nay seasons, of record-breaking rainfall, a drought has already scorched the lawn. We watch anxiously at the browning valley as we move our sheep from field to field to share the sparse rations. The sprinkler is working overtime as borders wilt in the heat. And yet we cannot but celebrate summer and sunshine at last.

At the end of July, I persuaded a group of gardens in our village to open their gates for the second time to visitors in aid, once more, of the National Garden Scheme (NGS). Meetings were held, plans made, signs put up, a beautiful map produced, an extra car park and community bus made available. Gardeners gardened, nay manicured for the occasion. Volunteers manned the car park, helped with the teas, took the money at the garden gates, sold plants. Artists and craftspeople displayed their work.

Dittisham is such a beautiful village. It overlooks the widest stretch of the River Dart just three miles upriver from Dartmouth. In the past, it has always been protected from the worst weather by rolling hills and the temperance of the Gulf Stream – a gardener's paradise. Thatched cottages with gardens filled with all the old-fashioned favourites, look out across the river to Dartmoor in the distance. There are modern gardens too with contemporary planting, one even now under construction. Terraced gardens cling to the hillside, and cream teas to be served on the sweeping lawns at Middle Meadow. The famous Dit'sum plum orchards flourish still and Agatha Christie's house, Greenway, is to be seen across the river, among the trees.

Was it Paul, chatting on *The Potting Shed*, on Radio Devon in the morning? Or maybe people read about us in the local press or read the *NGS The Yellow Book*; one thing's for sure they arrived in droves. Gardens filled with admiring, aspiring gardeners; cream teas flew out of the village hall; the bus trundled breathless people back and forth. 'How do you manage these steep hills?' they asked, time and time again. Villagers just smiled while our wonderful gardens and their hardworking owners glowed in the sunshine! All in all, it turned into the most incredible weekend. I counted all the money over and over. I couldn't believe my sums! This year we have broken the county record for any group village garden opening. All the money goes to the NGS who pass it on to the nursing charities: Macmillan Cancer Support, Marie Curie, Help the Hospices, and the Carers Trust plus related guest nursing charities. A truly wonderful weekend!

MISS MILLICENT ARRIVES

Miss Millicent has joined us. On Sunday 1 November, a day so unseasonably warm and sunny, we stopped with Mr Porter for lunch in a pub garden en route to Camborne to collect our new eight-week-old black Labrador puppy.

It is years since we last had a puppy; Wellie was the last, the year we struggled to restore the farmyard after the big flood of Christmas 1999. Daughter of our doughty sheepdog Meg, she was one of a litter of nine collie lurcher-cross pups. A dear dog, she had a long, happy and eventful life.

Next, Mr Porter joined us, a skinny, frail eighteen-month-old black lab with sticking-out ribs and underdeveloped muscles in his hindquarters. He is the fellow we rescued through Labrador Rescue Trust – he had been kept in a crate without food or water, without any exercise. Slowly with love, food and gentle exercise he has grown into a big, loving, funny, boisterous fellow.

Next, came Sam, also a rescue dog. This time we were not so successful. Sam had been so cruelly treated he was not going to learn to trust us or anyone else, nor was he to settle happily with Mr P whom he bullied relentlessly. Despite a professional dog training course in Cumbria, he continued to chase our sheep. He frightened our grandchildren and finally, he turned on me. Devastated we had to return him to Labrador Rescue. The charity told us that sadly, sometimes the early cruelty is so unimaginably bad and the damage, therefore so deep-seated, it cannot be overcome by any amount of love and patience; poor dog.

Next, came the beloved Barney, a funny yellow Labrador, also a rescue dog belonging to a dear friend of ours. He joined us when our friend became too ill to keep him. Mr Porter adored Barney and they were like two old companions running through the fields together then curling up in front of the fire. We had Barney for ten wonderful months until severe ill health got the better of him. He was eleven years old.

So once again Mr P was alone and, without wishing to anthropomorphise, he was without doubt, a very sad lonely dog. He needed a companion and so did we. So, this time a new Labrador puppy it would be!

Labrador Retrievers are the descendants of St John's water dogs used in the nineteenth century by the fishermen of Newfoundland. The second Earl of Malmesbury brought the breed to England in 1830, so impressed was he by their agility in the water. It was as well he did because by the 1880s the breed was nearly extinct due to a swingeing government tax on dog ownership resulting in many dogs being destroyed. However, thanks to the Earl, the breed flourished this side of the Atlantic. In order to avoid confusion with the huge indigenous Newfoundland dogs, they soon became known as Labrador Retrievers after the sea they had worked, off Newfoundland.

These steady, gentle, intelligent, loving dogs have become one of most popular breeds in this country, recognised by the Kennel Club as early as 1916. They can be trained to help in so many ways: as guide dogs, assistance dogs, sniffer dogs and, of course, gun dogs. Their waterproof coats, webbed feet and rudder-like tails make them great swimmers and they can cover the ground very fast indeed, reaching 12mph in 3 seconds! Labrador owners don't need the gym! Labradors have such soft mouths they can carry an egg without breaking it and retrieve birds without damage.

A tiny new puppy is so different from taking on a rescue dog. Millie knows no right or wrong. She is not naughty; she simply doesn't know what is good or not so good, safe or unsafe. It is entirely up to us and, of course, Mr Porter, to show her how life is. As we play our part, he plays his quite fascinatingly well. He is her hero. She watches his every move and copies him, for better or worse, regardless. Sometimes it is very funny indeed.

He has cheered up no end and plays with her for hours until he's has had enough and growls a gentle instruction to be left alone.

It is a joy to see her learn, but also a sobering reminder of the damage done to both Mr P and poor Sam by their terrible treatment as small innocent puppies. It takes me back to my previous life in psychotherapy and the heart-rending similarity to the lifelong damage caused by the early experiences of badly neglected children. Bowlby's famous Attachment Theory applies just as well to animals as humans. I so agree with him that no variables have more far-reaching effects on personality development than a child's experiences within the family. Starting during a child's first months in his or her relation to both parents, the little one builds up working models of how attachment figures are likely to behave towards him or her in any of a variety of situations, and on all those models are based all expectations, and therefore all plans, for the rest of the child's life – a sobering thought indeed.

So as we go to our family in Bath for Christmas, Mr P will introduce Millie to his beloved 'cousins': a crazy, adorable Cocker Spaniel and another rescue Labrador, a sweet gentle girl, saved from a dreadful puppy farm by the RSPCA. Millie's socialisation will continue as she learns to play with other dogs, meet the children and doubtless try to chew the presents! We look forward to a happy, boisterous few days of huge family fun!

ENDINGS AND NEW BEGINNINGS

The seasons rotate relentlessly; round we go and here we are again. Another year ends; a new year waits in the wings. Endings and new beginnings; the cycle continues. Last winter dragged its feet into a wet and freezing spring. Slowly a glowing summer crept up on us, bathing the valley in sunshine at last. Autumn followed, gentle and mild, leading us round once more into winter.

Now naked trees swirl eerily in a wintery mist, days are short. We catch our breath in the freezing early morning air, in the half light of dawn, as we trudge up to the yard across fields white with frost. Christmas approaches oblivious to the tragedies and triumphs of the past year.

Things come to an end regardless of whether we are ready or not. Sometimes the end is abrupt, sometimes gentle. Sometimes we're left in shock and grief struggling with sadness and pain. Sometimes we see the end approaching far away on the horizon and have time to plan. This year we have suffered both: two loved ones dying suddenly and violently and then an old friend leaving us on the other side of the world.

Yet another shock awaited us. Stephen left us suddenly to return to his Kentish roots after twenty years working with us a day a week, here at Bramble Torre. We miss his quiet reassuring presence, his gentle humour and extraordinary ability to anticipate exactly what needed doing ahead of time. His departure was very abrupt, which made things so much worse: the inevitable conditions of selling one's house means there is no room for manoeuvre if you want to hang on to a keen purchaser. The buyer calls the tune. So it was with Stephen. And ten days from exchange of contract, he was gone without warning. It felt like yet another bereavement.

Dear old Bunty finally left us too, some three weeks ago. I miss the gentle little donkey but her end was peaceful and the last fifteen years of her life here so much better than that which had gone before. The two other donkeys watched her passing. They paced about eeyoring loudly but seemed to settle as they saw her go to her resting place in Sunday Orchard to be with her erstwhile companions, Dandy and old Sweep. It's strange just having two little donkeys after all these years.

But it was not all negative. Old friends married, babies were christened, birthdays celebrated. And we spent another lazy week in the Isles of Scilly gazing at the ocean and walking in the autumn sun.

And so to new beginnings – a skip graces the yard now heralding a fresh start. Methodically we work our way through the great sheds removing rubbish accumulated over years and years, some still the legacy of our predecessors, some ours and some indeed Stephen's! Oh, how cathartic it is to see it all go!

The pigs have gone too, their short but happy life ended! I miss them but know that without Stephen's help I can keep pigs no more.

The rams have left the ewes, their job done. Now they stare wistfully at the harem through the fence. The other day as I climbed the hill to the top barn, I caught the girls gambolling like overgrown lambs – great pregnant bundles of wool dancing and leaping and spinning in the air. Suddenly they spotted me laughing and stood quite still staring as if to say '*qui moi*': so much for 'the secret lives of sheep' I thought

George comes on Monday mornings now. He speaks to the donkeys in Romanian, the sheep too, as, smiling quietly, he brings them gently down the hill to the farmyard.

Life changes, life goes on, lambing will begin soon, chicks will hatch – new life waiting in the wings! The cycle continues; soon it will be spring.

'We shall not cease from exploration and the end of all our exploring will be to arrive where we started and know the place for the first time.'

T.S. Elliot

LIST OF RECIPES

Note: All our ovens vary so much that I tend to refer to a hot, moderate or cool oven on the basis that you will know better than me how that translates to your own oven, be it Electric, Gas, Fan-assisted or a Range! As a general guide, a hot oven would be around 200°C (180°C fan) Gas 6, moderate 160°C (140°C fan) Gas 3 and cool 140°C (120°C fan) Gas 1.

READING LIST

Acton, Eliza, *Modern Cookery for Private Families,* Longmans, 1845.

Beeton, Mrs, *Book of Household Management,* S.O. Beeton Publishing, 1880.

Carluccio, Antonio and Priscilla, *Complete Italian Food* Quadrille Publishing Ltd, (New Edition) 2002.

Corrado, Vincenzo, *Il Cuoco Galante* [The Gallant Cook], Naples, 1773.

David, Elizabeth, *French Provincial Cooking,* Michael Joseph, 1967.

Dimbleby, Josceline, *Book of Puddings, Desserts & Savouries,* Penguin Handbooks, 1979.

Everard, Mary A., *The Handy Dictionary of Cookery,* James Nisbet & Co., 1888.

Fearnley-Whittingstall, Hugh, *The River Cottage Meat Book,* Hodder & Stoughton, 2004.

Gerard, John, *The Herball or General History of Plants* [1597]; *Gerard's Herbal,* ed. Marcus Woodward, Senate, 1994.

Gray R. and Rogers R., *The River Café Cookbook,* Ebury Press, 1996.

Grigson, Jane, *Fruit Book,* Michael Joseph 1982.

Grigson, Jane, *Charcuterie and French Pork Cookery,* Grub Street Publishing, 2001.

Henderson, Fergus, *Nose to Tail Eating: A Kind of British Cooking,* Bloomsbury Publishing, (New Edition) 2004.

Jaine, Tom, *Making Bread at Home*, Phoenix 2005.

Larousse Gastronomique, Hamlyn 2001.

Leyel, Mrs C. F., and Hartley, Olga, *Gentle Art of Cookery*, Quadrille Publishing Ltd, 2011.

Markham, Gervase, *The English Huswife*, McGill–Queens University Press, 1994 [1615].

Picture Post, Morning After the Blitz, 3d. 3 May 1941.

Royal Horicultural Society (RHS), *The Vegetable Garden Displayed*, RHS, *c*.1941.

Roden, Claudia, *Mediterranean Cookery*, Random House, 1987.

Slater, Nigel, *Kitchen Diaries*, Fourth Estate, 2007.

Spry, Constance, *The Constance Spry Cookery Book*, Grub Street Publishing, (2nd Edition) 2011.

Surflet, Richard, *La Maison Rustique [A Countrie Farme]*, London, 1600.

Svendsen, Dr Elisabeth, *For Love of Donkeys*, Whittet Books, 1993.

Toussaint-Samat, Maguelonne, *History of Food*, WileyBlackwell, (2nd Edition) 2008.

Tusser, Thomas, *A Hundredth Good Points of Husbandrie*, Trübner, 1557; *Five Hundred Points of Good Husbandry*, Kessinger Publishing, 2010.

Uttley, Alison, *The Tales of Little Grey Rabbit*, Macmillan Children's Books, (New Edition) 1991.

Washington, Martha, Hess, Karen (ed), *Booke of Cookery and book of Sweetmeats*, Columbia University Press, 1996.

Wolfert, Paula, *The Cooking of South West France*, John Wiley & Sons, (2nd Edition) 2005.

ACKNOWLEDGEMENTS

Huge thanks first to Paul of course, for his constant unwavering support. And then to Josceline Dimbleby who, not only encouraged me to soldier on, but also wrote a foreword for me and introduced me to Bryony Hill who, in turn, put me in touch with the wonderful RedDoor Press. I am so grateful, in particular, for the patience and support of Heather Boisseau at RedDoor who has helped me through an enormously steep learning curve! And, of course to my dear friend, Gay, she of many publications, who has been a stalwart support throughout. Without them all this book wouldn't exist!

Thank you, too, for all the support of my family and friends and all those wonderfully encouraging farmers, especially to Phil Bond, Mark Lobb, Stephen, Ali, George and Eva. Thanks to Will, Jasmine and Claire at The Anchorstone Café and so, so many more. Thank you to all my gardening friends who step in every year to help us open for the National Garden Scheme. Without your help we couldn't possibly raise so much money for the nursing charities.

But above all, the biggest thanks goes to our son, Tom, living in Japan, who started it all by emailing me one day, all those years ago, saying, 'Why don't you write a blog, Mum, about what farming is *really* like?'

I had no idea what he was talking about. What on earth was a blog?

INDEX

Find out more about RedDoor
Press and sign up to our
newsletter to hear about our
latest releases, author events,
exciting **competitions**
and more at

reddoorpress.co.uk

YOU CAN ALSO FOLLOW US:

 @RedDoorBooks

 Facebook.com/RedDoorPress

 @RedDoorBooks